CARING & S

The Centenary History of the Co-operative Women's Guild

by

Jean Gaffin, M.Sc., B.Sc.(Econ)

and

David Thoms, Ph.D., M.A., B.Sc.(Econ)

To Ann & Girla

with love

Jean

March
1985

CO-OPERATIVE UNION LTD

Holyoake House, Hanover Street, Manchester

First published in 1983

I.S.B.N. 0 85195 133 3

Printed in Great Britain by the
Nottingham Printers Ltd, Stadium Works,
Nottingham Road, Basford, Nottingham NG7 7FE.

Contents

Preface

I am delighted as a Guildswoman in this the centenary year of the movement to be asked to write this foreword to "The History of the Co-operative Women's Guild".

My memories of "our guild" as I like to call it go back only 55 years, but nevertheless are vivid ones. I can recall being taken by my mother to her local guild branch meetings. This was the highlight of the week, and come rain or shine she and I rarely missed a meeting. As I grew up and joined young co-operators' groups I realised the strength of the Co-operative Movement and how it sustained the interest of women of my mother's time.

In the 1920-1930s we were going through difficulties not dissimilar to those of today — recession, mass unemployment, deprived families — to name but three. Yet with all these difficulties the guildswomen kept faith with their movement, which was increasing in numbers. They fought for changes in legislation to improve conditions in both home and family life, by raising the trading standards of their local Co-operative shops and a greater involvement in the education and political facilities that were available. They joined in demonstrations both for improvements in their own country and for peace throughout the world. It was with great pride that I wore my mother's white poppy to my first peace demonstration.

Reading their book will remind my generation of the work we and our predecessors carried out. It will also serve as an indication to the younger generation of the need to fight and to hold on to these achievements and regain those we have lost.

There is still a great deal to be done. We need more women to take an active part in the planning of the country's economy, in the running of local community affairs and the establishment of a successful and highly competitive Co-operative trading movement.

Women who are concerned about these things will find a place to air their views at a local branch of the Co-operative Women's Guild. The past 100 years have shown we can triumph over adversity and the way forward lies in a strong women's movement.

My message to all who read this book is remember the past, fight to improve the present standards under which we live, and look forward to security and peace for all in the future.

Norah E. Willis
Co-operative Congress President, 1983

Foreword

To compress 100 years into the pages of a small book has been difficult. We have been forced to leave out more than we put in. We have failed to pay tribute to so many who have devoted a life-time to the Guild, keeping the Rainbow Flag flying all through these 100 years, up to and including many still active today. We have had to omit many of the campaigns fought and issues argued for in order to give adequate space to those chosen for discussion.

More detail has been given about the period since 1939 for two reasons. First, much of the early history of the Guild has been told in Catherine Webb's book "The Woman with the Basket", and secondly because we hope guildswomen will recognise and recall their own experiences as they read about the more recent past.

As we have read and learnt more about the Guild and guildswomen in the past and present, we have been impressed by their energy and activities, awed by their achievements and proud to have been chosen to write about the Guild's first century.

We would like to thank the many people, mostly guildswomen, who wrote to us, or gave their time for an interview.

We have written this book primarily for guildswomen but we hope it will reach a wider audience who may come to share with us our admiration for the past hundred years of effort, and our hopes for renewed vigour in the century about to start.

Jean Gaffin
David Thoms

Acknowledgements

It is invidious to name a few from so many, but special thanks must go to Kathleen Kempton, who joined the Guild in 1935, aged 21 and who has become part of its history. Ken Hulse, Chief Information Officer, Roy Garratt, Librarian and Information Officer, and Joyce Darlington of the Co-operative Union, have been particularly helpful, as have so many other Co-operative employees, and David Douglas at the Fawcett Library, City of London Polytechnic. Sheila Knight helped with the Index.

Books have to be typed, and we are grateful to Rosemary Daly, Kate Thoms, Peggy Boardman and Anne Finnerty for coping with our handwriting. Books also have to be written, and for those who work full-time and write, like we did, in their time-off, a special thanks for sparing us must go to:-

Alec, Rachel and Mike Gaffin
Kate, Rachel and Hugo Thoms

CHAPTER 1

FOUNDATION AND FIRST STEPS: 1883-1889

Introduction

The foundation of the Women's Co-operative Guild was a major landmark in the history of the women's movement and a remarkable achievement in a strongly male dominated society. Economic dependency and a discriminatory legal framework relegated most women in the 1880s to second class citizenship. Evelyn Sharp later recalled that when the Guild first began 'the wife of the wage-earning workman had no recognised rights of her own, no independence, and no cultural leisure.'[1] For a substantial number of women, however, the retail Co-operative Movement provided a focus of interest and a network of relationships which in 1883 came together to produce the Women's League for the Spread of Co-operation, later the Women's Co-operative Guild (1884). As one of the first separatist organisations for working class women the formation of the Guild was of great significance, but its subsequent development raised its importance, becoming as it did an articulate and influential protagonist for women's rights as well a vehicle for personal and communal development. From a position of individual obscurity, the Guild came to provide working class women with the opportunity to voice their opinions from a national platform and to enjoy the satisfaction of helping to shape social change rather than merely respond to its whims.

The early history of the Guild is associated with the "Women's Corner", a section of the "Co-operative News" specifically devoted to items of interest to the newspaper's women readers. The "Corner" first appeared in January 1883 and was the direct product of a friendship between Mrs Alice Acland, the "Corner's" first editor from 1883-6, and Samuel Bamford, a well known and respected personality in the Co-operative Movement, and the editor of the "News". Mrs Acland was an educated and articulate woman, capable of writing with great fluency and style, who by 1883 had already contributed an impressive series of articles to the "News" on 'Women's Lives'. Like her husband, an Oxford don, her

1

interest in Co-operation stretched beyond retailing to encompass the Movement's broader political and social aspects. Mrs Acland's support for a separate women's organisation and her ability to use the "Corner" to unify and mobilise isolated pockets of interest provided the necessary platform from which to launch the Guild. In her first editorial Mrs Acland emphasised that her aim was to link Co-operative women all over the country and, although the "Corner" was to be concerned with homecraft — cookery, child care, needlework and so on — the question of women's rights was already raised as an issue of singular importance. While recognising that this controversial subject was beyond the scope of her first contribution, Mrs Acland set the tone of future development by her rhetorical question that:

> what I want to know is — why are we held in such little esteem among men? Why is the feeblest type of man called an old "woman?" Why do our lecturers dislike to speak to a "parcel of women?" Why is "woman-hearted" a term of reproach?[2]

These comments are a perfect illustration of Mrs Acland's wry sense of humour, powers of expression and deep concern for the honour of her sex, qualities which made her such an important force in the Guild's early development.

Mary Lawrenson, the Guild's General Secretary from 1885-9, and a teacher by profession, deserves to be ranked with Mrs Acland as co-founder of the League. Although sometimes regarded by her friends as an amiable dreamer, she was a most persuasive public speaker and her contribution to the Guild's development was based upon a healthy mixture of ideological commitment and pragmatism. She was deeply committed to the values associated with nineteenth century Co-operation and was personally much influenced by her father, a Woolwich printer, (active in both the Trade Union and Co-operative Movements) and also by the work of the early Christian Socialists. Mrs Lawrenson later claimed that the idea of a women's organisation linked to the Co-operative Movement had been in her mind for some time but that the appearance of the "Corner" gave her the opportunity to express her views to a wide audience. However, her formal involvement in the Guild's birth came in February 1883 when she suggested through the "Corner" that Mrs Acland, with help from others, should establish an independent body to promote instructional and recreational classes for mothers and single girls. Mrs Acland's response was immediate and supportive.

> *If we women were to form an association, or guild of women,*
> *bound over to do all we could to help in the cause of*
> *co-operation, I think we might do a great deal. We all do*
> *something already, no doubt, but we should get a sense of*
> *support from our association. We should not feel that our*
> *efforts were isolated, and of little value — we should have others*
> *to consult, in case of difficulty — we should have something to*
> *invite other women to join — we should have wherever we went,*
> *friends ready made, with whom we should have a starting point*
> *at meeting, which would give us a sense of that "old friendship"*
> *which is so cheering and helpful in our lives.*[3]

From Small Beginnings

Yet Mrs Acland's call for suggestions regarding the aims and
rules of a 'Woman's League for the Spread of Co-operation'
elicited little response so that by the end of March 1883 she could
record only 'some degree of encouragement.' To some extent
this may be explained by the restricted readership of the
relatively expensive "Co-operative News", though more
importantly perhaps some potential recruits were deterred by
the independent, even robust, tone of the early correspondence.
Mrs Newman of Norwich for instance, suggested that

> *Now none of us must be idle, we must all have something to say*
> *to one another, and let men see we are interested in something*
> *more than housekeeping and nursing babies.*[4]

In their hearts, many of the "Corner's" readers must have
agreed with Mrs Newman that

> *Women want more than they have now.*

though such sentiments challenged the contemporary view of
womanhood and must have induced apprehension and even
fear of the consequences. Perhaps it was with this in mind that
Mrs Acland reassured her readers with the soothing words that

> *we can move in a quiet womanly way to do true woman's work.*[5]

The personal contacts of Mrs Acland and others
supplemented the "Corner" in helping to build support for the
formal introduction of an association of Co-operative women.
Mr. Acland was a popular speaker who, accompanied by his
wife (who often sang at her husband's meetings), travelled
extensively in the North of England, meeting Co-operative
leaders and their wives. Such engagements provided Mrs
Acland with the opportunity to establish friendships with other

3

women co-operators, but also helps to explain why a number of leading Co-operative men such as Vansittart Neale, Abraham Greenwood and Samuel Bamford came to lend their support to the Guild.

Some of Mary Lawrenson's experiences illustrate the practical difficulties and hidden pitfalls of gathering support for the formation of the League. Mrs Baker, a domestic servant before marriage and one of Mrs Lawrenson's neighbours, was one of the first to respond to her letter in the "Corner". Mrs Baker praised the suggestion, but doubted its practicability amongst the members judging from her own impressions. Although she was prepared to help, Mrs Baker said

> she was afraid of being "responsible for people".

In fact this concern was misplaced since she was an assiduous worker for the welfare of the local community, but, according to Mrs Lawrenson, was

> A proof how careful well meaning people have to be in trying to draw up schemes for others who are not on the same level of life.[6]

This is a good example of the fact that in the 1880s working class women were not a unified entity, but rather a collection of sub-groups with different material circumstances, interests, aspirations and levels of education. Not even every Co-operative working class wife had the inclination or the confidence to join let alone organise a women's guild.

Mrs Lawrenson next attempted to recruit another of her neighbours who, because of her involvement with the Woolwich Society and her training as a pupil teacher, was a particularly attractive target. Her wide circle of acquaintances rendered her a potentially fertile recruiting agent, while her education qualified her for an administrative role. Negotiations stumbled, however, when in return for her support, the lady in question demanded certain favours, including the presidency of the new organisation.

By the middle of April the League could still muster only seven committed supporters, though towards the end of the month Mrs Acland felt sufficiently confident to declare through the "Corner" that 'The woman's league for the spread of Co-operation has begun.' The real turning point, however, came in May when, during the Co-operative Congress, which in 1883 was held in Edinburgh, the League convened its first formal meeting. The members deliberated in private but some fifty ladies talked for over an hour until the discussion was prematurely terminated by the fact of the men having concluded their own business. Nevertheless, the meeting confirmed Mrs Acland as organising secretary for one year and arranged for the appointment of a number of local secretaries on a temporary basis. It was also agreed to introduce a subscription of 6d a year, plus donations from those who could afford it. With the League formally established, possessing an outline organisational structure, an independent source of finance and with an increase of membership from 14 to 50, the focus of attention moved to events at branch level.

The Guild Begins to Grow

Although still highly limited in size, by May 1883 the League's membership was widely dispersed with representation in Manchester, London, Oxford, Rochdale, Stowmarket, Market Harborough, Aberdare and Gloucester. Three branches were functioning at the end of 1883 and in June of the following year this had doubled, with a total membership of 195 distributed between

Hebden Bridge	60
Rochdale	42
Woolwich	43
Norwood	20
Chelsea	14
Coventry	16

By 1889, when Margaret Llewelyn Davies became General Secretary and the Guild was poised to embark upon its second phase of expansion, the number of branches had increased to 51 with a total membership of approximately 1800.

The first branch, that at Hebden Bridge, was formed at a meeting held on September 17 1883 with 40 members present. In terms of scale of membership and range of activities, Hebden Bridge was one of the Guild's most successful outposts. When, in February 1884, the branch held its first combined tea and public meeting over 200 people joined in the festivities. The branch benefited from a lively Co-operative Society which became something of a showpiece for the Movement. In "My Apprenticeship" Beatrice Webb recalled three happy days spent at Hebden Bridge in March 1881.

My interest was in the vigorous Co-operative life of the place; I saw many co-operators and attended their meetings. Young

5

Oxford men are down here; and they and the co-operators form
a mutual admiration society between intellectual young Oxford
and co-operative working class.[7]

One of those young Oxford men was Arthur Dyke Acland who in January 1883 addressed an enthusiastic audience on the subject of Co-operation. Mrs Acland accompanied her husband on this occasion and no doubt took the opportunity to sow the seeds of the Guild's later development.

During the opening period of its development however, the Guild's greatest successes were achieved in the South of England so that by 1889 only 7 of the 51 branches were located in the north of the country. Similarly, it was easier for Guild members in the south to participate fully in the activities of the Co-operative Movement. For example, in the early 1890s Mrs Lawrenson and Miss Catherine Webb, the founder and first Secretary of the Battersea branch, were elected members of the Southern Section of the Co-operative Union's Central Board, an achievement that was not paralleled in the Midlands until 1917 and even later elsewhere. According to Miss Llewelyn Davies, the Co-operative societies in the south were more receptive to new ideas than their counterparts in the north, while the male membership was also more flexible in its attitude to women's roles. She noted that

In the South, the women were more easily and quickly accepted
as fellow workers, and such an expression as "Let my wife stay
at home and wash my moleskin trousers" would not have been
heard at a Southern Conference.[8]

The experience of the Coventry branch illustrates the importance of a friendly environment to the Guild's success. From its inception in 1867 the Coventry Perseverance Society had freely allowed women full membership and, when the Guild held its first meeting in November 1884, the Society placed a room at its disposal. Membership quadrupled in the next two years and an accommodation crisis soon developed, but the Society came to the rescue by arranging for the premises to be extended to meet the additional pressure.

The Coventry branch benefited from the fact that its first President, Miss Shufflebotham, was the daughter of Charles Shufflebotham, one of the pioneers of the Co-operative Movement in the city. Indeed a significant feature of branch formation seems to have been the role of women connected by family with the Movement's local and national leadership. Miss **Holyoake,** the daughter of the veteran co-operator

G.J. Holyoake, was a founder member of the Brighton branch, while Miss Greenwood, daughter of Abraham Greenwood, the first Chairman of the Co-operative Wholesale Society, was the founding Secretary of the Rochdale branch. It was Miss Greenwood who in August 1884 suggested that the League's name be changed to that of Guild. The enthusiasm of ordinary co-operators, such as Mary Lawrenson's father in Woolwich, also encouraged many wives and daughters to take an interest in the Movement and thus to be among the Guild's pioneering members.

Co-operation in the Nineteenth Century

The Co-operative Movement provided the inspiration and means for the foundation and development of the Women's Co-operative Guild. It was also a central feature of the working class struggle for an improved material and intellectual experience. Yet nineteenth century Co-operation was a complex phenomenon, the characteristics and meaning of which were modified by the passage of time and the interpretation of its followers. The structured and expanding Co-operative Movement of the late nineteenth century was directly linked to the ideas which Robert Owen had preached fifty years before. But it was more practical, less concerned with moral regeneration than the benefits of efficient shopkeeping. Yet working class aspirations cannot be explained without reference to Owen, and certainly his influence may be traced within the aims of the Guild and the evangelicalism of its members. Indeed, lectures on Owenism remained for some time a prominent feature of the Guild's educational programme.

Owen was a prolific writer but he is perhaps best remembered for his practices as an enlightened mill owner at New Lanark, near Glasgow, and for the moral and social philosophy which he contributed to the Co-operative communities of the early nineteenth century. As an employer, Owen demonstrated that production could occur efficiently and without brutality and acrimony, provided that the conditions of work were designed to provide a happy and co-operative atmosphere. He believed, too, that some of the great social problems of his day, such as urban poverty, could similarly be alleviated by positive intervention in the economic and social environment. Despite his success in business, Owen was unable or unwilling to provide

7

the finance or the organising skill to launch successfully the utopian communities for which his ideas were the inspiration. The failure in 1846 of Queenswood in Hampshire, the last great community experiment associated with Owen, brought to a sad and rather ignominious conclusion that phase of endeavour which largely defined Co-operation in the first half of the nineteenth century.

Despite the intellectual limitations of his ideas and the difficulties of their practical implementation, Owen was perhaps the outstanding contributor to the development of nineteenth century English socialism. Owen challenged the underlying tenets of the capitalist system, advocating an economic and social order which stressed co-operation and harmony rather than competition and discord. He believed that personality and behaviour were shaped by the environment and that the village or small community represented the ideal circumstance for the development of happy and moral lives. They were to be the New Jerusalem, democratic, non-sexist, classless and conflict-free. Owen also attached great importance to education and at New Lanark children were not permitted to work before the age of ten and were required to pursue carefully organised courses of study. Owen's emphasis upon collective responsibility and the mental and moral development of the individual has direct links with the Co-operative Movement of the later nineteenth century and with the Women's Co-operative Guild, both of which sought to develop the higher qualities of the human personality. In addition, Owen's hope that Co-operative retailing might help to provide the funds for community building provides a tangible connection with the shopkeeping activities of the Rochdale Pioneers and their disciples. Yet the distinction between Owen and the Rochdale Pioneers was fundamental. It contrasted the anti-capitalist and capitalist perspectives since the Rochdale Pioneers sought not to overthrow the existing economic framework but to make it work more effectively for the benefit of the working classes, or at least the upper layers of that social grouping. Robert Owen's 'Co-operative Commonwealth' was to provide a production orientated utopia, while the prime concern of the Rochdale Pioneers was the welfare of the consumer. Interestingly, the radicalism of the Women's Co-operative Guild, particularly during Margaret Llewelyn Davies' period as General Secretary, was in some respects intellectually closer to Owenism than the gentlemen stalwarts of the late nineteenth century Co-operative societies. When she spoke of the 'transformation of society' Miss Llewelyn Davies was evoking the spirit if not the substance of Owen's ideas.

Many of Owen's followers were working class men and women whose circumstances were often those of abject poverty, with little hope of rising above the daily experience of uncertain employment, low wages and poor health. The economic depression which had given force to Chartism began to recede after 1842 and the 1850s and 1860s were generally prosperous times as economic fluctuations became less severe and the developing industries of the industrial revolution led to significant improvements in the quality of life. Even during the years 1828-34 when Owen's influence was at its greatest some, particularly skilled, workers had prospered, but during the middle decades of the nineteenth century the spoils of industrial capitalism, including the opportunity for self advancement, came to influence the living standards and attitudes of a wider section of the urban working class. The 1840s witnessed a substantial acceleration in the growth of real wages, and the development after 1844 of the consumer orientated Co-operative Movement was in part a response to the financial experience of artisan workers who now had a growing margin of income to spend. With characteristic exaggeration, Engels could declare in 1844 that the social war was already being waged, whereas the reality, as Bagehot later pointed out, was that the English were becoming a deferential community.

The new style Co-operation of the Rochdale Pioneers was both result and example of this change in climate: it illustrated the self help spirit of an increasingly confident upper stratum of the English working class. The Rochdale Equitable Pioneers Society, whose famous store in Toad Lane was opened in 1844, had direct personal links with Owenism, but its revolutionary aspect was not a desire to restructure society but to pay a dividend on purchases, having first met the necessary financial obligations to shareholders. The dividend separated the Owenite Co-operative Societies from the new model, since it meant that in practice funds could not be accumulated to finance community projects. The commercial success of the Rochdale experiment led to it being copied elsewhere and by 1850 over 200 societies had been established. In the next two decades the retail Co-operative Movement spread rapidly, especially in Yorkshire and Lancashire, though the period of dramatically accelerated growth occurred during the last quarter of the century when the membership of all Co-operative societies grew three times as fast as the population of the United Kingdom. Following the foundation of the Co-operative Wholesale Society in 1863, this latter period also witnessed the diversification of Co-operative activities beyond retailing to include banking and the provision of mortgage and insurance facilities. It was within this framework of a prosperous and expanding Co-operative Movement that Mrs Acland, Mary Lawrenson and others established the Women's Co-operative Guild.

Women and Co-operation

Although the "Corner" paved the way for the creation of the Guild, it was the Co-operative stores which justified and facilitated its existence. Thus the key relationship between the Co-operative Movement and the Guild is that without the former the latter would not have existed. In its early, rather uncertain days, the Guild received crucially important support from the Co-operative Union and some of its most prominent personalities. In September 1886, for example, E. Vansittart Neale, the Union Secretary, assured Mrs Lawrenson that

> I am much pleased to do anything to further the action of an institution so valuable as the Women's Co-operative Guild actually is — still more promises to become.[9]

In the same year the Union contributed its first grant to the Guild of £10, which increased steadily in subsequent years reaching £200 by the end of the century. The modest nature of these grants enabled the Guild to retain its independence, and they were useful in helping to meet essential administrative expenses. Even so the Guild's initial progress was handicapped by a shortage of funds to meet the costs of travel, postage and printing inevitable to such an undertaking. Mrs Lawrenson noted how in the early days she was frequently out of pocket, complaining that

> the actual expense of management should be borne by our own members.[10]

However, Mrs Lawrenson was equally aware that branches were often most unwilling to provide financial support for a central administration, commenting in 1888 that

It is a fact that the Woolwich women do not see why they should give anything to the Central Fund.

The situation gradually improved, though it was not until 1892 that the Winter Circular could declare with any degree of confidence that the Guild operated on a sound financial basis. However, adequate funding remains a problem for the Guild in 1983.

Perhaps the most important service which the Co-operative Movement rendered to the formation of the Guild was that of publishing facilities, particularly through the columns of the "Co-operative News." The "Corner" was the brainchild of a number of women who met informally during the Oxford Co-operative Congress of 1882, but was given practical reality by the generous support of the editor of the "News", Samuel Bamford, who faced considerable opposition from his Board dominated, as Miss Webb described it, by masculine preferences. The early pages of the "Corner" were largely concerned with matters of household management, but with the emergence of the Guild the paper came to serve as the main source of communication, with conference and branch reports and in 1893 'Notes from the Central Committee' helping the widely dispersed membership to keep in touch. The sound journalistic quality of the "Corner" under the direction of successively Mrs Acland, Miss Amy Sharp, Miss Catherine Webb and Mrs Vaughan Nash was of immense importance in establishing the Guild's credibility during its formative years. Frequently the wit and pace of the "Corner" contrasted sharply with the more prosaic style of the "News". The fine literary skills of these women was the perfect complement to the persuasive oratory of Mary Lawrenson, Sarah Reddish and other leading pioneers. With the Movement's support the Guild began to publish a large and varied selection of pamphlets and leaflets concerned with administrative, educational and policy matters. This use of the printed word was instrumental in cementing the Guild and advancing it to a position of influence, both within and beyond the Co-operative Movement.

While attachment to the Co-operative ideal no doubt attracted many women to the stores, the practical advantages, particularly the dividend, was probably the more powerful magnet. The dividend was distributed quarterly, half-yearly or yearly and was a proportion of the societies' profits in relation to the members' purchases made during the relevant period.

11

One of the attractions of the dividend was that, together with interest on shares, it could be left to accumulate as additional shares earning interest. The dividend thus became a form of saving which could be used for major purchases, including even housing, or left as insurance against hard times. Margaret Llewelyn Davies fully appreciated the attractions of the dividend but regretted that it frequently resulted in a rather restricted view among women of the aims of the Co-operative Movement.

Yet the commercial practices of the societies and their store managers were not free of criticism and from its inception the Guild served as an effective consumers' organisation, eventually using its members' "basket power" to influence Co-operative policy on a range of issues, from credit sales to wholesale production. In September 1883 Mary Lawrenson criticised the goods sold in her local ·store in Woolwich, informing the manager that

> *I have reason to suppose that I have always been charged in excess of the value judging from the prices of fairer tradesmen.*[11]

She also claimed that some manufactured goods were poorly produced, soon requiring a return to the store for repairs. With just a hint of trouble to come, she concluded that

> *it is not surprising if I think with other ladies that it is time things were looked into.*

Further north, at Hebden Bridge, Guild members soon arrived at similar conclusions as regards price and responded by convening a deputation of three members to meet the Society's Drapery Committee. Pricing policy remained a sensitive aspect of Co-operative shopping, one of the criticisms being that it deterred the poorest classes from patronising the stores, and it was this which, towards the end of the century, encouraged the Guild to adopt the radical policy of taking Co-operation to poor neighbourhoods. Yet pricing did place the societies in something of a dilemma since if dividends were to remain attractive and capital be available for future development, profits had to be maintained at a respectable level, which meant relatively high prices in the shops. Some societies, however, accumulated more funds than they required, which led them to invest in outside activities and this was another issue which the Guild seized upon as worthy of debate.

One of Mrs Lawrenson's hopes in the early 1880s had been to resurrect the ideals of the early co-operators by using the League to help establish co-operative workshops of women who would share in the profits of their collective activity. As Miss Webb noted, .

> *In the very early days the sympathies of the Guild were strongly attracted to the ideals of profit-sharing and co-partnership forms of production, and many dreams were indulged in of establishing workshops on these lines for women and girls.*[12]

However, apart from its many practical difficulties, this notion was out of keeping with the spirit of the period and seems even to have contributed to Mrs Lawrenson's reputation as an eccentric, fond of building 'castles in the air'. In 1891 Miss Llewelyn Davies produced a discussion document which finally resolved the issue, for it pointed to the undoubted benefits of the federated system whereby production was under the control of the distributive societies but co-ordinated by the Co-operative Wholesale Society. In practice though, even as Mrs Lawrenson wrote to the "Corner" in 1883, the end of such profit sharing schemes had already been signalled with the formation in the previous year of the Co-operative Productive Federation.

Women in the Nineteenth Century

In her first contribution to the "Corner" Mrs Acland, perhaps as much for the benefit of her male as her female audience, assured readers that at present she had no intention of raising the 'much-vexed' question of women's rights. She did suggest however, that male guilt at having for so long monopolised the "News" was one of the reasons for the introduction of the "Corner", adding that while the paper had provided 'sound, instructive reading' it had been 'ten times more difficult for women to take an interest in it than for men.' Over time the Guild's interest in feminist concerns came to be broad based, committed and expressed with great determination and force, but the women's movement also contributed to its foundation and early development. Conversely, the strong anti-feminist sentiment which prevailed during much of the nineteenth century, involving as it did, a sharp distinction between the role of men and women, was one of the major obstacles facing the Guild during its infancy, and indeed this remained a serious problem well into the twentieth century.

Throughout the nineteenth century immense legal and social barriers restricted the rights of women and limited to very narrow boundaries the scope of their ambition. Even middle class women were technically little more than chattels, for until 1891 a husband was perfectly entitled to kidnap and imprison his wife. Even prominent male supporters of female rights often faced vehement opposition from the anti-feminists. The "Saturday Review" was a consistent opponent of the women's movement and in November 1859 stated its case against reform of the law as it affected women.

> It is not the interest of States, and it is not therefore, true social policy, to encourage the existence, as a rule, of women who are other than entirely dependent on man as well for subsistence as for protection and love ... Married life is a woman's profession; and to this life her training — that of dependence — is modelled. Of course by not getting a husband, or by losing him, she may find that she is without resources. All that can be said of her is, she has failed in business, and no social reform can prevent such failures.[13]

The "Review" thus condemned married women to a life of dependency, and unmarried women to a state of financial hardship. If this was an exceptionally harsh view of the female role, it was not untypical, and serves to illustrate the kind of opposition which, even by the 1880s, challenged the Guild's very existence.

While middle class women complained of their inability to vote in parliamentary elections and to retain legal title to their property after marriage, their working class counterparts were probably more concerned not to offend the conventions of their married state. The comments of one of the Guild's founder members provides instructive reading in this connection.

> It was unheard of, when I was a child, for a woman's hand to be idle. My own aunt used to keep a half-knitted sock near the front door, so that, if a knock came, she could catch it up and open the door looking as though she had been interrupted in the middle of her work. At the early meetings of the Guild, the women used to bring their sewing with them, unable to rid their minds of the notion that there was something wrong in sitting with their hands in laps while they listened to speeches or took part in discussions. It has taken us fifty years, you might say, to get over the idea that a woman is idling and wasting her time when she is using her brains without her hands, and doubly so if she is a married woman.[14]

Deviation from their traditional pattern of behaviour could subject working class women to considerable abuse. As Mrs Acland later recalled, even the personal appearance of the

Guild's founding members could provoke strenuous male opposition.

> The women who were fighting for the rights of women (in 1883) were sometimes strange in their personal appearance.
> Co-operative menfolk were fearful that I intended to lead their wives and daughters to adopt similar styles of dress and speech.
> So I had to walk with the most wary caution.[15]

No doubt it was to help alleviate the fears and suspicions reflected in these comments that the Edinburgh meeting in 1883 decided that there should be 'no platform speaking, no advertising, no going out of our woman's place.'

By 1904 Miss Llewelyn Davies could report that male co-operators were generally supportive of their wives' participation in the Guild's activities. This was probably also true of many couples in the 1880s, though the balance of opinion, particularly in the North of England, was likely to have been against women developing unnecessary commitments outside the home. This would have been consistent with middle class values, which often formed the model for the higher groups among the working class, and which idealised the home as the very bedrock of society. Indeed, issues central to the women's movement in the nineteenth century, female suffrage, for example, revolved around the key problem of how change would affect the stability of family life. Anything which, it was suspected, would vitiate that experience was widely condemned as immoral. The domestically orientated nature of the female role often threatened the Guild's early development. For example, it was customary in many families for wives not to leave the home unaccompanied by another member of the family. Thus the Secretary of the Norwich branch of the Guild reported in 1885 that

> It has been my painful experience in asking mothers to come out for an hour or two to enjoy themselves, they nearly all make one answer — Oh, thank you but I never go out, but my daughter will come, or my husband and children will come.[16]

A life independent of the home was for many women in the 1880s a mere pipedream, and it was one of the great achievements of the Guild that it brought a sense of freedom to lives previously incarcerated within extremely narrow emotional and intellectual confines.

Even when a husband agreed with his wife's membership of the Guild it was often difficult for her to find the time to attend meetings, much less take on administrative responsibilities. As

15

Miss Llewelyn Davies commented,

With so much work, and so many lives depending on them, it is not surprising that we often find women who hardly ever leave their homes, whose lives become very monotonous and restricted and whose spirits and health suffer severely.

This particular problem was not unique to the Guild and was, for example, a factor in the slow development of women's trades unionism. However, in supporting the introduction of Co-operative laundries, wash houses and other labour saving arrangements, the Guild did make positive recommendations to free women from the excessive physical burden of their daily round and create the opportunity for their full participation in the Guild's educational programme. Catherine Webb summarised these objectives when in 1893 she stressed that

We desire to remove from the life of the working woman some at least of the toilsome drudgeries which too frequently fill her days and hinder the development of these higher duties.[17]

In practice the birth and subsequent development of the Guild was made possible because, despite the sacrifices, large numbers of women were prepared to rise above the drudgery of their daily routine.

Some of the opposition which the Guild encountered in its early days was a consequence of the challenge to male dominance which the women's movement in general represented. This movement assumed many forms, though for the most part it was dominated by middle class women and was a reaction to long standing discriminatory practices as well as new difficulties which emerged in the wake of the Industrial Revolution. The belief that the Victorian family provided the perfect environment for social and moral development was, even for the middle classes, an idealised myth which came to be exposed by the women themselves and by their male sympathisers. In reality the Victorian middle class family was strongly hierarchial, with the economic role of fathers, husbands and brothers justifying their dominant position. With relatively few opportunities for education and employment, women found it difficult to escape from what for many of them was a claustrophobic and unfulfilling experience. The often dreary nature of the female role was made worse as the nineteenth century progressed by suburbanisation and by the accumulation of middle class wealth. The former resulted in a loss of the wife's contact with her husband's business as the place of work and residence became physically separated, while the growth in employment of domestic help, facilitated by the expansion of incomes, further diminished the active role of women within the home. Middle class women thus became identified as creatures of leisure, sheltered by their male protectors, but with relatively little opportunity for personal development or the expression of talent other than that of a purely domestic nature. These are generalisations and for some middle class women the experience of instructing servants and tradesmen no doubt represented an interesting and even stimulating challenge, but many, perhaps the majority, would have preferred a greater sense of personal freedom and self development.

Women Feel Their Feet

Yet it was the limitations of this domestic limbo, coupled with specific issues, particularly the legal title to one's own property which initiated and fuelled the women's movement. The early women's organisations were middle class, relatively moderate in their demands and concerned particularly with economic issues. One of the first organised groups was the Society for the Employment of Women which developed from a small committee originally formed in the mid 'fifties to petition for a Married Women's Property Bill. The Society acquired its own magazine, "The English Woman's Journal", which began publication in 1858 and became an important forum for the discussion of feminist concerns. The middle decades of the nineteenth century saw the proliferation of organisations concerned with the administration and maintenance of the new industrial society. In many cases, housing associations and poor relief for example, women came to take an active part in their operation. These manifestations of female independence were assisted by the spread of improved facilities for both secondary and higher education, but, because of its broad implications, perhaps the most significant spur to the women's movement was the growth from the 1860s of the female suffrage campaign. The franchise issue attracted wide interest and the activities of the National Society for Women's Suffrage, founded in 1867 (and its successors), provided a focus for the debate on women's rights: it was a constant reminder that, compared with men, women enjoyed only partial citizenship.

The limitations of the female role and the battle for greater freedom and equality undoubtedly influenced those of the early leaders whose middle class backgrounds gave them, in the words of Miss Webb, 'the advantage of scholarship and culture.' Yet it is difficult to assess how far the women's movement motivated the rank and file of Guild members, though Mrs Acland implied that there was a connection when she noted that

> *People charge me with stirring up unrest and discontent amongst the women, but one knows now that one only voices the unrest — the desire for a wider outlook — that was rising in the minds of all women.*[18]

The growth of female trades unionism in the 1880s would suggest that many working class women were refusing to accept their inferior economic status and were beginning to appreciate the benefits of collective action. Indeed some of the male opposition which the Guild encountered may well have derived from this more general assertion of the rights of working class women.

As time progressed, Guild members became involved in a wide range of feminist concerns, including suffrage rights, conditions of women's employment and maternity services. But to begin with they largely ignored these issues and even failed to interest themselves in the specific debates of the period, such as that concerned with family limitation, about which there was much publicity in the 1880s. The explanation for this relates to the Guild's association with the Co-operative Movement and from the social composition of its membership. The prime justification for the Guild's existence was its role as a vehicle for the spread of Co-operative principles: initially it was an organisation with a single purpose and only later did it become a pressure group with more broadly based interests. The limitations of the female role played a significant part in the Guild's foundation but it was specifically linked to Co-operation, being concerned with degrees of influence within the Movement. Miss Webb noted that the drive for open membership was one of the very first campaigns undertaken by the Guild and her comments, reading rather like the report of a war correspondent, reflect the profound importance which was attached to this issue:

> *One of the first concerted "campaigns" within the Movement undertaken by the Guild was for "Open Membership", and the campaign lasted long, for the menfolk did not welcome the intrusion of women, and a certain amount of jealous fear as to*

18

the positions women might win in the Movement kept this door shut against them. Even when this element was absent it was no light task to persuade a Society to change its rules on "sentimental" grounds (as the men were inclined to regard the wish of the women for personal membership), which seemed to them as though it could hardly increase the bulk of trade.

The battle was sometimes sharp and successful, sometimes tedious and the result disappointing, but the Guild stuck to its guns until time and circumstances wore down all opposition, and today, not only is "open membership" the general rule of the Movement, but there would be consternation indeed, if women members did not appear in good numbers at quarterly meetings.[19]

Miss Reddish provided the theoretical justification for this campaign, arguing that although women may not always be producers, they were nevertheless entitled to equal rights

for the simple reason that they assist in production by enabling others to devote their time and energies more entirely to the earning of wages in production and distribution.

She added that

Women help to build up, to strengthen, and maintain co-operative societies and establishments, and therefore have equal right to equal power and representation in controlling and managing them.[20]

The open membership battle was eventually won and Guild members also became increasingly involved on Co-operative society committees. As late as 1933 Evelyn Sharp noted that

there is still some anti-feminist prejudice lingering in the Movement;

but added in happier vein that

there is probably less in the Co-operative Movement than elsewhere, and this may be fairly attributed in a considerable degree to the position women have established for the members by their advisory and executive work within the Guild.[21]

Early Guild Members and the Labour Aristocracy

In common with the first trade unions for women, the Guild's early leadership had a substantial and highly important middle class element, though rank and file membership was predominantly working class. However, since the Co-operative societies, with their membership fees and relatively high prices, attracted the more secure artisan families, the Guild's membership was biased towards the upper bracket of the manual wage earning group. Most of the early Guild members were married and the majority were without paid work, a characteristic of working class married women as a whole since female employment was scarce, except for the textile areas of Lancashire and Yorkshire. In 1880 only about a quarter of all women worked so that many working class wives, like their middle class sisters, were confined by circumstances to household duties. In 1904 Miss Llewelyn Davies summarised the Guild's social composition:

> The members who form the Guild, are almost entirely married women belonging to the artisan class, and are associated, through their husbands and relatives, with all the prevailing trades of the localities in which the Guild branches are situated. We find husbands of Guild members among weavers, mechanics of every kind, miners, railwaymen, Co-operative employees, dock labourers, country labourers, bricksetters, printers, joiners; and every sort of miscellaneous tradesmen and worker is included — cement and quarry workers, warehousemen, draymen, not omitting chimney sweeps, gardeners, painters, van-drivers, coachmen, etc. It will thus be seen that the Guild stands ..... for the organised purchasing or consuming power of the working-class community of the country.
>
> As regards the Guild women themselves, a certain proportion, especially in Lancashire, work in the mills, while others go out to nurse, wash, clean, and some are teachers and dressmakers. But for the greatest number, their homes are their workshops.

A substantial proportion, probably the bulk, of Guild members were thus married to men who possessed a relatively high degree of occupational skill, the so-called labour aristocrats. Although the Industrial Revolution gave birth to the modern concept of social class, it did not immediately produce a sharply defined three tiered structure. Degrees of skill created a number of subtle distinctions within the working class as a whole which in turn were reflected in material conditions and future prospects. The economic growth of the nineteenth century supported an elite, perhaps ten per cent of all manual workers, who had higher and more regular earnings, men whose occupational scarcity not only protected them from all but the most severe economic fluctuations, but gave them the opportunity to develop the first national and effective trade unions. As regards both place of employment and residence, the labour aristocrats had an important degree of choice, but above all they regarded themselves as respectable and it was this respectability which separated them from the remainder of the working class. In terms of status, skilled artisans and their families merged with the lower level of the middle class and frequently enjoyed better financial circumstances and a more opulent standard of living.

The expansion of the metal and engineering trades in the last quarter of the nineteenth century created more opportunities for occupational and social mobility. However, the increase in purchasing power during the same period meant that all but the poorest sections of the working class enjoyed a prosperity never experienced before. From the 1870s, but more particularly the 1880s, cheap cereals and meat (aided by a fall in the cost of marine transport), flooded into Britain from the United States and elsewhere. This dragged down the cost of living and provided a growing margin of income for consumers to spend.

Working class prosperity in the 1880s, especially that experienced by the families of skilled men, is relevant to the Guild for two principal reasons: it allowed them to copy middle class modes of behaviour and it accentuated the economic power of consumers. The association of status with a leisured wife influenced working, as well as middle class, families and the growth of income made it possible for an increasing number of skilled men to cast their wives in the role of full-time homemaker. The late nineteenth century thus witnessed a further decline in the employment of married women, though marked regional variations occurred according to job availability. From the male point of view, this arrangement had the added benefit of increasing homely comforts since wives now had more time to devote to the domestic round. It probably meant too that more women felt the need for some activity outside the limited confines of the home, while for others more leisure time enabled them to pursue personal interests.

In the early 1880s there were relatively few opportunities for women to meet and enjoy the friendship of other women and the appearance of the Guild was in part a response to this social vacuum. In addition however, the growth of incomes accentuated women's basket power, making shopkeepers more sensitive to the wishes of their customers. In the last thirty years of the nineteenth century the number of shops increased by some 56 per cent, significantly greater than the rise in population. This was a period when growing competition between retailers forced them to resort to advertising and other promotional techniques in order to retain or increase their share

21

of a rapidly expanding consumer market. As the authority of purchasers increased, conditions developed for some form of consumers' organisation, and as the largest retail complex, with its special form of customer relationships, the Co-operative Movement was ideally suited to provide the necessary inspiration and organisation. The Guild was a product of many forces, but its creation owed much to the particular economic and social circumstances of the early 1880s.

Conclusion

The broad currents of change in the nineteenth century provide the framework against which the foundation and early development of the Guild may be understood. The motivation of individuals is more difficult to analyse, particularly in an organisation whose success depended upon the commitment of dozens, hundreds and eventually thousands of women whose activities for the most part went unrecorded. The study of history necessarily produces selected aspects of the past rather than the full canvas. However it is clear that many of the Guild's pioneers were inspired by some of the most profound intellectual debates of the nineteenth century. For example, the work of the early Christian Socialists was of great significance in the lives of Mary Lawrenson and Margaret Llewelyn Davies, while Sarah Reddish, the mill girl from Bolton who became Guild Organiser in 1893, was greatly influenced by the rekindling of socialism in the 1880s. Mrs Acland and Miss Tournier, the Guild's President in 1891 and 1892, saw it as a champion of women's rights, a role taken up with increasing enthusiasm towards the end of the century. If some Guild members were apathetic towards or unaware of the great political issues of the day, the majority valued the educative and social functions which their membership provided. For many, perhaps the bulk, of its members the Guild was more than the manifestation of theory or the utilitarianism of more effective shopping, it provided a unique retreat from the day to day tribulations of working class life. As Miss Llewelyn Davies put it

The testimonies of the health-giving properties of the Guild could almost rival those of Beecham's Pills.

The formation of the Women's Co-operative Guild and its ability during the period of its infancy to overcome a frequently hostile environment was a magnificent achievement. Yet in

1889, when Margaret Llewelyn Davies became General Secretary, its aims were still relatively modest and its future by no means secure. During the next twenty years it burgeoned into a powerful advocate of women's rights and its membership expanded rapidly to make it the most representative voice of working class female opinion. It is doubtful whether Mrs Acland or Mary Lawrenson appreciated the significance of their progeny at the time, but both deserve special recognition for their vision and humanity in giving so many women the chance to rise above the narrow confines of Victorian domestic life, while the members themselves merit praise in having the courage to seize the opportunity afforded to them.

Notes to Chapter 1

1. E. Sharp, Buyers and Builders (1933).
2. *Co-operative News,* 6th January 1883.
3. *Co-operative News,* 17th February 1883.
4. *Co-operative News,* 20th January 1883.
5. *Co-operative News,* 31st March 1883.
6. Mary Lawrenson Collection, Co-operative Union Library, Manchester.
7. B. Webb, My Apprenticeship (1926).
8. M.L. Davies, The Women's Co-operative Guild, 1883-1904 (Kirkby Lonsdale 1904).
9. C. Webb, The Woman with the Basket (Manchester 1927).
10. Mary Lawrenson Collection, op.cit.
11. Ibid.
12. *Co-operative News,* 6th January 1883.
13. Quoted by J.A. and O. Banks, Feminism and Family Planning in Victorian England (Liverpool 1964).
14. Sharp, op.cit.
15. Webb, op.cit.
16. Davies, op.cit.
17. C. Webb, Co-operation as Applied to Domestic Work (paper read at the Guild's Leicester Conference, 1893).
18. C. Webb, op.cit.
19. Ibid.
20. S. Reddish, The Right of Women to Membership of Co-operative Societies with Reference to Suplus Capital (Published by W.C.G. 1896).
21. Sharp, op.cit.

The Late Miss Greenwood,
Vice-President (Rochdale).

Mrs. M. Lawrenson
(Woolwich).

The Late
Mrs. B. Jones
(Norwood).

Mrs. Acland, *President.*

Miss Shufflebotham
(now Mrs. Trotman),
Treasurer (Coventry).

Mrs. Helliwell
(Hebden Bridge).

Miss Allen (now Mrs. Redfearn),
General Secretary, Manchester.

*The first Central Committee in 1884 includes
Mrs. Alice Acland, who was previously General
Secretary 1883/84, Miss Allen 1884/85 and
Mrs. M. Lawrenson, General Secretary 1885/89.*

Miss Margaret Llewelyn
Davies,
General Secretary
1889-1921

Mrs. Eleanor Barton,
General Secretary
1925-1937

Miss A. Honora Enfield
General Secretary
1921-1925

CHAPTER 2

MARGARET LLEWELYN DAVIES AND THE DRIVE TO MATURITY: 1889-1921

The Guild's Golden Age

Margaret Llewelyn Davies succeeded Mrs Lawrenson as the Guild's General Secretary in 1889. Her period of office, which lasted for 32 years, witnessed a rapid expansion of membership, from approximately 1,800 to over 51,000 while the number of branches increased from 51 to 1,077. Significantly, these years were also characterised by major innovations in the Guild's administrative structure, and by a pronounced radicalisation and broadening of its aims and activities. In many ways, this was the Guild's golden age when a whole series of issues of fundamental concern to women were debated and pressure applied to produce a society more responsive to the needs of women. It was a time of high excitement when the women's movement at last came to realise some of the fruits of its long and often bitter struggle. A number of circumstances contributed to the Guild's successful development during these years. The rise in membership, for example, was associated with the expansion of the Co-operative Movement itself, while external developments, such as the suffragette campaign, also served as catalysts of change. But Miss Llewelyn Davies herself made an enormous intellectual and practical contribution to the Guild's success, and her presence provided an important element of continuity within the organisation's leadership. The purpose of this chapter is to evaluate the Guild's structure and aims during this crucial period of its history, while the following chapter examines the issues and campaigns with which it became involved.

A cynic might argue that the numerically male dominated character of the Davies family, Margaret was outnumbered by her brothers six to one, was sufficient to thrust her into the women's movement, whereas in truth she benefited from a supportive atmosphere of advanced thought and social commitment. Two of her brothers, Crompton and Theodore, were friends of Bertrand Russell at Cambridge, who described them as 'able, high-minded and passionate.'[1] Theodore became

Private Secretary to a number of Conservative Chancellors of the Exchequer until in 1905, at the age of 34, he was tragically drowned in a swimming accident near Kirkby Lonsdale in Westmorland.

In common with his sister, Crompton had strong views on the role of the state. While rejecting socialism and supporting capitalist free enterprise, he attacked monopoly power, believing in the overriding importance of an environment which allowed free rein to the energy of the individual. In his economic and political thinking, Crompton was in many senses a typical product of the nineteenth century laissez-faire philosophy. However, he also believed that society had a responsibility to champion the rights of the disadvantaged and in this respect he was strongly interventionist. Bertrand Russell said of him that 'he was a crusade in himself, for Ireland against England, for small business against big, for the have-nots against the haves, for competition against monopoly.' It is difficult to imagine that a man of such ability and passion, as well as wit and humour, had anything but a stimulating effect upon his sister, even if she did not always agree with what he had to say!

Yet the overwhelming male influence in Miss Llewelyn Davies' life was almost certainly her father, the Reverend John Llewelyn Davies, for some time Rector of Christ Church in Marylebone, London, before moving north in 1889 to the parish of Kirkby Lonsdale. John Llewelyn Davies was a man of considerable intellect, a translator of Plato's Republic, and a strong advocate of Christian Socialism. He was a Broad Churchman whose liberal views, derived in particular from Frederick Denison Maurice, were said to have restricted his progress within the church. Maurice was one of the most significant contributors to the Christian Socialist movement of the mid-nineteenth century, and indeed its theology largely derived from his teaching. He rejected the Victorian attempt to restrict religion to narrow issues of individual morality and personal salvation, arguing that the church should concern itself with the secular world and the condition of society at large. In this respect, Maurice's influence may be detected in the growing concern of many late nineteenth century churchmen with matters of social welfare, particularly the plight of the poor. Maurice's essential humanitarianism, like that of other Christian Socialists of his period, came to influence the development of the Co-operative Movement at large.

According to Catherine Webb, John Llewelyn Davies shared in this contribution for he was 'one of the band of Christian Socialists whose ideals had helped so largely to shape the spirit, if not the actual organisation, of modern Co-operation.'

Other members of Miss Llewelyn Davies' family also no doubt contributed to her intellectual development and the formation of her attitudes. One of her aunts was Emily Davies, the founder of Girton College, Cambridge, at which Margaret was herself a student, while an uncle was an ardent supporter of the women's suffrage movement and a friend of John Stuart Mill. Emily Davies was one of the most prominent and dedicated of Victorian feminists. She was for a time associated in a literary capacity with the "English Woman's Journal", though her principal interest was the promotion of equality of educational opportunity for women.

Miss Llewelyn Davies enjoyed a sheltered but highly stimulating upbringing. She was an intellectual, but also highly practical, and possessed the gift of mixing happily with all social classes. She was clearly an outstanding personality, shown by her meteoric rise in the Guild: in the space of two years from branch to General Secretary. She was still only in her late twenties when she assumed responsibility for the second phase of the Guild's development, but she approached her task with a high degree of intellectual and emotional maturity, qualities that were to serve her well during the next three decades. G.D.H. Cole, the historian of the Co-operative Movement, acknowledged that: 'In terms of personal quality and disinterested idealism, Margaret Llewelyn Davies is, to my thinking, by far the greatest woman who has been actively identified with the British Co-operative Movement. From the moment when she assumed control of the affairs of the Co-operative Women's Guild it began to become a really powerful progressive force.'[2] Miss Llewelyn Davies was also highly popular among guildswomen, regularly topping the poll in votes cast for membership of the Central Committee, some margin ahead of her nearest rivals.

When her retirement was announced in 1921 she received a flood of letters which conveyed a mixture of shock and dismay. Many correspondents said quite plainly that they simply could not conceive of the Guild without her, whilst most found it difficult to conceal their sense of personal loss. At the Port Clarence branch Miss Llewelyn Davies' resignation was 'read

27

out among tears' and its Secretary, Mrs Ethel Duffy, perhaps voiced the feelings of Guild members in general when she said that

> Although to many of us you are known only by your work and name, it is enough to inspire us with the Co-operative Spirit & Ideals you so nobly stand for.[3]

Part of the reason for Miss Llewelyn Davies' popularity among Guild members was the obvious energy and enthusiasm which she brought to her work. The histories of individual Co-operative societies reveal that she travelled extensively in all parts of the country, meeting members and promoting the Guild's activities. Although not a natural orator — she had to prepare her speeches carefully in advance — Miss Llewelyn Davies was capable of rousing an audience and winning its admiration and affection. One member recalled hearing the General Secretary speak at a meeting in Liverpool, commenting that

> I came home full of the Guild and my love for it has never waned.[4]

Guildswomen with whom she came into contact, whether at public lectures or less formal gatherings, must have been impressed by her striking presence for she was a tall, gracious woman, with a deep pleasant voice and a strong personality. Yet Miss Llewelyn Davies' influence must have derived in large measure from her written output, which was not only prodigious in scale, but carefully researched and closely argued. Her reports and discussion papers were a model of clarity and persuasive argument and in this way she reached a much larger proportion of members than was possible through public speaking engagements. Mabel Ridealgh, who joined the Guild in the early 1920s, told the authors that Miss Llewelyn Davies was very good at explaining things in a straightforward and down-to-earth manner. One of the most fascinating aspects of the Guild's history is that some very complex issues were communicated, apparently with considerable success, to an audience whose educational background was at best moderate and at worst almost non-existent. This would not have been possible without the verbal and literary qualities of women such as Margaret Llewelyn Davies.

Miss Llewelyn Davies' appointment as General Secretary coincided with her father's move to Kirkby Lonsdale so that in 1889 the Guild office was transferred from the south of England to Westmorland, where it remained until the family returned to London in 1908. Sarah Reddish recorded that when she first visited Kirkby Lonsdale

> *I was soon introduced to the guild office, where there are letters, papers, and work almost unlimited in amount to be attended to daily on behalf of the guild.*[5]

It seems remarkable that it was not until 1906 that the Guild employed an office clerk. However, Miss Llewelyn Davies was greatly assisted by the practical and organising capacities of her friend over many years, Lilian Harris, who became the Guild's Cashier in 1893 and served as its Assistant Secretary from 1901-1921. Miss Harris soon came to supervise the whole of the Guild machinery and her special knowledge was put to particular use in 1912 when the General Secretary's illness kept her from the office for several months. Neither Miss Llewelyn Davies nor Miss Harris was paid, which was itself a valuable contribution to the Guild's financial health, particularly in its early days when it was desperately short of funds. Miss Llewelyn Davies felt strongly that administrative duties should be undertaken on a voluntary basis, believing this to be an integral part of the Guild's democratic structure, though she apparently failed to appreciate that this precluded less financially independent women from standing for office.

The Guild's First Employees

In 1893 Miss Sarah Reddish became the Guild's first paid employee when she was appointed Guild Organiser at a salary of £1 per week, plus expenses. The minutes of the Central Committee reveal that a 'friend of the Guild' donated £100 to assist with the work of organising its activities. However, since the 'friend' in question was Miss Llewelyn Davies' mother, it seems likely that the gift was intended to relieve her daughter of some of the more burdensome administrative tasks, particularly that of promoting branch formation, in order to allow her to concentrate more fully upon the problems of management and the formulation of policy. Miss Reddish was a conscientious employee, fully committed to the Guild's aims and activities. Her work involved long hours and a great deal of travel. In one period of twelve months between 1894 and 1895 she attended over 100 Guild meetings, a formidable task at a time when transport facilities, though improving rapidly, were still far from perfect. Miss Llewelyn Davies said of her that she was one of the organisation's 'most honoured names' who contributed 'much to the progress of the Guild, to the increase in branches, and the improving quality of their work.'

Miss Reddish was succeeded in 1895 by Miss Mayo, a prominent member of the Huddersfield branch. Again Miss Llewelyn Davies was full of praise for her contribution to the Guild's welfare, commenting in particular upon her great enthusiasm and perseverance despite 'wearing journeys, and varying fortunes and misfortunes.' The anecdotes which follow belong to Miss Mayo and, although fairly long, are worth quoting since they bring to life the experiences of the many women, including Miss Llewelyn Davies, who were prepared to devote their time and energy (frequently in the most adverse circumstances), to the promotion and consolidation of the Guild and its work

> *Once upon a time I was drawn by a pony, I hardly think it could have been a Co-operative one, that ambled at the pace of a goat, taking an hour and a half for six miles, and that insisted on stopping at each public-house we passed. Wet driving snow was falling, and on arriving at the station I looked like Lot's wife; from the shawl over my head to my feet I was white. Before I could thaw or scrape the snow off, my train came up, and I had several hours' journey to the next meeting, after which I was nursing a cold for a fortnight.*
>
> *Another day, while trudging two miles from tram to meeting one dark winter's night, and while being guided across a ploughed field by way of a short cut, the bottom came out of the slide box, and all the slides slithered down among the furrows. Whenever I miss one, I always think it must have been lost then.*

And here is another experience:-

> *On visiting a town to speak at a branch in a new locality on its outskirts, I took the tram bearing the name of the suburb, and I alighted at the terminus in a dark residential quarter. When I asked for the Store it was pointed out to me in the distance, on the other side of a large sheet of water. The floods were out, and I ought to have taken a tram to the further and higher side, but no one had thought of mentioning it. It was late, and there was not time to go all the way back again. There were no cabs, and the nearest stand was a mile away. The water appeared to be six or eight inches deep; piles of stones, sticks, and a shed or two, and other signs of building, stood out of it. I inquired for a cart, but they had all gone away for the night. At last after much persuasion, a coke merchant at the corner of the street was*

induced to lend his coster's cart. A pony was produced from an outhouse, an orange box put up for me to sit on, and then, clasping my slides tightly, we started. It was just like going out to sea in a bathing machine. We bumped and splashed over stones and into holes, but at last arrived, and found all the audience on the pavement watching my progress with excitement, and wondering why I had chosen that route.[6]

The Guild and its Officers

In 1888 the Guild decided that, with the exception of the General Secretary, members of the Central Committee should hold office for a maximum of three years before retiring for a period of at least twelve months, a practice which also came to be followed by several branches. This was consistent with the Guild's democratic spirit, but it did result in a fairly rapid turnover of officials and a consequent loss of administrative talent and experience. A further consequence, however, was that for the vast bulk of its members Miss Llewelyn Davies came to personify the Guild and its activities simply because over the years she was the one national official to provide continuity. Moreover, as her experience increased, her stature and authority were also likely to overshadow those of her colleagues on the Central Committee. Perhaps it was for this reason that, when the occasion demanded, her diplomatic skills were employed in mediating between the Central Committee and the Sections. In the days before the use of the telephone became widespread, the location of the Guild office in a relatively remote area helped to facilitate Miss Llewelyn Davies' writing and perhaps protect her from excessive bureaucratic intrusion. It also released the Guild from its early association with London and Oxford.

One of the consequences of moving the office to Kirkby Lonsdale was that the number of branches and Guild membership in the north increased quite rapidly. More generally, the growing strength of the Guild during the late nineteenth and early twentieth centuries was related to the efficiency which Miss Llewelyn Davies brought to her work. There is clear indication that one of the reasons for Mrs Lawrenson's retirement from the General Secretaryship was that she found it increasingly difficult to cope with a set of administrative duties which expanded daily. Miss Amy Sharp

31

spoke plainly when in February 1889 she informed Mrs Lawrenson by letter that:

> It appears to me that you have double too much on your hands, and that this whirl of meetings is incompatible with the Secretarial work proper. I fully recognise the value to the Guild of your gifts of speech, but the attempt to combine functions seems rather disastrous.[7]

Mrs. Lawrenson's independent approach also brought a pointed rebuke from Edith Wilson, author of one of the Guild's early histories, who reminded her that it was not the function of the Secretary

> to have ideas and start new plans as to be the servant of the existing members of the Society.[8]

Miss Llewelyn Davies was also fond of pursuing her own inclinations but she was a more practical and well organised woman, quite capable of taking both the membership and her committee with her.

Mrs Lawrenson was plainly vexed at the circumstances of her departure from the Secretaryship and this surfaced in a petulant and rather sad note to Miss Llewelyn Davies which she wrote shortly before the Guild's Manchester festival in 1892.

> Since you brought forward (I suppose it was **your** proposal) the suggestion of a 'big' meeting of the Guild, I would have thought that really the Festival would have offered a fine opportunity for such a meeting. Of course I don't suppose you will take any notice of the suggestion. I simply mention it here, as I should have done long ago, had any expression of opinion been asked from me.[9]

These comments reflect Mrs Lawrenson's personal bitterness, but they also demonstrate the growing influence which Miss Llewelyn Davies was already exerting over the Guild's activities. Mrs Lawrenson's formal involvement with the construction of Guild policy was brought to a conclusion in 1893 when she lost her place on the Central Committee. She remained popular with guildswomen, though even in old age she was a subject of controversy to the national leadership. In 1931 the Central Committee received a number of letters suggesting that she should be offered the freedom of the Guild, but refused on the rather dubious grounds that 'she had not given many years continuous national service to the Guild'. However, in the face of strong pressure from the membership, the Committee eventually capitulated and Mrs Lawrenson's new status was duly conferred at the 1931 Congress.

Social Class and the Guild Leadership

Mrs Lawrenson's contretemps in the late 1880s with other prominent members of the Guild's hierarchy also raised another important issue, namely the relationship between a strongly middle class leadership and a predominantly working class membership. Mrs Lawrenson's personal papers again provide evidence of the tensions which occasionally surfaced. For example, she became increasingly irritated by the treatment she received from Miss Amy Sharp in her capacity as editor of the "Corner", complaining in 1888 that

> *I appreciate as highly as it is possible to do the presence of*
> *educated women amongst us, but I am not disposed to place*
> *myself in the position of "Your humble obedient servant".*[10]

One of the most important reasons for Miss Llewelyn Davies' success as General Secretary was her ability to relate to working class women, among whom she had many close friends, and to understand their problems. She was not patronising and her genuine pleasure at meeting with and helping less privileged women must have communicated itself to her working class sisters. Her obvious delight at returning to the experimental Co-operative store in Sunderland which catered specifically for the poorer sections of the working class, and which she had helped to establish, is reflected in the following passage from May, 1903.

> *As I came down the street on my arrival, I could not fail to*
> *notice that no other shop in the street could boast of awnings,*
> *and our gay striped window shades were most conspicuous. The*
> *usual groups of children were playing at the corner, and when*
> *they recognised me I was soon surrounded by an excited little*
> *crowd that quite blocked our doorway for some minutes. But*
> *very soon I was busily at work, visiting my own street again,*
> *helping at the various meetings, or sitting at the desk.*

Yet Miss Llewelyn Davies was aware of the reality of the Guild's middle class leadershp and the problems which could ensue from it. In a most revealing and candid passage in her Guild History she writes of those women with time at their disposal, who are connected with the Guild as

> *Editors of "Women's Corner", as Organising Secretaries and as*
> *occasional Branch Presidents or Secretaries .....whose*
> *sympathies attracted them to a working class organisation rather*
> *than to philanthropic work. These women must stand for*
> *election on equal footing with other members and must identify*

themselves with working-class interests, and come as interpreters of the needs and wishes of the workers. The Guild does not seek outsiders of 'position' to preside over its functions or direct its councils.

No doubt some working class women resented Miss Llewelyn Davies' status and financial security but the overwhelming majority probably agreed with the correspondent who in 1921 praised her for having

found out our capabilities and drawn them out without us knowing it.

At a more practical level, others would have accepted the view of another admirer that the Guild's success

would not have been possible without strong personalities at the head.[12]

Miss Llewelyn Davies was not only profoundly committed to enhancing the dignity of all women, but she was also far too radical to join that army of middle class ladies narrowly motivated, in the judgement of Beatrice Webb, by a 'class consciousness of sin'.

The Guild's Administrative Structure

One of the Guild's most impressive achievements was to build an administrative structure which welded together the interests and ambitions of thousands of women distributed throughout the entire country. As Laurie Pavitt MP said to the authors,

The foundations were built to last.

To begin with, the Guild's administration was simple and was conducted in a relatively informal manner. As membership increased and its activities and objectives broadened, it became necessary to strengthen the organisation's management structure and its way of working. This was a formidable task for women who were largely unschooled in organising. As Miss Webb noted:

Amendments to rules have been responsible for a 'certain liveliness' at more annual meetings and congresses than any other topic of discussion, and it has not infrequently fallen to my lot to help pilot changes of rules through Congresses which seemed capable of reaching the maximum of muddled misunderstanding.

Indeed the Guild owed a substantial debt of gratitude to Catherine Webb for her patient and thorough compilation and revision of the rules of the Guild. For her part, Miss Webb, who was an expert on the structure of the Co-operative Movement, benefited from the guidance of her father, a Director of the Co-operative Wholesale Society, and from her family's long association with the Co-operative society in Battersea. This reinforces the important point made earlier that the Guild's formation and development was inextricably linked to the Co-operative Movement which, in this case, provided the administrative model upon which Miss Webb and others could base their constructions.

Rules for the guidance of the Central Committee and model rules for the assistance of branches were formulated in 1885. The major administrative innovation, however, occurred in 1889 when it was decided to sub-divide the organisation into sections and districts, the areas chosen being those of the Co-operative Union. Miss Webb attributed this development to the pressures created by a rising membership and the advent of Miss Llewelyn Davies as General Secretary. In practice, credit should also go to Mrs Lawrenson who as early as May 1888 informed Miss Llewelyn Davies that

I think the time has come when some advanced reorganisation might be attempted — and the Guild divided — either into Sections with officers in each Section responsible for local work — or divided according to lines of work as above or perhaps both could be arranged.[13]

The administrative areas established in the 1890s were subsequently modified until by 1915 seven sections, corresponding to the structure of the Co-operative Union, supervised the Guild's activities. Although both section and district boundaries were subsequently modified, the pattern established by the early twentieth century has remained the basis of the Guild's administrative framework. In 1981 Congress rejected proposals to change this basic framework.

Mrs Benjamin Jones, President from 1886-91, and Miss Llewelyn Davies seem to have shared responsibility for introducing the notion of Guild conferences. Mrs Jones was a popular figure within the Guild and her premature death in 1894 provoked widespread sorrow. Her contribution to the Guild's work was commemorated the following year by the inauguration of the "Mrs Jones Convalescent Fund" (see Appendix 1), which was designed to finance periods of rest and recuperation for sick guildswomen. The Guild's first annual meeting was held in tandem with the Co-operative Congress of 1885. In 1893 the Guild took the significant step of holding its own separate meeting, an important innovation which symbolised its independence within the Movement. The annual conference became the focus of Guild policy-making, though in practice the Central Committee exercised enormous influence.

One of the most important aspects of the Guild's national and sectional conferences was the sense of occasion they provided to the delegates and to guildswomen in general who read in the "Corner" and later the "Wheatsheaf" of important decisions taken and campaigns mounted. The national conferences provided the Guild with a focus of attention and contributed to its unity of purpose. They were also a marvellous social event for those women fortunate enough to attend in person, and, as Catherine Webb pointed out in 1927,

Every year, even today, there are delegates who have never before left their homes and families, and quite a number who have never been so far from home in all their lives.

The keynote of the Guild's administrative structure was democratic participation since branches, districts and sections were all governed by committees elected from among the membership, while for their part members were expected to contribute to the effective operation of the organisations to which they were attached. The overall control of the Guild rested with the annual meeting, which in 1900 formally assumed the status of Congress. The Central Committee was the Guild's executive arm and comprised seven members elected by the branches. According to Miss Llewelyn Davies,

The object aimed at in this organisation is healthy independence in local work, combined with response from the centre. When the Guild was started, the only regular meetings which working women used to attend were of a religious or philanthropic character — "mothers' meetings" — where the promoters might be described as working for and not with the people, and where no ideas of working women's rights and wrongs or of their citizenship, ever crept in.

One of the great achievements of the Guild was to promote the feeling, which became widespread among members, that their participation in its activities bestowed on them an equality of status and a greater sense of personal dignity. As one pioneer member noted, the outstanding feature of the Guild was

its splendid democracy, for the humblest member can feel that she stands on an absolute equality with the most lofty.

36

Although the Guild's constituent elements enjoyed a significant measure of autonomy, in practice the Central Committee exercised a strong controlling influence. Miss Webb hinted at this in her Guild History when, with tongue in cheek, she noted thàt

> The period covered by the present record ends in 1927 with 1,227 branches, a live and active body of 57,874 guildswomen effectively organised into eight sectional and 50 district areas, all circulating, like moon and stars, round the centralising and animating forces emanating from the General Secretary and Central Committee.

Perhaps this was alien to the Guild's democratic spirit, but it did introduce an important element of discipline and uniformity which was necessary for stability in such a diffuse organisation. It also strengthened its position as a force for social reform since it meant that all its elements were normally pushing in the same direction. One of its great strengths as a reformist body was the Guild's concentration upon specific issues at particular times which meant that its energies were not dissipated in unplanned adventures, but rather channelled to where they could be used most effectively. As one Guild member expressed it

> we must conserve our energy for the really important things and not allow it to be dissipated by trying to do a little of everything.[14]

A good example of the practical implementation of this strategy occurred in 1911 in connection with the campaign for maternity benefit.

For six weeks the energy of the Guild was thrown into the work. Branches showered resolutions on their MPs, Guild members worked hard in the lobbies securing support, and attended the meetings of the Standing Committee.[15]

Despite the enthusiasm of the majority of its members, the Guild has always encountered a number of obstacles, some of which have threatened its very existence. The often virulent male opposition of the pioneer days has already been recounted, but another serious, if less vocal, problem was that of weak or even non-existent leadership at branch level. This manifested itself in a variety of ways, the most extreme of which was inadequate branch formation in areas where well established Co-operative societies apparently provided a fertile source of recruitment. For example, in 1904 the Northern Section contained 154 Co-operative societies and yet could muster only 24 branches. According to Mrs McBlain, the Guild's President at the time,

> *The reason for so few branches is not, perhaps, so much the fault of the women, who are willing to become members, but rather of the fact that so few women are sufficiently interested and willing to take the position of secretary, which is the most important office for the successful working of the branch.*[16]

It is interesting to note that in the 1960s and 1970s branches began to close because of inability to find members willing to accept official positions with the branch.

Petty squabbling was a less serious aspect of leadership failure, but was one which could nevertheless have a destructive influence. Thus it was reported in the early 'nineties that the Plumstead branch in South London worked smoothly because the members pulled harmoniously together, but the Secretary of the South Metropolitan District added flatly that not all branches worked with the same spirit.[17]

An indication of how seriously the Guild regarded the efficient conduct of secretarial duties was provided in 1909 when the Central Committee responded to the alleged incompetence of one of the Sectional Secretaries by authorising Miss Llewelyn Davies to write to her

> *asking her to resign, saying that we should be obliged to point out her inability to Branches, if she declined.*

Yet the most common problems were those of poor attendance and fluctuating membership. Miss Reddish reported in 1893 that as Guild Organiser she had spoken at many meetings where the audience was disappointingly thin. Sometimes this reflected an apathetic membership rather than an incompetent administration.

> *At Walkden, on March 29th, I had my first experience of going to a place and having no audience, in spite of a thousand handbills having been distributed. Only five persons were present, and these represented the two families of the president and secretary of the society.*[18]

Sometimes local membership became so small that disaffiliation occurred and by the close of the nineteenth century about a dozen branches a year suffered this fate. However, this was more than compensated for by the creation of new branches. In 1921, the year of Miss Llewelyn Davies' retirement, six branches ceased to exist but approximately 150 new ones were in the course of formation or had already been affiliated. Indeed by 1910 recruitment was so healthy that the

Central Committee could afford to double the minimum number required for affiliation from ten to twenty members.

In part, the Guild's administrative network was specifically intended to remedy the problems associated with a fluctuating and sometimes indifferent membership. Thus in reporting the structural innovations in 1889, the Annual Report explained that

> We hoped by placing a secretary over each section and district that the number of our branches might increase more rapidly, that more help might be given to those already in existence, and that a more vigorous joint life might be secured.

Yet the directing influence of the Central Committee was of paramount importance in the attempt to produce a more vigorous Women's Co-operative Guild. Membership was stimulated in a variety of ways. For example, flourishing branches were encouraged to act as missionaries, promoting the Guild's activities in less responsive areas. The Jubilee History of the Bridge End branch illustrates how successful this practice could be.

> In September, 1893, a visit was paid to Bridge End by Miss Bamford, of Manchester, accompanied by Mrs Crossley, Miss Clegg, and others, from the Todmorden Society, where a branch of the Guild was already established. Miss Bamford spoke on the duties of women to the Store, and showed how opportunities were lost to them from defective organisation. The enthusiasm of these women for the Guild as a means of educating and increasing their interest in Co-operation resulted in the formation of a branch at Bridge End.[19]

A more forceful method of recruitment introduced in 1895 was that of house-to-house canvassing. The Annual Report for that year records that 45 branches were involved in the initial campaign, with the most dramatic success being achieved at Accrington where membership zoomed from 190 to 537. One of the Central Committee's most sophisticated approaches to recruitment concerned the attempt to publicise the Guild's work among trade unionists, a section of the working class movement which was itself expanding rapidly in the last two decades of the nineteenth century. In September 1890 the Committee decided to make

> a special effort to spread our work among trade unionists' wives, and women trade unionists, by means of meetings arranged if possible by Educational committees and Guild branches.

This became official policy at the annual conference in 1892 and, apart from its impact upon recruitment, helped bring the Guild and sections of the trade union movement into a fairly close working relationship.

As its activities assumed a more complex form, the Guild's progress became increasingly dependent upon adequate financial support. Donations and fund raising programmes, including the sale of postcard portraits of Miss Llewelyn Davies, helped to keep the Guild afloat, but membership fees represented the principal source of income. However, the Central Committee had to contend with the fact that branches and their members did not always show unqualified enthusiasm for meeting their annual subscriptions. In 1894 the Committee simplified the Guild's accounts by basing subscriptions upon the calendar rather than financial year. They also attempted to increase the proportion of income received on time by making the right to vote dependent upon monies received in the previous, rather than current year. With the boom in recruitment during the late nineteenth and early twentieth centuries, financial problems abated, and in 1903 the Guild was even able to establish a special fund to assist weak branches. Even so, the Minutes of the General Committee indicate that inadequate resources restricted its activities and remained one of the Guild's major headaches that even Miss Llewelyn Davies, portraits and all, could not cure.

The most important way in which the Central Committee came to impose its stamp upon guildswomen was through its authority to determine the topics for debate by the sections and branches. Reinforced by the Guild's educational and publications programme, this placed the Central Committee in a unique position to direct and influence both the members' interests and the policies adopted by Congress. To begin with, branches enjoyed complete autonomy in the conduct of their meetings, but according to Miss Webb this liberalism soon proved counter-productive since it frequently gave rise to rather aimless and mundane discussion.

In 1889, however, the Central Committee issued its first Winter Circular in which it was recommended that branches study Arnold Forster's Laws of Everyday Life, thus setting the precedent of centralised control over branch meetings. This practice was reinforced three years later when the Winter Circular for 1892 announced the publication of 'Guild Popular

Papers', obtainable on loan from the General Secretary, to serve as a basis for discussion throughout the movement. These arrangements appear to have been accepted without significant local dissent, though some women may have relinquished their Guild membership rather than face the demands of a more structured and challenging experience.

In 1910, however, it came to the attention of the Central Committee that some sections were debating issues other than those on the official programme and it was decided to remind section councils that while they were entitled to recommend topics for conference discussion, the ultimate choice of both subject and speaker rested with the central administration. It was also to be pointed out that:

> as a rule, the same subject will be taken throughout the Guild, because experience has shown (1) that this is the most effective plan for securing that unity of action which is part of the strength of the Guild's work, (2) that it secures discussion of progressive subjects in every section, and (3) that it greatly lessens the cost of printing papers.

In general, during Miss Llewelyn Davies' period of office the Central Committee seems to have taken a firm line with recalcitrant branches and sections, even when this resulted in some loss of membership.

Ideas and Policies

Miss Llewelyn Davies' appointment in 1889 as General Secretary was an important turning point in the Guild's administrative development, but even more significant was her profound impact upon policy, which she both broadened and radicalised. The liberalism and strength of her intellectual development, allied to a passionate admiration for the ideas and practical achievements of the Co-operative pioneers, made Margaret Llewelyn Davies one of the outstanding social commentators of her day. She was an ardent believer in the importance of human dignity and devoted her life to constructing a society in which women enjoyed not only personal development and happiness, but economic, social and political equality. These aims were to be realised through the twin vehicles of the state and the Co-operative Movement.

Although sympathetic to many of the aims of late nineteenth century socialism, Miss Llewelyn Davies rejected as essentially

41

undemocratic a social and economic system dominated by the intrusive power of the state. She believed that government should be used discriminately to protect individual freedoms and to remedy social evils. Thus in connection with the campaign for maternity benefits, the theme of her policy was that

> *charity and philanthropy will be expected to make way for national provision.*[20]

Yet the central feature of Miss Llewelyn Davies' economic and social philosophy was her interpretation of the Co-operative ideal which, she believed, was capable of producing a fundamentally democratic and harmonious society. Thus she argued in 1890 that a democratic industrial structure should be the root of modern Co-operation, for it would lead to a more equitable distribution of wealth and

> *the production of it without the warfare in the industrial world.*[21]

She admitted at the time that the structural framework for this development had not yet presented itself and, though she always remained rather vague on this, she did come to argue that the socialised control of money power was a fundamental precondition of a Co-operative economic structure. In common with many other Co-operative pioneers, Miss Llewelyn Davies was a revolutionary, but she was also a great humanitarian and at heart a pacifist. Indeed her influence was a major factor in the campaign for peace and international harmony which formed such an important aspect of the Guild's work during the 1920s and 1930s. Although prepared against the background of economic decline and social decay, the passage below, which was written after her retirement, neatly encapsulates Miss Llewelyn Davies' views on the process of social change which she held during the whole of her adult life.

> *Capitalism and Class Society have broken down. They have to go, and their place has to be taken by the Rule of the People. And we Co-operators believe that Co-operation is the way we can secure this revolution without bloodshed. And think what power our United Women can have! Through our baskets, through our municipal and parliamentary votes, through refusing to be carried away by scares and panics, we can and must dismiss armed force as a means to the Co-operative Commonwealth.*[22]

Miss Llewelyn Davies was a complex mixture of Owenite idealism and Rochdale pragmatism. She had, in the words of Miss Clara Collet, one of the Board of Trade's first women officials, "the finest vision before her of any woman of my time".

Miss Llewelyn Davies identified a more substantial role for the Co-operative ideal than did the Co-operative Union itself, and one of the Guild's major accomplishments between 1889 and 1921 was that it became the most progressive and intellectually fertile element within the Movement as a whole. Indeed its radical medicine for social evils was something which the Union occasionally found difficult to swallow, and in 1914 the Guild's President and General Secretary voiced their frustration at this by complaining that

> even in our strictly Co-operative campaigns, on behalf of anti-credit, extension of co-operation to the poor, minimum wage, it has seemed often as if the official movement preferred us to work apart.[23]

The Guild's founding pioneers identified as its prime objective the dissemination of Co-operative principles and practice. This was reflected in the published aims of the Women's League for the Spread of Co-operation which appeared in the "Co-operative News" in May 1883.

1. To spread the advantages of Co-operation.
2. To stimulate among those who know its advantages a greater interest in the principles of Co-operation.
3. To stir up and keep alive in ourselves, in our neighbours, and especially in the rising generation, a more earnest appreciation of the value of Co-operation to ourselves, to our children, and to the nation.

Some branches adopted these precepts with enthusiasm. In Coventry, for example, Miss Shufflebotham, the local Secretary, explained in 1886 that the aim of her branch was

> to gain a greater knowledge of Co-operation, and to do our best to spread this knowledge among others so that we may become more united and useful to each other in self-help and independence.[24]

Moreover, from their earliest days some branches developed the theme of basket power, often taking an independent and sometimes highly critical view of their parent society. However, some practices quickly attracted criticism from the Guild's national leadership, particularly the provision of coal clubs, clothing clubs and sick visitors, since these, it was said, were more appropriate to the generalised activities of mothers' meetings. In practice, the nature and quality of branch life must have varied enormously according to the members' inclinations and abilities, though the Guild's first Winter Circular detected in 1889 a distressing tendency for some meetings to descend into mere sewing classes. This was soon to change, however, since, as Catherine Webb noted,

From now onward we see the guiding hand of Miss Davies in turning the attention of the guildswomen more and more definitely towards specialised studies on practical social reforms, and gently, but persistently, pushing into the background the popular domestic subjects and occupations.

The impact of this change may be illustrated by reference to the Winter Circular of 1895 which contained a list of 73 topics, complete with lecturers, recommended for discussion at branch level. Many of the subjects, 'Sick Nursing' or 'The Life and Times of George Eliot' were of a domestic or cultural nature, but others were firmly geared towards a better understanding of the social, economic and political environment. Thus members were able to benefit from talks on:

Women's Work in Local Government
Women's Present Position, Social and Political
Women as Factory Inspectors
Robert Owen's Influence and Work at New Lanark
Women and Labour Legislation
Women's Suffrage
Women's Trade Unions
Technical Education for Girls
Women as Poor Law Guardians
Explanation of Factory and Workshop Acts
Deductions from Wages and the Trade Act

The effect at local level of the new emphasis in educational work was recorded by the historian of the Coventry Co-operative Society who noted in 1917 that the branch had relinquished sewing and similar domestically orientated classes and

an entirely educative Co-operative work is aimed at, such questions as the abolition of credit trading and entrance fees, women's work on committees, suffrage and divorce law reform receiving consideration at the guild meetings.

The revised approach to Guild meetings must have been a wonderfully liberating experience for many women. As one of Miss Llewelyn Davies' admirers reflected in 1921

I often wonder what my life would have been but for the Guild, and its influence.[25]

However, few women could have the commitment of one member in the Midlands who appears to have surprised even the usually unflappable General Secretary for

She had read through the whole of Henry George's "Progress and Poverty" while she nursed her baby, and had herself written to the late William Morris to ask him to come and address a meeting in her village, and knew the writings of Edward Carpenter.[26]

There was, of course, an alternative response to the challenge of a more demanding and politically focused Guild. Some branches, for example, refused to discuss certain controversial issues, such as credit trading and divorce law reform, while others wanted to keep to Co-operation pure and simple. Miss Llewelyn Davies reported in 1893 that

The Suffrage is barred out by one or two Branches, and I have even heard of two or three members walking out when it was decided to read a paper on the White Slave Traffic.[27]

The Annual Report for 1890 drew attention to another common problem, that of stimulating interest in topics which appeared unexciting or intellectually taxing:

One of the most common difficulties is found in trying to arouse the interest of members in anything of at all a serious character. They have a great distaste for what they consider "dull and dry". We have to face the fact that Co-operation and all economic subjects are difficult, and require thought and attention.

To some extent these problems were alleviated as Forster's Education Act of 1870 took effect, and also by the collective efforts of the women themselves, though in practice the Central Committee appears to have been unconcerned by any loss of membership which resulted from the new policies.

Mrs Acland recalled how in the Guild's early days controversy surrounded the question of whether or not its members should engage in public speaking. She noted that

Mrs Lawrenson, Mrs Jones, who followed me as president, Miss Webb and others were in favour of public speaking, while I, because of the necessity I felt at this stage of conciliating those kindly folks who were afraid of women speaking in public, had to take the other side.[28]

Mrs Acland was defeated on this particular issue and public speaking became an important part of the Guild's training programme and its work as a reformist body. One of the reasons for the stand taken by Mrs Lawrenson and her supporters was that many of the Guild's pioneers were exceptionally talented communicators. Mrs Lawrenson was herself soon noted for her beautiful delivery and elegant language, while the magnetic eloquence of Miss Tournier and Miss Llewelyn Davies inspired enthusiasm whenever their voices were heard. More particularly, however, if women were to be influential within the Co-operative societies and supportive of the Labour movement in general, it was necessary for them to voice their opinions and to do so in an intelligent and convincing manner.

Preparation for public speaking began at branch level. This aspect of the Guild's work naturally caused trepidation in the hearts of some women, and one member recalled how, at her first speaking engagement, she was almost frightened to death.[29]

This was an enduring problem for guildswomen and some forty years later Mrs Gwendoline Teather remembered

the first time I had to make a speech at a Guild dinner, and I sat near the mayor — I was dumbstruck till I thought to myself, he's just a human being like me.

Yet in time, the countless women who spoke on the Guild's behalf came to make an invaluable contribution to the articulation of women's rights, both within and beyond the Co-operative Movement.

Although some women must have rejected the rigour of Henry George and William Carpenter and the ordeal of public debate, Miss Llewelyn Davies regarded the Guild's educational and training programmes as justifying its very existence. Part of her rationale for this was that she regarded serious debate as essential to the Guild's good health at branch level, arguing that it was the breadth of interest which kept the members fully alive, intelligent and open to the best Co-operative thought and work.[30]

More particularly, education contributed to the intellectual and emotional maturity of each member, which was both desirable in itself, but crucial to the Guild's success as an advocate of women's rights. Margaret Bondfield, for a time one of Miss Llewelyn Davies' closest colleagues in the Guild, summarised this position when in 1914 she explained that

An intelligent, educated motherhood, free to co-operate with and use civil and political forces, will strike at the root causes of many of our social ills.[31]

Miss Llewelyn Davies' redirection of the Guild after 1889 may have been viewed by some members with incomprehension, anxiety or even outright hostility, but the majority of women, as the growth in membership implies, supported her attempt to apply in a broad and highly practical manner the idealism of the Co-operative Movement to which she was so strongly wedded.

Co-operative Links and Clashes

One further aspect of the Guild's principles and practices during Miss Llewelyn Davies' period of office concerns its status within the Co-operative framework as a whole. Mrs Lawrenson was instrumental in establishing the first formal link between the Guild and the Union when in 1886 she persuaded the Co-operative Union to contribute its first grant of £10, though from the earliest days many societies had assisted with the provision of accommodation, heating and lighting. Regular contributions also came from the Co-operative Wholesale Society, while donations from other institutions and individuals also helped to keep the Guild solvent. Yet the Guild was and remains a self-governing organisation, and it was the primacy of its own internal sources of finance which, from the beginning enabled it to enjoy a jealously guarded independence, and provided its strengh as a reformist body. As Evelyn Sharp correctly observed:

This independence has been of great importance in enabling the members to become pioneers, introducing new progressive policies into the Movement.

When their autonomy was threatened, Miss Llewelyn Davies and the Central Committee acted decisively and with great determination to defend the Guild's position. In 1902 the Guild conducted the first of a planned series of investigations into the nature and causes of urban poverty. Work began in Sheffield, but the Co-operative Union, which funded the project, soon objected to the involvement of two Guild researchers from outside the city who, it was felt, represented an unnecessary expense. Miss Llewelyn Davies' response was sharp and uncompromising.

In my interview with the Office Committee, after which they agreed to recommend the United Board to make a grant, I expressly said in reply to Mr. Taylor's opinion that the local

Guild members could do whatever work was necessary, that this was impossible — that the kind of work I proposed needed to be done by special people. There should therefore have been no misunderstanding on this point. We should certainly not have undertaken the work unless free to conduct it in such a way as would obtain the best results possible, with the people available. Sheffield was the first and a heavy piece of work and I felt it advisable that two people should do it.[32]

As this passage indicates, Miss Llewelyn Davies did not succumb easily to male, or indeed, female pressure, but was an adversary of the most determined kind.

The Guild's independent approach to its affairs brought it into conflict with the United Board on a number of other occasions. In 1907, for example, the Board made known its displeasure at the Guild's stand on the anti-credit and franchise issues, but the most serious rift occurred in 1914 when the Union withdrew its grant, a sanction which it maintained for the next four years. This drastic action was precipitated by the Guild's radical position on divorce law reform, which it set out in its evidence to the Royal Commission on Divorce Law Reform established by Asquith's Liberal Government in 1909.

The Commission's report was published in 1912 and immediately attracted considerable publicity and controversy. As the only contribution from a working class women's organisation, the Guild's evidence, which was vigorously attacked in the Minority Report, received a great deal of attention. This came particularly from the Manchester and Salford Catholic Federation, which objected not only to the Guild's point of view, but to its very involvement in what to the Federation was a purely religious issue. The opening skirmishes occurred in October 1913 when the Federation wrote to the Guild objecting to its role in the divorce reform issue on the grounds that a proportion of its funds originated from the societies, some of whose members were Catholics and disapproved of divorce altogether.

In rejecting this line of argument the Central Committee set in motion the most traumatic experiences in the Guild's history. The Federation increased the intensity of its pressure by warning the United Board of possible 'disruption in the Movement'. This was no empty threat since in some areas Catholics made up a substantial proportion of the membership, perhaps as much as 80 per cent, and the withdrawal of their support could easily have precipitated a society's collapse.

Alarmed by a sense of impending disaster, the Board informed the Guild that it objected to the divorce reform campaign and requested the Central Committee 'to consider giving up work in this direction', which in turn was unanimously rejected.

However, Miss Llewelyn Davies and the President, Mrs Gasson, prepared a detailed reply in which they rejected the right of an outside body to dictate to the Guild on an issue of such fundamental social and moral importance. They defiantly reminded the Union that they represented an organisation which acted independently and not in the name of the Co-operative Movement. Thus by the Spring of 1914 the battle lines were drawn and the two sides had manoeuvred themselves into a position from which it became increasingly difficult to identify an honourable exit.

Matters came to a head in June 1914 when the Central Committee received deputations from both the Federation and the Co-operative Union. Again the Federation pleaded that divorce was a religious issue and 'as such should not be dealt with by the Movement', while the United Board proposed 'that the Guild should waive its agitation on Divorce for a year, and that a referendum should be taken among the members as to whether it should be continued'. The Central Committee, however, held its ground, refusing to be moved by either party, a position which was endorsed without dissent at the Guild Congress later the same month.

When the Union implemented its threat to withdraw financial support, which by 1914 had reached £400, the Guild established an Independence Fund, which by mid October totalled £150. In addition, Miss Llewelyn Davies supplied the Guild with a loan from her own resources, while attempts were made to economise on campaign expenses. Although the Union was able to embarrass the Guild, it could not silence its voice on the divorce issue, though finance did become a serious problem. The adverse impact of the economies upon the maternity campaign must have been particularly distressing and perhaps it was for this reason that in May 1915 the Central Committee proposed retaining their position on divorce while at the same time using the Union's grant solely in support of subjects approved by the Board. This suggestion failed to bear fruit and the controversy deteriorated into a prolonged and acrimonious dispute harmful to all concerned. Both the Union and the Guild published articles and pamphlets in support of their respective positions, while the Salford Federation stepped up its campaign in the Manchester area, which the Central Committee recognised to be highly damaging. At one stage of the dispute the Central Committee was forced to provide special financial assistance to branches which had received the Federation's particular attention.

The dispute simmered on during the war years, though it lost some of its force after 1915. Each year a renewal of the grant was offered, but on terms which the Guild considered to be incompatible with its democratic principles. In 1918, however, at the Union's request a meeting was convened with Guild officials which led to the renewal of financial support on the basis of the work undertaken by the Guild during the previous year.

The Board's withdrawal of grant had never enjoyed the unqualified support of the Co-operative Movement and its reinstatement in 1918 was in part an attempt to heal the divisions of the previous four years. Moreover, the status of Co-operative women had been enhanced by the war since the events of these years

> helped to prove to the Movement that its voluntary women's organisation was capable of placing at its service a body of well-trained Co-operators not afraid of working for the cause either within or outside the Movement.[33]

By 1918 the public debate on divorce reform had also lost some of the rancour which accompanied the publication of the Royal Commission's Report in 1912. In addition, as Catherine Webb shrewdly noted, the formation of the Co-operative Party in 1917 and the extension of the franchise in 1918 to females over 30

> improved the status of the women as potential supporters in a wider field than simple "buying".

The bulk of guildswomen now enjoyed political as well as basket power and their value to the Co-operative Movement and influence within it rose accordingly.

As part of its attempt to legitimise its battle with the Union, the Central Committee decided in January 1915 to attribute to it the official title of the 'Self-Government Campaign'. This symbolised the Committee's position which throughout the dispute centred upon the primacy of free speech and the Guild's independence within the Co-operative Movement. In addition, Miss Llewelyn Davies pleaded the case for free debate on the basis that it was this *which has been the source of the vitality and progress of the Guild.*[34.]

As the Union's attitude hardened, the Guild was put into a position of defending not simply its stand on the divorce issue, but its fundamental right of independence. Thus the Co-operative Congress of 1914 resolved that 'the application of the English Women's Co-operative Guild for a renewal of the grant of £400 be agreed to on condition that they cease the agitation in favour of Divorce Reform and that in future the Women's Co-operative Guilds take up no work disapproved by the Central Board'.

The dispute had swiftly escalated into a direct challenge to the right of free speech in general and is an interesting reflection of the way in which the Guild's activities had become a painful thorn in the Union's flesh. The Guild was dragging a reluctant Co-operative Movement into the twentieth century, but at considerable financial and emotional cost.

The controversy over divorce reform, including the issue of self-government, brought some internal dissent to the Guild, though one of the most remarkable aspects of the affair was the high degree of unanimity which the membership displayed. When, in the summer of 1914, the dispute evolved into outright war, a mere 30 of the Guild's 611 branches opposed the Central Committee's defiant stand. Similarly, by May 1917 only 4 branches had used the divorce issue as a reason for failing to comply with the increase in the membership subscription which had been agreed the previous year.

The Guild also enjoyed substantial support within the Co-operative Movement. In 1915 for example, a motion was tabled at the Union Congress by 16 societies which recommended that the grant be restored on the usual terms. The justice of the Central Committee's stand had been widely recognised while, at another level, the Guild had been instrumental in raising the tempo of public debate on an issue of outstanding social importance. The Guild had taken on the might of the Co-operative Union, and won. It had gained in self confidence and demonstrated its importance and independence within the Co-operative Movement. Its performance during these most unsettling times exemplified and was a tribute to the sound organisation and liberating influence which had developed in a period of little more than twenty years.

The Women's Co-operative Guild reached its structural and intellectual maturity during Margaret Llewelyn Davies' period as General Secretary. Her influence was profound and enduring and her appointment in 1922 as the first woman President of the Co-operative Congress was a fitting recognition of the Guild's status within the Co-operative Movement, and of Miss Llewelyn Davies' contribution to its development. Yet her efforts should not obscure, nor would she have wished them to do so, the many thousands of women who devoted the necessary time and energy to making the Guild a success. In researching this Centenary History, however, one cannot fail to have been impressed by Miss Llewelyn Davies' enormous zest, ability and influence, and it seems entirely appropriate to associate this period of the Guild's development with her name.

Notes to Chapter 2

1. B. Russell, The Autobiography of Bertrand Russell, 1872-1914 (1967).
2. G.D.H. Cole, A Century of Co-operation (Manchester 1944).
3. London School of Economics, Miscellaneous Collection.
4. Ibid.
5. Annual Report, 1893.
6. M.L. Davies, The Women's Co-operative Guild 1883-1904 (Kirkby Lonsdale 1904).
7. Mary Lawrenson Collection, op.cit.
8. Ibid.
9. Ibid.
10. Ibid.
11. LSE, Miscellaneous Collection, op.cit.
12. Ibid.
13. Mary Lawrenson Collection, op.cit.
14. Anon. The Relation of the Guild to other Organisations (1924).
15. WCG. Handbook (1916).
16. The Consett Co-operative Record, March 1904.
17. Annual Report, 1893.
18. Ibid.
19. F. Pickles, Jubilee History of the Bridge End Co-operative Society Ltd. (Manchester 1902).
20. M.L. Davies, Motherhood and the State (1914).
21. Statement for the use of delegates to the North Lancashire District Conference, November 1890.
22. Draft speech, April 1934, LSE Miscellaneous Collection, op.cit.
23. Quoted by J. Gaffin, 'Women and Co-operation' in L. Middleton (ed) Women in the Labour Movement (1977).
24. Anon. Jubilee History of the Coventry Perseverance Co-operative Society Ltd. (Coventry 1917).
25. LSE Miscellaneous Collection, op.cit.
26. Davies, The Women's Co-operative Guild, op.cit.
27. M.L. Davies, The Education of Guildswomen (1913).
28. C. Webb, The Woman with the Basket (Manchester 1927).
29. LSE Miscellaneous Collection, op.cit.
30. Davies, The Women's Co-operative Guild, op.cit.
31. M.G. Bondfield, The National Care of Maternity (1914).
32. LSE, Miscellaneous Collection, op.cit.
33. Webb, op.cit.
34. Davies, The Women's Co-operative Guild, op.cit.

CHAPTER 3

ISSUES AND CAMPAIGNS:1883-1918

Introduction

Although the Women's Co-operative Guild shared some of the characteristics of the other organised feminist groups of the late nineteenth and early twentieth centuries, it enjoyed a refreshing individuality which is reflected in the debates and campaigns associated with its formative years. Unlike the suffragists, for instance, it concerned itself with a broad range of issues, the conservative outlook of its early days soon yielding to a wider and more radical interpretation of society's problems. From a narrow preoccupation with home management and Co-operative shopping, the Guild came increasingly to extend its interests and involvement to some of the most significant and contentious issues of the period.

Like other bodies with a large middle class leadership, the Guild displayed philanthropic characteristics common to the evangelical tradition. Thus it was concerned with moral and material welfare and the promotion of legislation to protect the vulnerable, particularly women and children. Yet the Guild was more than a mere appendage to Victorian philanthropy, for most of its leaders were motivated by a strong belief in the unfairness of the existing economic and social fabric. Their political perspectives were far too radical for the bulk of their middle-class sisters. The Guild was not militant in the physical sense epitomised by the suffragettes, but its policies and activities nevertheless posed a serious challenge to the existing order.

Another distinguishing feature of the Guild's role as a pressure group was its special links with the Labour Movement, many of whose leaders, such as Keir Hardie and George Lansbury, were strong feminist sympathisers. In contrast to the Conservatives and Liberals, the Labour Party was generally supportive of the women's movement. The Guild thus benefited from its political connections which were strengthened after 1919 by the advent of the Co-operative Party. In the years before the First World War the Guild became the most strongly feminist of all the women's groups within the

Labour Movement and, together with other bodies such as the Women's Labour League, was influential in persuading the Labour Party to move to an ever more fully committed position on women's rights.

Although the Guild's strategy and tactics were less dramatic and colourful than those of some other women's groups, the Guild expressed its opinions in a constructive and effective manner. Its members spoke on street corners and at more formal gatherings, presented petitions and gave evidence to public bodies, lobbied Members of Parliament and debated with Ministers. Guildswomen became involved in both local and national administration, from election to Poor Law Unions to membership of wartime emergency committees. By 1918, the Women's Co-operative Guild was a widely respected advocate of women's rights whose voice was heard in the Labour Movement and on a variety of central and local government committees. In the space of 35 years it had developed from an insignificant women's organisation with purely sectional interests to a body of national reputation and influence.

Battle for Equal Pay in the Co-operative Movement

As we have already discovered, one of the reasons for the Guild's foundation was its members' concern with the quality and price of goods sold by Co-operative stores, whilst some of the fiercest of its early battles were fought over open membership and female involvement in the management of both the societies and the Union. But the Guild's involvement with the operation of the Co-operative Movement did not end there for in the 1890s a campaign was initiated to improve the conditions of service, particularly wages, of its women employees. The prelude to this was a growing suspicion that, despite its high ideals, the Co-operative Movement exploited a large number of women by obliging them to work exceptionally long hours for relatively low wages. This distressing situation was confirmed in 1896 by the results of a systematic enquiry conducted by Miss Reddish into the employment practices of 169 societies, which provided the evidence for a campaign to upgrade the wages of female Co-operative workers.

Guild pressure contributed to the Movement's acceptance in 1907 of the principle of a Co-operative minimum wage. The Guild quickly seized this opportunity of establishing a women's scale and, helped by the Amalgamated Union of Co-operative

Employees, produced recommendations for submission to the societies and to the C.W.S. These scales were subsequently approved by the United Board and confirmed by the Co-operative Congress of 1908. However the new arrangement was received without enthusiasm by the employers and during the next four years the Guild attempted to cajole a rather unresponsive Co-operative Movement into improving the wages of its female workers.

In 1908, the Guild presented its case for the introduction of a women's scale in 'A Co-operative Standard for Women Workers' which circulated in thousands. The pamphlet attacked as fallacious the view that family responsibilities justified higher wages for male employees, since many men had no such commitments, while, conversely, women were often the family's sole or principal breadwinner. The plight of single women was identified as a particular concern, for in providing financial assistance to their families and relatives 'they are not only hard pressed at the time, but are unable to put by for their old age, when they will themselves very often be without the aid of children's wages'. This was a very real and growing problem since at the time an imbalance in the sex ratio increased the number of spinsters in relation to bachelors. The pamphlet also noted that not only did Co-operative enterprise pay women less than men but that the level of remuneration varied considerably from one society to another, with the main explanation being the degree of competition for labour rather than variations in the cost of living. Thus Co-operative wages tended to be relatively generous in Lancashire since alternative employment for females was normally available in the textile industry. The Guild rejected the view that improved wages for women would bring higher prices, lower dividends or a combination of the two, arguing that low pay simply reflected inadequate management which, given the will, could be easily corrected. The Guild's approach was uncompromising for the 1908 pamphlet noted that 'if we are told that a small and struggling society or certain departments (such as Drapery, Dressmaking or Packing) could not exist if a decent minimum wage were paid, then we must boldly say that it is better they should not be carried on'.

The Guild Congress of 1908 insisted on equal pay for equal work and attacked the practice of differential rates on the grounds that low pay for women could foster immorality, while

Mrs. Cecily Cook,
General Secretary
1940-1953

Mrs. Mabel Ridealgh,
General Secretary
1953-1963

Mrs. Kathleen Kempton,
General Secretary
1963-1983

*Miss Lilian Harris
was cashier of the
Guild in 1893 and
Assistant Secretary
from 1902-1921*

*Mrs. Norah Willis, an
active Guildswoman
and co-operator since
1945, and the third
woman President of
the Co-operative
Union Congress —
in 1983*

*Miss Catherine Webb
chaired the first Guild
Conference in 1886
and wrote the Guild's
History, ''The
Woman with the
Basket'' published in
1927*

equality of treatment brought 'the power and dignity of independence to mind and body'.[1] A campaign strategy was developed and placed before guildswomen in the Winter Circular of 1908-1909. It invited discussion of the principal issues at the Guild's sectional conferences and outlined a plan for pressurising both the societies and the CWS. Efforts were to be made to encourage the Amalgamated Union of Co-operative Employees to adopt a more forceful policy on pay scales for women, while employees were to be pressed to join the Union. Pressure was to be applied to Management Committees in the form of deputations or special conferences. During the course of the next two years the Guild conducted a lively and inventive campaign. Articles appeared in the "Co-operative News", leaflets were distributed, speeches made at Guild and Co-operative Union conferences and in March 1910 a petition containing more than 13,000 signatories supporting the principle of a national pay scale for female Co-operative employees was deposited with the Directors of the Co-operative Wholesale Society in Manchester by the Guild President personally.

The Guild Congress of 1909 passed a resolution calling upon the Co-operative Union to include in their model rules for societies a provision that all employees should be paid trade union rates. The Union refused, but the Guild enjoyed greater success at local level for, by 1911, 64 societies had adopted the pay scale and others gradually came into line. When a rather ambiguous response was produced to the Guild's petition, local societies were encouraged to apply their own pressure to the Co-operative Wholesale Society. As a democratic body, the Co-operative Movement was particularly vulnerable to the tactics of attrition used by the Guild at both central and local level. Victory was finally achieved towards the end of 1912 when the Co-operative Wholesale Society carried a resolution to place all its women workers on the scale by 1914.

The campaign for a minimum pay scale for women was one of the Guild's major successes within the Co-operative Movement. It was, as the "Manchester Guardian" observed, 'a triumph for the progressive power of democratic organisation and a vindication of women's capacity for politics'[2] The Guild had bravely criticised the societies in the North, with their huge profits and dividends, and attacked the United Board and the Directors of the CWS for their intransigence. But the campaign had not been intemperate or unreasonable; it aimed at guaranteeing women little more than a subsistence income. On a broader plain, the Guild was concerned that the Co-operative Movement should set an example, for by putting its own house in order it would help to raise the standard of wages and industrial conditions for all women workers. The strategy had been orchestrated from the centre by Miss Llewelyn Davies and in 1913 she received the Central Committee's formal congratulations. But it was a collaborative effort, and provides a good example of the application of the talents and determination of hundreds of women widely dispersed throughout the country.

The Guild and Trade Unionism

The basket power of its members, together with the democratic structure of the Movement in general, gave the Guild its leverage with respect to the pay and working conditions of female Co-operative employees. Yet the Guild's interest was not confined to Co-operative stores and workshops since for a time it became closely involved with the broader current of trade union and industrial affairs. Since the Trade Union Movement aimed to eradicate the abuses identified with capitalist employment, the Guild's support of it was fully consistent with the ideals of the producer-orientated communities of the early nineteenth century, which sought to construct an economic system that did not exploit labour. Moreover, unlike their craft predecessors, the general unions of the 1890s were concerned to improve working conditions for a broad section of the working class, including women, rather than simply an occupational elite. In this they accorded well with the spirit of a Co-operative Commonwealth. In addition, as we have already noticed, the Central Committee recognised in 1890 that association with the Trade Union Movement could have a beneficial effect in terms of membership, while a joint approach to selected problems could enhance the influence of both parties. Some of the Guild pioneers in the north, such as Sarah Reddish and Selina Cooper, were themselves inspired by trade union ideals, and their influence also helped to draw the Guild into a concern for the welfare of working class women in general.

The industrial action in 1888 by the match girls employed by Messrs. Bryant and May and the London dock strike of the following year aroused widespread public sympathy and support, and it was in this atmosphere that the Guild began to develop its relationship with the Trade Union Movement. At the suggestion of Miss Llewelyn Davies, a series of meetings between trade unionists and men and women co-operators was held in London in the winter of 1891 under the auspices of the Women's Co-operative Guild. The sessions were suported by some of the leading trade unionists of the period, including Tom Mann of the Engineers and Ben Tillet of the Dockers' Union. Although these meetings achieved few practical results, they did help to foster more cordial relationships between the two Movements.

More significant was the campaign introduced in the following year in conjunction with the Women's Trade Union League to promote unionisation among factory girls. The League, which like the Guild, had a strongly middle class leadership, sponsored the formation of women's trade unions and assisted their development. Initially a rather conservative body in the philanthropic mould, under the guidance of its able Secretary, Clementina Black, the League gradually became more radical in its outlook, pressing its views upon MPs and male trade unionists and demanding a voice in any discussion which involved the welfare of female workers. Miss Black became well known to many guildswomen and indeed spoke at their first delegate conference. It seems likely that she provided at least some of the inspiration for the Guild's pay scale initiative for she had long been a staunch advocate of equal pay for equal work.

The Guild's Annual Report for 1892 shows that during the course of the year many branches became actively involved in promoting female trade unionism. Battersea branch, for example, played a prominent role in assisting girls employed in a local bon-bon factory to form a union in order to resist a reduction in wages. Similar attempts elsewhere in the country also appear to have borne fruit for the League's third annual report recorded appreciatively the work of the Women's Co-operative Guild in 'helping to organise women's unions', adding that the 'prospect of their assistance is one of the most encouraging facts in the year's history'. The Guild and the League also co-operated in other ways. In 1894, for example, the two organisations joined forces in the formation of the Women's Industrial Council, which, through its committees, conducted a number of significant enquiries in respect of female employment, and became an important and progressive influence upon industrial legislation. It is worth recording that Catherine Webb served for some years as the Council's General Secretary. One final example of the joint efforts of the Guild and the League is that in 1916 both were accorded representation on the Standing Joint Committee of Women's Industrial Organisations, which was regarded by both the Government and the Labour Party as the main voice for women in industrial employment. The Guild is still represented on its successor, the Standing Joint Committee of Working Women's Organisations.

As economic conditions worsened, placing pressure on employment and wages, and employers became increasingly resistant to trade union activities, the collaboration between the Guild and the League lost its early momentum. By the mid 1890s the Guild's interest had switched from the unionisation of female labour to the regulation of working conditions. This was encouraged by the formation in 1893 of the Labour Department of the Board of Trade, one of the functions of which was the collection of employment data, including that relating to women. With a significant proportion of its members either in employment or with recent experience of paid work, the Guild was in a strong position to assist the Department with its enquiries. The Department's correspondent for the Women's Section, Miss Clara Collet, quickly enlisted the aid of guildswomen in the composition of her reports. Some fifty years later Miss Collet recalled that

In the Labour Department of the Board of Trade from 1893 onwards the branches of the Guild were always the first to be asked for aid, and to give it, on every social question affecting women.[3]

The Guild's contribution to the Department's work is exemplified by those guildswomen who provided monthly returns on the amount and regularity of female employment in the textile trades for publication in the Labour Gazette. The scheme was introduced in 1894 and in the first year of its operation the Department enlisted the services of 33 correspondents, of whom 29 were Guild members.

The Guild devoted considerable care to publicising their members' rights under current industrial law and were also prominent in campaigning for new protective legislation. Following the Factory Act of 1894 the Central Committee arranged for the publication of explanatory pamphlets, while a team of 36 speakers was used to visit and provide specialist advice to branches. The Guild's policy on female employment was agreed at the annual meeting in 1896.

1. Reduction of non-textile hours to those of textile trades
2. Further restriction and ultimate abolition of overtime for women
3. Inclusion of laundries under the Factory Acts
4. Replacement of home by factory work
5. Increase in the number of women factory inspectors
6. Appointment of women as certifying surgeons
7. Annual examination of the health of factory children

The Guild's special relationship with the Labour Department, and Miss Collet in particular, gave it some influence in promoting industrial reform, though with other organisations pursuing similar objectives it is difficult to assess the Guild's precise significance. One campaign in which the Guild was especially prominent and appears to have enjoyed considerable success, albeit of a negative kind, concerned the Factory Bill of 1900 which contained several clauses objectionable to guildswomen, including a shift system which would have legalised factory work on Sunday. Branches were encouraged to hold meetings and to besiege MPs and the Home Office with resolutions. Guild members responded with vigour and enthusiasm and after a short time the Bill was withdrawn and its successor contained none of the offending measures.

As the 1890s drew to a close, relations between the employers and the trade unions deteriorated with strikes and lock-outs becoming common place, and the courts adopting an increasingly hostile attitude towards organised labour. This bad publicity may have been one reason why the Guild moved away from the close relationship with the Trade Union Movement which had been promised following the collaboration in 1893 with the Women's Labour League. The Guild was generally supportive of the industrial action taken by trade unions, including the famous coal strike of 1894, the first dispute to be resolved by Ministerial intervention so damaging did it become to the nation's economy. Guild members assisted miners and their families by providing for the care of needy children, helping with relief committees and collecting money for a strike fund. By the late nineteenth and early twentieth centuries the range of activities which consumed the Guild's energies was expanding rapidly to include retail credit, employment conditions in the Co-operative stores and the Movement's social responsibilities to the poorer sections of the working class. The Guild's resources were becoming dangerously stretched and it was principally for this reason that the Guild failed to develop fully its relationship with the Trade Union Movement and its concern for matters of industrial welfare.

Taking Co-operation to the Poor

One of the Guild's chief priorities by the turn of the century was that of taking Co-operation to the poorer sections of the working class. With their relatively high prices and entrance fees the Co-operative stores were normally beyond the reach of low income families. This meant that the poor remained largely untouched by the Movement's broader, more philosophical aims. These issues had been discussed by co-operators for some time, but one delegate to the Co-operative Congress of 1889 made the specific point that:

If we are to go down to the level of winning those who have not joined our Movement, there was no agency which would do this better than the Women's Guild.[4]

The Central Committee regarded this remark as something of a challenge with the result that within the space of a few months Miss Llewelyn Davies had produced a paper entitled 'Co-operation in Poor Neighbourhoods', which was swiftly despatched for discussion by the sectional conferences. The paper set out the financial obstacles which prevented poor families from joining the societies and outlined a number of ways in which these might be overcome. The suggested innovations were of three main types and revolved around the introduction of a 'People's Store' to be located in the less affluent urban districts. The central marketing strategy of these stores was that they should supply wholesome food and other articles in small quantities but that saving should occur automatically through low prices rather than high dividends. It was also proposed that the stores should have a Loan Department which, with adequate security, would fund customers' purchases during periods of personal misfortune. Apart from its welfare benefits, Miss Llewelyn Davies argued that such an arrangement would discourage the poor from engaging in fraudulent behaviour and would also undermine the practice of weekly pawning. Finally, one of the most interesting suggestions concerned the provision of club rooms or a settlement, with propagandist work being conducted by resident helpers. It would be a centre of Co-operative activity in the district, as well as weaning people from undesirable leisure habits, especially over-indulgence at the public house.

The Guild soon introduced a most active campaign in support of Miss Llewelyn Davies' scheme. More pamphlets were published, conferences held and letters and articles appeared in the "Co-operative News." In 1902, with the aid of a grant of £50 from the United Board, the Guild conducted an investigation into the relationship between the commercial practices of the Co-operative stores and the shopping habits of the poorer elements of the working class. Concurrently, surveys were made in a number of urban locations of the nature and causes of poverty. The results of these enquiries were published in a report entitled, 'The Open Door', which became the watchword for the attempt to take Co-operation to the poor. The Guild's investigations revealed once again the importance of relaxing the financial constraints which all too frequently prevented low income families from joining the societies. The first enquiry into urban poverty took place in Sheffield in January 1902. Interviews were conducted with the Medical Officer of Health, the School Attendance Officer, the head woman sanitary inspector and members of the Education Committee, while visits were made to a number of homes in the poorer areas of the city.

The investigations revealed a horrifying picture of squalor and ill-health. It was noted that the 'low physical condition of children of the poorest classes, borne out by both statistics and observation and the numbers of young people applying to enter the army and rejected on account of not coming up to a very moderate standard, are indications of the painfully low standard of health pervading amongst the poorer classes of the community.'[5] By the middle of 1902 the Guild had responded enthusiastically to the challenge put to it at the Co-operative Congress of 1899. It had produced numerous discussion papers, supported by careful research, and had made a number of valuable suggestions concerning the most appropriate method of extending Co-operation to the weakest sections of the working class community.

A few societies had attempted to take Co-operation to the

poor even before the publication of Miss Llewelyn Davies' paper in 1899, but the majority objected to the radicalism of the new initiative, while both the United Board and the CWS were non-committal. However, the Sunderland Society took up the challenge and opened a store in Coronation Street, Sunderland, in October 1902 which was based upon the principles Miss Llewelyn Davies had outlined some two years before. The site chosen by the Society was famous for its high incidence of disease and crime. The store was carefully constructed to meet its special functions and, in addition to its grocery and cooked food departments, included an upstairs hall with accommodation for 500, plus a kitchen, scullery and two bedrooms for resident workers. The decoration was bright and cheerful, while plate glass windows and electric light served to display the goods on sale to their best advantage. The hall was painted in red and white, had pictures on the walls and bright red fustian curtains provided by the Hebden Bridge Society. Miss Llewelyn Davies, who organised the community work for the first three months, commented that

> anyone might forget the outside surroundings were it not for the rain of big black smuts, the loud voices of the children, the street fights, the "Hallelujah Chorus" on an organ, the trumpet of a little man exchanging rag and bones for whiting and candy, or the cries of the neighbouring butcher to the unresponsive passers-by.

This was a happy period in the General Secretary's life and when she received the Freedom of the Guild in 1922 she recalled how

> several of us lived in rotation, sitting behind the counter taking deposits and making members and selling cake on Christmas Eve, carried on meetings, clubs and concerts, and took the good news of the store into the homes.[6]

By early 1903 some six meetings a week were held in the hall with a total attendance of 300-400. Monday evening was given over to a club for young men which had both educational and leisure aspects to it, for members sometimes practised their handwriting, while on other occasions they played football. Tuesday evening was restricted to those above school age and had a strong musical flavour, but with the occasional lecture. Sunday was devoted to discussion of a more serious nature. Even so, the men 'in their seedy garments, sucking their pipes in the Hall on Sunday evenings' were said to be 'grateful for such a good exchange for the public house.'[7]

The "Daily News" defined the project as 'a mission to help the poor to help themselves', adding that 'ladies show how to keep out of debt ... no patronage, no charity but a centre of real neighbourliness and absolute social equality.' The article concluded with the observation that if this form of Co-operation could succeed in Sunderland 'it can make its way anywhere.'[8] Yet in September 1904 the Directors of the Sunderland Society proposed to the Quarterly Meeting that the settlement should be jettisoned, which was agreed and the shop consequently became a trading store only. Thereafter, although some societies opened new stores in poor neighbourhoods and there was also a general reduction in entrance fees, the collapse of the Sunderland project effectively concluded the attempt to carry Co-operation to the more underprivileged sections of the working class community.

A number of reasons explain the Guild's enthusiasm for taking Co-operation to the poor. For some fundamentalists the Co-operative tradition centred upon the provision of comfort and aid to the most vulnerable sections of the community. One speaker reminded delegates to the Co-operative Congress of 1902 that:

Robert Owen, whose memory we all revered, intended that Co-operation should enable the very poor to help themselves.[9]

This position was well summarised in 1904 by Sarah Bennett.

It is very shocking to me that we should now-a-days be discussing how to take Co-operation to the poor. Why, it is the heritage and birthright of the poor, their own peculiar possession, because the fruit of their best powers of mind and body. But it has been filched from them, as everything worth having is, in these cruel machine days.[10]

Miss Bennett argued that poverty was socially divisive, while charitable handouts merely exacerbated the problem by undermining personal independence. According to Miss Bennett

anyone who remains outside social influences is a danger and a sore in our midst.

She was thus able to justify Co-operative intervention in the lives of the poor on the grounds of both political expediency and social justice.

Miss Llewelyn Davies agreed with the general spirit of Miss Bennett's remarks, but she was also greatly influenced by the social theorists and investigators of her time. The final decades of the nineteenth century witnessed a growing public interest in the plight of the poor and a realisation that poverty was often a product of circumstances beyond personal control rather than simply the result of feckless or imprudent behaviour. The investigations of Charles Booth in London and Seebohm Rowntree in York pointed to the particular problems of uncertain employment, ill-health and low wages as major contributors to the extreme financial hardship experienced by many working class families. Miss Llewelyn Davies was personally influenced by Rowntree's work and the Guild's own urban surveys of 1902 were a practical demonstration of this.

The development in the late nineteenth century of group social work and community organisation was partly a response to the research findings of the early social investigators such as Henry Mayhew and Andrew Mearns. However religion was also a powerful influence, particularly in the establishment of the settlements, the first of which, Toynbee Hall, was set up by Canon Barnett in 1884. Like the Sunderland experiment, Toynbee Hall was based upon the principle that social reformers should go to the poor rather than expect the poor to come to them. Toynbee Hall and the settlements which followed aimed at promoting harmony between rich and poor. Although they were not concerned with retailing, their social activities were similar to those of the Coronation Street branch of the Sunderland Co-operative Society. The settlements shared some of their inspiration with the Co-operative Movement, particularly the ideas of F.D. Maurice and John Ruskin. In addition, Toynbee Hall was named after Arnold Toynbee, who was not only a prominent Oxford academic and social reformer, but a well known co-operator. It is also worth recording that Miss Llewelyn Davies was associated with the Toynbee family and it seems clear that the notion of a 'People's Store' which she expounded in 1899 derived its intellectual origins from the ideas about community work exemplified by the settlement movement.

The collapse of the Sunderland project was precipitated by the resignation through ill-health of Miss Partridge, the resident worker. However, towards the end of 1904 the "Co-operative News" reported that a faction within the Sunderland Society objected to the basic principle of extending Co-operation to the poor. To some extent this derived from a concern over dividends, but more important was the commonly held view that democracy in Co-operative trading required that

66

no one district received special consideration. There was also a feeling, reflected in a more general way by the harshness of the nineteenth century Poor Law, that imperfections of character were responsible for the financial hardships of the lower sections of the working class. Moreover, the Sunderland project did not fully conform to the self-help tradition associated with the Co-operative Pioneers. Indeed it savoured of soup and blankets rather than thrift, saving and sensible shopping. In practice, the community aspect of the Coronation Street branch was incompatible with the views held by a large section of Co-operative members and this explains why the project not only collapsed in Sunderland, but also failed to take root elsewhere. These views are encapsulated in the comments of one delegate from Sheffield to the Co-operative Congress of 1902.

He knew about the poor, and attributed their poverty to want of thrift. They found money to pay fines in the police-court. Co-operation was not founded on philanthropy, but on self-help.[11]

In the face of the Movement's general apathy and occasional hostility the Guild's interest in extending Co-operation to poor areas eventually petered out to be replaced by new campaigns, some of which achieved a more lasting success, though few reflected more accurately the essential humanity of guildswomen.

The Guild and Social Policy

During the first two decades of the twentieth century there were considerable innovations in the provision of public welfare benefits and facilities. The introduction of old age pensions in 1908 and health and unemployment insurance in 1911 were directed principally at adults, while a number of measures, such as those concerned with school meals and the school medical service, involved the welfare of children. The period was also characterised by important local initiatives, particularly the provision of council and voluntary infant welfare clinics, and the employment of health visitors. As the foundations of the early welfare state were laid, government spending on social services increased sharply, rising from under two per cent of Gross National Product in 1890 to over four per cent in 1913. Old age pensions were too small and came too late in life to have much impact upon the health of the elderly, while medical insurance under the 1911 Act did not apply to dependants. However, the maternity and child welfare provisions appear to have yielded an immediate return since the infant mortality rate fell quite markedly during the Edwardian period, a phenomenon which can be only partially explained by general improvements in living standards and medical care.

The new welfare initiative owed something to humanitarian concerns, for the surveys of Booth, Rowntree and other social investigators revealed widespread working class deprivation, especially among the elderly, the sick, the unemployed and those with large families. This was also a period of falling birth rate, a trend which some contemporaries attributed to an alleged decline in the nation's physical powers. This general hypothesis was given added strength by the poor health of many of the army's potential recruits during the Boer and First World Wars. In 1899, for example, some 60 per cent of men who attempted to enlist at the army depot in Manchester were rejected as unfit for military service. This and similar revelations resulted in the establishment of an Inter-Departmental Committee on Physical Deterioration which, when it reported in 1904, gave much emphasis to the importance of protecting the health of the next generation. Indeed, the Edwardian period saw the rise of a national efficiency movement dedicated to producing, in the words of Lord Rosebery,

a race vigorous and industrious and intrepid.[12]

At a time when industrial production and military warfare were still far from fully automated and when a large Empire required to be governed, it is understandable that the health of a relatively small population should receive substantial public attention.

Campaigns for Improving Maternity Provisions

The Guild became actively involved in the social policy debates of the early twentieth century, though it was particularly concerned to press for improved maternity and infant welfare facilities, and the payment of maternity benefit direct to the mother. The Central Committee orchestrated a series of determined, sophisticated and effective campaigns which made the Guild the chief protagonist of the welfare rights of working class expectant mothers and their infants. Evelyn Sharp argued that perhaps

> *the most spectacular political achievement of the Guild was its campaign for securing the inclusion of the Maternity Benefit in the Insurance Act, and afterwards for getting it made the wife's property.*

Although reforms in the provision of facilities for maternity and infant care were more of a shared success, the pressure applied by the Guild was again of fundamental importance in persuading central and local government to recognise and meet their responsibilities to working class women.

Although the Guild's contribution to the welfare debate of the early twentieth century was linked to the broad social and political problems of the period, it derived its particular impetus and characteristics from its own researches and campaigns and the experiences of its members. The investigations in 1902 into the nature and causes of urban poverty provided first hand evidence of the health problems of poor working class mothers and their children, while the minimum wage campaign also revealed the difficulties encountered by low income families. The Guild was unable to compel the adoption of its social welfare initiatives, but when allied to other pressures it became a powerful and progressive force for policy innovation.

The National Insurance Act of 1911 introduced a limited scheme of health and unemployment insurance. When the Insurance Bill was still in its formative stages the Guild submitted to the Chancellor of the Exchequer a fully costed scheme of maternity benefit. The plan evidently made a considerable impression for a deputation was invited to the Treasury to discuss the matter and when the Bill was eventually published it incorporated a number of the Guild's proposals. During the Bill's passage through Parliament the Guild's main effort was directed at securing payment of maternity benefit direct to the mother and to widening the scope of health insurance to include dependants. The Guild also emphasised the need for a general increase in medical care facilities, particularly as they affected women and children. The Guild's case rested upon the contribution of wives and mothers, including those not in paid employment, to the well being of the family unit. Miss Llewelyn Davies argued that

> *by her work as mother and housewife, the woman contributes equally with the man to the upkeep of the home and the family income in reality is as much hers as the man's.*[13]

The Act incorporated many of the Guild's suggestions, including a voluntary health scheme for non-wage earning women, but, while it conceded maternity benefit, it did not make such payments the property of the mother. Lloyd George's belief, as Chancellor of the Exchequer, that the financial burden would have been unacceptable seems to have been the main reasons why the Guild's proposals concerning the extension of health care were not accepted in full. The Guild's contribution to the Insurance Act was formally recognised when it was invited to provide representation on the committees set up to advise on the scheme's day to day administration.

The Guild's attempt to influence the shape of the Insurance Bill reflected a high degree of organisational maturity. Not only was the maternity scheme costed by a professional actuary, but the deputation to the Treasury was also armed with the results of a major enquiry among guildswomen concerning health care. In the Spring of 1911 MPs received a letter from the Guild pointing out the Bill's deficiencies and protesting in particular at the allocation of the maternity benefit to the husband as his property.

Miss Llewelyn Davies debated personally with Lloyd George and expressed her views with clarity and force in the letter pages of "The Times". Yet the Guild's most vigorous onslaught was reserved for the Amending Bill to the 1911 Insurance Act when it came up for discussion in 1913. Once again pressure was focused upon the payment of maternity benefit direct to the mother.

In August 1912 the Central Committee set up a small group to watch for and promote new legislation or administrative arrangements relevant to the Guild's interests, and it was this body which orchestrated the maternity campaign. The sub-committee, which contained four members, including the General Secretary, was chaired by Margaret Bondfield. Miss Bondfield had joined the Guild in 1911 and immediately assumed a most prominent role in the health and maternity benefit campaigns of that year. Miss Llewelyn Davies said of her that

> no workers in any movement ever had a colleague who was more single-minded, generous and loyal.[14]

These qualities seem to have been most usefully employed in 1913 since the Minutes of the Central Committee reveal that she was the Guild's major force in the attempt to modify the existing scheme for the payment of maternity benefit. The Guild arranged for the lobbying of MPs, letters to the press and representation of its views to a variety of public officials. Although passed in Committee, the Clause which would have secured the Guild's position was opposed in the House of Commons when it returned there. The Guild quickly organised a petition appealing to MPs to support the Clause. Catherine Webb recalled that this memorial was a triumph of rapid organisation for

> within the space of five days, 565 signatures were secured of women councillors, midwives, nurses, members of insurance committees, sanitary inspectors and health visitors, poor law guardians, officials of political and other women's organisations, educationists, doctors, social workers and others.

The Government allowed a free vote on the issue and the Guild's efforts were vindicated when Lord Robert Cecil's amendment making it possible for the husband's signature to be accepted only if authorised by the wife was carried by 21 votes. The affair generated considerable public excitement and the reports in the columns of "The Times" leave no doubt that the Guild was chiefly responsible for the new arrangements for the payment of maternity benefit.

The Guild also fought for an improved scheme of health care for mothers and infants to be organised through the public health services. This topic had received considerable discussion following a visit to France and Belgium by Guild representatives in 1905-6, who reported on the impressive medical care arrangements for women and children in those two countries. In 1910 the Guild conducted a campaign designed to encourage local education authorities to provide school clinics. Meetings were arranged and papers read on the subject at 211 branches, resolutions were sent to 19 local education authorities and, in conjunction with other organisations, local committees were formed to keep the matter in the public eye.

However, when Margaret Bondfield became chairman of the central administration's sub-committee in 1912 she helped to direct attention once again to the care of mothers and infants and in 1913 this was adopted as the group's special subject for that year. Miss Bondfield and Miss Llewelyn Davies toured the country speaking to health visitors, doctors and local government officials. The Guild pressed for public Maternity Centres to be financed in part by the Treasury, and the appointment of municipal midwives. Miss Bondfield also argued for the creation of a Ministry of Health with a special department responsible for maternity and infant care, with a woman at its head and provided with female inspectors. She demanded that the state provide working class women with the same standard of health care that could be purchased by their middle class counterparts. Miss Llewelyn Davies pointed out that infant mortality was still far too high among working class families and that the reason for this was a combination of low incomes and ignorance of pre- and post-natal hygiene. She argued that Maternity Centres should be within easy reach of working class residential areas and that maternity hospitals should also be readily available, noting that in many districts the workhouse infirmary remained the only refuge offered.

In 1914 a deputation visited Herbert Samuel, the President of the Local Government Board, to press for implementation of the proposals outlined by Miss Bondfield and Miss Llewelyn Davies. By June of that year a government Circular was issued to Public Health Committees recommending adoption of most of the Guild's programme. The Circular provided an incentive for local authorities to respond positively by offering a grant of 50 per cent towards expenditure incurred on health and welfare work. By the end of January 1915 the Guild's sub-committee was concentrating solely upon the medical care issue, encouraging branches to apply pressure to their local Public Health Authority and enlisting the co-operation of other organisations sympathetic to the cause.

"Maternity: letters from Working Women" was published in 1915. This was a collection of letters from Guild members describing their own experience of motherhood. The book presented a distressing and moving picture of women exhausted and made sick by a succession of births and miscarriages and whose problems were often exacerbated by poor diet and heavy domestic toil. Miss Llewelyn Davies quoted the sad experience of one respondent to the Metropolitan Branch of the Society of Medical Officers of Health.

I received your paper on Maternity Scheme, and I can assure you it brought back to me many painful hours of what I have passed through in 21 years of married life. For one thing, I have had a delicate husband for 15 years and I have had nine children, seven born in nine years. I have only one now, some of the others have died from weakness from birth. I only had a small wage, as my husband was then a railway porter. His earnings were 18s. one

72

week and 16s. the next, and I can say truthfully my children have died from my worrying how to make ends meet and also insufficient food.[15]

"Maternity" received considerable public attention, both in Britain and America, and, despite the war, two editions were sold out within months of their appearance. "The Times Literary Supplement" said of it: 'A book of notable interest and of singular distinction. The whole book deserves careful study. The letters are human documents, straightforward, outspoken and quiet.'[16]

The Guild's campaign for improved maternity and infant health care was strengthened by the onset of war. In his preface to "Maternity", Herbert Samuel noted that a substantial part of the nation's potential population was lost before birth and in infancy, a forceful point at a time of falling birth rate and military carnage. The Maternity and Child Welfare Act of 1918 provided statutory support for several of the Guild's proposals, though the financial crisis of 1921 threw the health lobby on the defensive and undermined much of the good work which had already been accomplished. Nevertheless, in the space of some seven years the Guild had played a crucially important role in improving the public provision of maternity benefit and health care for mothers and their children. It had demonstrated in the words of Herbert Samuel,

that it is the duty of the community, so far as it can, to relieve motherhood of its burdens, to spread the knowledge of mothercraft that is so often lacking, to make medical aid available when it is needed, to watch over the health of the infant.

The Guild and the Reform of the Divorce Laws

The Guild's important contribution to the debate on maternity and infant care suffered from having coincided with its research for the Royal Commission on the Reform of the Divorce Laws and the subsequent battle with the Salford and Manchester Catholic Federation and the Co-operative Union. Margaret Bondfield's efforts on behalf of the Guild, particularly between 1911 and 1915, was one of the main reasons why it was able to carry such a heavy administrative and propagandist commitment during this key period. In January 1915 Miss Bondfield's heavy duties in connection with the Central Employment Committee for Women forced her to relinquish the secretaryship of what had now become the Guild's Citizenship Sub-Committee, to be replaced by the equally indefatigable Lilian Harris. Although Miss Llewelyn Davies was intimately concerned with the maternity and health campaigns, the tireless efforts of Miss Bondfield and Miss Lilian Harris released the General Secretary to organise the Guild's courageous and controversial stand on the reform of the divorce laws.

By the opening years of the twentieth century divorce facilities were available to men and women with sufficient resources to finance what was still an expensive and unsavoury procedure. Moreover, women were at a considerable disadvantage since, while adultery remained the sole grounds for divorce, a wife was required to show that her husband's offence had been aggravated by other wrongs, such as desertion or cruelty. The high cost of divorce deterred most working class couples from using this method of ending an unhappy union. However, the Matrimonial Causes Act, 1878, empowered magistrates to grant orders of non-cohabitation, maintenance and custody of children where a husband had been found guilty of assault upon his wife. This procedure was relatively inexpensive so that by the early twentieth century the magistrates courts were dispensing some 8,000 separation orders a year. The more affluent middle and upper classes made use of the central divorce court which at approximately the same time granted about 600 divorces and 80 judicial separations per annum. Thus, when in May 1911 the Guild was invited to contribute evidence to the Royal Commission on Divorce the existing matrimonial legislation discriminated on grounds of both sex and social class.

The Guild's initial reaction to the invitation extended by Lord Gorell, the Commission's Chairman, is recorded in the Minutes of the Central Committee for 5 May, 1910. A long discussion took place, in which the need for an equal law for men and women, and for cheapening divorce proceedings was brought out. The difficulties of women in finding the money necessary was expressed, and also the need for extending the grounds for divorce, failure to maintain the wife and family being specifically mentioned.

The Committee eventually decided to circularise branches requesting members to express their views on whether the grounds for divorce should be the same for men and women, and whether the cost of matrimonial proceedings should be lowered. Replies were received from 429 branches; 414 supported the principle of equality before the law, while 364 reported in favour of cheaper divorces so as to bring the facility within the reach of the low paid. Only 40 branches specifically declared their opposition to divorce. An additional questionnaire seeking members' views on extensions to the grounds for divorce was sent to 124 Guild officials. Over 80 per cent of the respondents regarded cruelty as sufficient justification for terminating a marriage, while over 60 per cent supported the much more radical notion of divorce by mutual consent. The replies to the Guild's enquiries formed the basis of its evidence to the Gorell Commission, and also appeared in book form in 1911 under the title 'Working Women and Divorce'.[17] The Guild's evidence was important because it was the first substantial public expression of female working class opinion on the operation of the marriage laws.

In its evidence before the Commission, the Guild reported that its enquiries had 'brought out in a striking way an overwhelming demand amongst married women belonging to the artisan class for drastic reform in the divorce laws' and added that no 'other subject in the life of the Guild has aroused such immediate response, and elicited such strength and earnestness of feeling.' It was also made plain that while only a minority of working class women actually wished to terminate an unhappy marriage, they were deterred from doing so by the stigma and expense. The expense of legal representation normally excluded working class couples from the divorce court, even when both parties desired to end their union. It was also noted that in their small dwellings 'they cannot get away from each other as rich people can', and that in the majority of cases working class couples were unable even to distance themselves by sleeping in separate bedrooms.

The Guild's evidence offered many justifications for the reform of divorce proceedings. Financial deprivation was a major problem and indeed it was argued that 'the commonest sign that a husband does not care about his wife is his leaving her without money.' Another major issue was that of physical and mental cruelty, which assumed a variety of forms. There were, for example, complaints of men boasting to their wives of their extra-marital conquests, while some husbands even brought another woman to live under the family roof. In one case where the wife had sold all her property to help her husband in business, and to "save his name being dragged through the court in an affiliation case," the man brought into the house another woman and made her sit at the head of the table.

Physical cruelty included the transmission of sexual diseases, though violent behaviour was its most common and obvious manifestation, including even attempts to induce miscarriage.

> She had eleven children, and told me that during the periods of pregnancy he would do all sorts of things to frighten her and bring on a miscarriage. He has even crept down the cellar grate and then rushed up the steps and burst into the kitchen with a great yell. Still she was obliged to stay with him, because she had no means of supporting herself and children.

Guildswomen recognised that even major reforms in matrimonial legislation would still leave many problems, particularly of a financial kind. In discussing the view that easier divorce would result in an increase in the number of matrimonial cases, the Guild argued that 'the real danger is not that women will seek divorce for trivial cases, but that reform of the marriage law without changes in their economic position may be of little use to many whose lives are being ruined by marriage.' It was claimed, however, that for many women personal self respect demanded that they should have the divorce option available to them. The Guild also expressed the opinion that easier divorce would make for happier wedlock since marriage would be cemented by love and respect rather than the cold hand of the law. This hope was summarised by the 1911 Sectional Conference Resolution in favour of easier divorce, which stated that 'such a law would prevent widespread suffering and degradation, would stimulate to better behaviour, would result in happier home life and higher standards of morality, and would strengthen what is best in married life'.

The Guild suggested a number of specific reforms to the existing legislation. It proposed an extension of the grounds for divorce to include desertion, cruelty, serious incompatibility and mutual consent, the latter being based not on the opinion of a judge or jury but 'on the sense of the sufferer himself, or herself, that the marriage was unendurable.' Divorce expenses were to be reduced by extending the venue of matrimonial proceedings to include county courts. In addition, it was suggested that maintenance should be collected by the court and legal restriction placed against arrears to help ensure the financial security of divorced women and their children. There was too, a suggestion that free legal advice and litigation should be available where necessary. Finally, guildswomen were also anxious to see women brought into the legal administration since it was felt that they would bring personal insights to the problems of married women and also encourage them to be more candid in the submission of evidence.

As we have already noted, the Guild's evidence and recommendations on divorce provoked considerable alarm within the Co-operative Movement, particularly in response to pressure from Catholic interests. Moreover, when the Royal Commission's Report was published in 1912, the Minority Report contained a specific attack on the Guild's objectivity and reference was made to 'a comparatively few individuals selected by a witness who shared their opinions.'[18] Much of the criticism emanated from Cosmo Lang, Archbishop of York and a member of the Commission, who believed the evidence of the Mothers' Union to be a more reliable guide to female attitudes on the reform of matrimonial law. In rejecting accusations of personal bias, Miss Llewelyn Davies contrasted the Guild's independence with the status of the Mothers' Union which, she emphasised, had strong links with the Church of England.

The Majority Report was welcomed by the Guild for it recommended equal treatment for men and women, a limited extension of the grounds for divorce, and the introduction of special courts to bring divorce within the financial means of the poor. The Report received considerable criticism from the more reactionary sections of public opinion and this, together with the onset of the First World War, prevented a speedy implementation of the Commission's recommendations. However, in 1923 men and women were granted equality of treatment and in 1937 there was an extension of the grounds for divorce to include desertion, incurable insanity and cruelty. Although the reform of matrimonial law was not one of the Guild's major interests during the interwar years, it continued to press for easier divorce, and probably contributed in some measure to the innovations of the period. Its chief significance, however, was that its liberal contribution to the Gorell Commission helped to set the tone of future debate. Some of the Guild's more radical suggestions were not adopted until after the Second World War. Thus financial assistance in support of litigation by poor families was introduced by the Legal Aid and Advice Act, 1949, while mutual consent as the basis for divorce was introduced in 1969.

In supporting social and economic change, whether it was higher wages for Co-operative employees or medical care facilities for mothers and children, the Guild employed a variety of powerful and intelligent campaigning strategies. As we have seen, one of the most effective techniques was the collection and publicising of the experiences of guildswomen themselves. "Maternity," for example, was a masterpiece of working class testimony, both moving and inspiring and offering a challenge, not just to its readers but to society as a whole. Yet guildswomen also recognised that direct involvement in the mechanisms of government, either as voters or elected representatives, could strengthen their reformist position. Margaret Bondfield summarised this view when she said that an

> intelligent, educated motherhood, free to co-operate with and use civic and political forces, will strike at the root causes of many of our social ills.

The Guild and Women's Suffrage

Since the Parliamentary franchise was restricted to men until 1918, attention in the early days focused upon local government where women had a role as both voters and elected representatives. Given its interest in the problems of women and children, it was natural that much of the Guild's attention should centre upon the new Poor Law. This topic was first raised for discussion at the annual meeting of 1894 when Mrs. Abbott of Tunbridge Wells read a paper which was subsequently distributed for discussion at branch level. Partly as a response to this initiative, 45 guildswomen presented themselves in December 1894 for election as Poor Law Guardians, 22 of whom were successful. Thereafter the Guild extended its educational programme to include the Poor Law and an increasing number of members took part in election campaigns, both as candidates and supporters. Guildswomen also came to be represented on local councils and their committees, including housing, education and maternity. The maternity campaign provides a good example of the potential value of such representation. In 1915 the 50 guildswomen who were represented on 36 Council Maternity Sub-Committees were in a particularly favourable position to apply direct pressure in encouraging local authorities to respond positively to Herbert Samuel's Circular on maternity welfare which had been issued the previous year. The outcome of such pressure is difficult to assess, but at least guildswomen had a further opportunity to voice their opinions and try to persuade others to join with them in support of their particular cause.

To begin with, the Guild's position on the wider issue of the Parliamentary franchise was rather uncertain, and indeed it was not until 1904 that Congress passed a resolution supporting full adult suffrage. Thereafter, however, as the political parties discussed the various permutations, the Central Committee had to decide whether or not to accept anything less than full adult suffrage. When in March 1905 the Committee met to consider this topic a long discussion ensued after which, with one member disagreeing, it was agreed to support the principle of a limited franchise. A Manifesto was issued to branches explaining the Guild's policy but reserving the right to support any measure which contributed to full womanhood suffrage. An invitation in June 1907 to attend a meeting organised by the North of England Suffrage Society illustrates the Guild's rather ambivalent position - it was decided to send a representative 'because of the vague form of the resolution to be proposed.' Nevertheless by that time the compromise of a limited franchise on the same terms as men had been accepted by the major women's groups, including even the highly militant Women's Social and Political Union led by Emmeline and Christabel Pankhurst. The Guild's view hardened in 1912 when the Central Committee adopted the policy of full adult suffrage. Once again Margaret Bondfield's influence seems to have been important for she had consistently opposed any limited extension of the franchise. She argued that common suffrage was the key to real equality between the sexes for it opened the way to reform across a broad front.

When in 1918 the franchise became the right of women over 30 the Guild immediately organised a scheme of political education for its members. In a paper published in 1918 Miss Llewelyn Davies emphasised the need for guildswomen to combine both locally and nationally to use their vote in the most effective manner. She urged members to support

the candidate who stands for Co-operation, for Trade

Unionism, for no taxes on food, for the taxation of land values and large incomes, for high wages, for the national care of maternity and infancy, for the children of the workers to receive as good an education as the children of the rich, for the abolition of slums and overcrowding regardless of vested interests, for the people's control of our relation with other countries, so that there may be no more wars.[19]

Perhaps the most energetic support among guildswomen for the suffrage campaign manifested itself at local level, particularly in the textile districts of Lancashire. In 1893, exasperated by their limited success, the middle class suffrage societies organised a giant petition. Within a year this special appeal had been signed by a quarter of a million women, including 25 per cent of Guild members. Yet the petition failed to make a decisive political impact and after the initial euphoria had ebbed away it became clear that the suffragists still faced an uphill struggle. In Lancashire, however, the petition signalled the start of a new initiative by working class women that was to last for the next twenty years and in which Selina Cooper, who joined the Guild in 1897, took a prominent part.

Selina Cooper was born in 1868 and began work in a Lancashire cotton factory when she was ten years of age. Like many other female industrial workers in Lancashire, Mrs. Cooper was greatly influenced by the power of the Trade Union Movement, though she later recalled how her interest was redirected towards the suffrage movement.

I carefully watched the proceedings and the policies pursued by such great unions as the Miners, Cotton Spinners, and Engineers, who all pressed for State interference with the object of improving their industrial conditions. I was compelled to recognise the power of Parliament - a power that can and ought to be utilised for the public good. Those well organised industries had the ballot box as a lever to raise their standard of life, but the women workers, however well they combined, had no such lever to help them in their demand for the redressing of their grievances.[20]

Mrs. Cooper soon became a most active and ardent supporter of the suffrage movement in Lancashire and in 1901 she was one of 16 women who presented to the House of Commons a petition containing some 67,000 signatures in support of the Parliamentary franchise for women. An article in the "Queen" magazine in April 1909 noted that 'She has taken part in 13 by-elections, and most of her speaking has been done at street corners and factory gates. Whether speaking in the open air, however, or under more sheltered conditions, Mrs. Cooper's utterances are so manifestly from the heart and from personal knowledge that they compel attention.'[21]

Another petition, also organised in 1901, further illustrates the drive of guildswomen at local level. Together with several other Guild members, Miss Sarah Reddish helped to organise and present to the House of Commons a petition on the suffrage issue containing the signatures of 31,000 women employed in the Yorkshire and Lancashire textile trades. These dramatic demonstrations of working class solidarity contrast sharply with the more prosaic approach of the Central Committee. However, votes for women was a highly sensitive political issue and perhaps Miss Llewelyn Davies' personal overtures to the Home Secretary in 1909 should be regarded as a more effective, if less exciting, form of pressure.

Miss Llewelyn Davies' resignation as General Secretary was a watershed in the Guild's history. Many of the great campaigns of its formative years had borne fruit and new challenges were already presenting themselves. Yet, although the Guild's interests and administrative style were modified in the period between the two World Wars, it would be wrong to deny the enduring influence of its pioneering members.

Notes to Chapter 3

1. Anon. A Co-operative Standard for Women Workers (Kirkby Lonsdale 1908).
2. Quoted by C. Webb, The Woman with the Basket (Manchester 1927).
3. Monthly Bulletin, July 1944.
4. Quoted by Webb, op.cit.
5. London School of Economics, Miscellaneous Collection.
6. The Freedom of the Guild (London 1922).
7. *Daily News* February 1903. Cutting in LSE Miscellaneous Collection, op.cit.
8. Ibid.
9. Report of the Central Board of the Co-operative Union, 1902.
10. S. Bennett, Communities and Character (Kirkby Lonsdale 1904).
11. Report of the Central Board, op.cit.
12. Quoted by B.B. Gilbert, The Evolution of National Insurance in Great Britain (1966).
13. *The Times,* 24th June 1911.
14. M.A. Hamilton, Margaret Bondfield (1924).
15. LSE Miscellaneous Collection, op.cit.
16. Quoted by J. Gaffin, 'Women and Co-operation' in L. Middleton (ed) Women in the Labour Movement (1977).
17. The quotations which follow are taken from Working Women and Divorce. An Account of Evidence given on behalf of the Women's Co-operative Guild before the Royal Commission on Divorce (1911).
18. *The Times,* 14th November 1912.
19. M.L. Davies, The Vote at Last (1918).
20. *The Queen,* The Lady's Newspaper, 17th April 1909.
21. Ibid. See also J. Liddington, 'Women Cotton Workers and the Suffrage Campaign: The Radical Suffragists in Lancashire, 1893-1914', in S. Burman (ed), Fair Work for Women (1979).

CHAPTER 4

GROWTH AND ADJUSTMENT: THE GUILD BETWEEN THE WARS

Introduction

The 1920s and 1930s were decades of considerable growth and adjustment for the Women's Co-operative Guild - growth of membership and range of interests, and adjustment to the retirement of its long-serving General Secretary, and to the economic and political instability of the period. Yet in a changing and uncertain environment the Guild retained its traditional beliefs. Its essential rationale had not become outmoded by the passage of time, and it was with considerable justice that the Guild could proclaim in 1930 that 'The woman with the basket is still the finest symbol of the power that rocks the cradle of the world to be.' The appearance of Mrs Lawrenson and Miss Llewelyn Davies at the Jubilee celebrations of 1933 was more than a mere symbolic link with the past, for the values which they had promoted fifty years before were still central to the Guild's moving spirit.

After the short boom which followed the First World War the international economy collapsed and, as trade slumped, manufacturing production suffered and unemployment increased. Although the picture had brightened by the mid-'twenties, the onset of the world depression in 1929 brought another reversal of fortunes for both the industrialised and the third world nations. Britain's depression was not as catastrophic as that experienced by many other countries but unemployment in 1932 reached about two and a half million or 25 per cent of the work force. Thereafter, recovery set in, promoted by the growth of private house building and the new industries, such as motor cars, electrical products and aircraft. Even so, throughout the 'twenties and 'thirties, unemployment did not fall much below 10 per cent of the insured population, and away from the prosperous Midlands and Southern regions the situation remained much worse with workers in shipbuilding, coal and cotton textile industries being particular casualties of the harsher economic climate. This was in fact a period when Disraeli's two nations became a reality for while the majority of families prospered in the wake of technological innovation, a substantial minority whose fortunes depended upon the staple industries of the Industrial Revolution experienced massive hardship. The prosperity of some members of the community was reflected in the acquisition of a new house, motor car and furnishings, while for others the interwar years offered unemployment, hunger and sickness. It was no coincidence that, in the 1930s, Jarrow, a town of severe unemployment, had a tuberculosis rate that was double the national average, and an infant mortality rate that was almost twice as great as that for the country as a whole. Significantly, by far the largest financial contribution to the Guild's miners' welfare fund of 1926 came from the Southern Section whose members were hardly touched by unemployment. This contrast of fortunes explains why, sandwiched between consideration of unemployment and poor living standards, the Guild Congress of 1938 could still recommend, in the style of Billy Butlin, the introduction of Co-operative Holiday Camps.

Political Battles of the Guild

The interwar period was also a time of considerable political flux. Abroad, the rise of the Dictators threatened international security, while at home the political parties were inhibited by internal divisions and a fickle electorate, as well as by an inability to tackle successfully the grave problems of financial stability and industrial decay. The Guild described Stanley Baldwin's period of office between May 1923 and January 1924 as a time when national life was 'unusually stagnant', whilst Ramsay MacDonald's National administration was dismissed in 1934 as 'the most reactionary Government of modern times.'[1] Even when Labour gained power for a few months in 1924 and for a longer period between 1929 and 1931 the Guild found it difficult to influence the course of social policy at national level. The contrast of atmosphere with the reforming period of the Liberal Government just before the First World War was sharp. In the two decades between the wars the Guild was forced to defend and consolidate the gains already made in an earlier and more supportive environment.

Yet the interwar crises in domestic and international affairs drove the Guild into a more political and radical position than it had ever held before. For example, while it was uncompromising in its condemnation of Fascism, the Guild's pacifist sympathies became expressed in an increasingly determined and vocal manner, culminating in the courageous White Poppy Campaign of the 1930s. The introduction of an economic system based upon a Co-operative form of production had always been one of the Guild's aims but the unemployment of the 'twenties and 'thirties seemed both to confirm the fundamental weaknesses of capitalism and to signal its imminent downfall. Against this background, the Guild's attacks upon free enterprise became more common and were expressed with considerable feeling. The Congress of 1926 elevated this particular aspect of its work by emphasising that 'The object of the Guild is to promote a new social order, in which Co-operation shall replace capitalism and women have equal opportunities with men.'[2] At the same time, it was decided to exclude from office members who were themselves or whose husbands were engaged in business which was in competition with that of the societies. In her presidential address to Congress in 1927, Mrs. Bird, to the accompaniment of loud cheers, looked forward to the time

> when consumers shall own and control the raw materials of the earth and the machinery of production and distribution for the benefit of the whole of the community and not of the few.[3]

These views were similar to those expressed earlier by Miss Llewelyn Davies but they had now become a more prominent feature of the Guild's interpretation of society's ills and of its own role within the Co-operative Movement.

With the emergence of the Labour and Co-operative Parties it is perhaps not surprising that the Guild should become more politicised. Moreover, the extension of the franchise to women provided its members with the incentive to take an active part in political affairs. The 1921 Congress set the tone of Guild politics in the interwar period when it declared 'its hostility to the Capitalist political parties, whether in coalition or apart.' It was also argued that 'the only hope for a new world order for the workers lies in Co-operation and Labour coming into power, with women as well as men represented in Parliament and the Government.'[4]

The 1926 Congress committed the Guild to support the aims of the Co-operative Party, and by the end of the decade well over 300 branches had cemented this relationship by formal affiliation. By that time, too, the executive of the Co-operative Party and the Guild's Central Committee were meeting jointly to discuss policy and strategy. Guildswomen supported the Labour and Co-operative Parties in several ways. They were particularly active at election time, canvassing, distributing literature and performing a variety of clerical duties. It was reported that during the general election of 1923 some branches in London and Sheffield closed for three weeks to enable members to help in the constituencies. Guildswomen also helped to promote and distribute Co-operative and Labour publications, particularly the "Co-operative News", "Woman's Outlook", "Reynolds' News" and the "Daily Herald".

In 1928 the Guild introduced a special fund to assist members in Parliamentary elections, provided that they supported the constitution and policies of the Co-operative Party. However, Co-operative women enjoyed little success in national politics, though on two occasions Mrs. Barton, the General Secretary, came close to being elected for the King's Norton Division of Birmingham. There was considerable difficulty in persuading constituencies to nominate guildswomen, while the electorate also failed to display the necessary enthusiasm for Guild candidates. It is worth mentioning however, that Margaret Bondfield, who had been so active in the Guild's maternity campaign, became a Labour Member of Parliament in 1923 and was the first woman to enter the Cabinet and to be sworn of the Privy Council when in 1929 she became Minister of Labour in Ramsay MacDonald's second administration.

Understandably, delegates to Congress appear to have been particularly well motivated in support of the Co-operative and Labour Parties. One guildswoman with Conservative sympathies had a particularly unhappy experience at the 1928 Congress.

> At one stage of the meeting such an uproar occurred that it was some considerable time before any sort of order could be restored. One delegate who was greeted with cheers was a second later hissed and booed to such an extent that she was compelled to sit down. This arose because she confessed that she was a Conservative.
>
> The audience yelled "Shame", "Rotter", "Down with her politics", hissed, booed and stamped.
>
> Mrs. Bedhall, the president of the Guild and Congress, rang a bell, waved her arms, and tried every other device to obtain silence.
>
> When she finally made herself heard she said that as the particular speaker still had three minutes to speak she would ask

her to resume.

There was a fresh uproar at this, and, although the speaker did get up and strive to continue her speech, it was with great difficulty, as she was interrupted continually.

"I have had to listen to more derogatory words and sentences on my party during these past three days than you have ever had to listen to against your Labour Party," she said.

"Our Guild should not be biased by political opinions. I am proud of being a Conservative."

At this the women rose again and shouted down the speaker.

The President asked for those who wished the speaker to go on to say "Ay" and those against to say "No". There was an almost unanimous shout of "No".

One other member got up to support the speaker, saying that those with differing opinions had a right to them and should not be shouted down. She was howled down.[5]

Yet the adoption of a more political orientation to the Guild's activities did not enjoy its members' unanimous support. Following Mrs. Barton's defeat at King's Norton in November 1922, the Annual Report chided some of its readers by observing that 'the Guilds in the locality and the co-operators generally did not as a whole rise to that standard of enthusiasm which is implied in the principles they profess.' There were, too, other signs of disapproval. Women were known to walk out on Guild meetings which became highly political, while some speakers prefaced their remarks by apologising for introducing into the proceedings an element of party politics. The most serious rift concerning the Guild's political commitment occurred in 1939 when several branches objected vigorously to the Congress decision of the previous year that any member holding office must undertake to support and work for the candidates of the Labour Party at municipal and Parliamentary elections. One of the Plymouth branches refused to accept this arrangement and in 1939 it received an ultimatum from head office that it must conform or disaffiliate. "The Times" reported that "Officials from London attended a meeting at Plymouth, but were excluded after an angry scene. Some members of the branch went with them, including the honorary treasurer. By a large majority the branch decided to accept disaffiliation and to carry on independently. There was some dispute about the possession of papers and funds, but, after negotiation between solicitors, these were returned to the branch, which has now reorganised itself, still on a strictly non-party basis."[6]

Undoubtedly the Guild's political commitment lost it some support during the interwar period, but it also added a new dimension to its work which many women must have found both challenging and rewarding. Indeed, in many respects the Guild was the Co-operative Party's most critical but stimulating partner in the Movement. Thus the male Chairman of the 1935 Co-operative Party Conference admitted that the Women's Guilds

> had invariably been in advance of the Co-operative Party in the matter of Co-operative policies.[7]

The Guild's Strategy

The Guild's links with the Co-operative and Labour Parties adds to the difficulty of assessing its impact as a reformist body. Indeed, increasingly in the interwar period the Guild's influence upon central and local government was exercised through committees representing more than one organisation. For example, the Guild was represented on the Standing Joint Committee of Women's Industrial Organisations when it was set up in 1916. During the First World War and after, the Committee developed as an influential voice on behalf of female employees in industry. Its interests were broad and by 1920 was involved with such diverse topics as women magistrates, old age pensions and the welfare of unmarried mothers. The Committee was influential because it represented the principal organisations concerned with female employment, but this very strength meant that the contribution and significance of its constituent elements becomes difficult to identify. Thus an important contrast between the pre- and post-war years is that after 1918 a substantial measure of the Guild's influence was channelled in a collective manner. The traditional methods of applying pressure were retained, such as deputations and letter writing, though the practice of investigating and publicising the personal experiences of guildswomen fell away. Members continued to be represented on public bodies and by March 1939 the list included two mayors, 18 mayoresses, 24 aldermen, 24 county council members, 255 city, town, or urban district councillors, and 137 magistrates. In the fashion of the period, marches became an increasingly important part of the Guild's campaign technique, particularly in relation to the peace movement.

The financial climate of the interwar period necessarily

Accrington & Church Co-operative Society.

WOMEN'S CO-OPERATIVE GUILD.

Maternity & Child-welfare Week,

In the Assembly Room, Oak Street, Accrington.

Opened by Dr. GREENHALGH, Medical Officer of Health.

EXHIBITION
—OF—
Hygienic
Clothing
For Children

LOVE
ORDER
PROGRESS

To promote
Healthy
Motherhood
—AND TO—
Save the Babies.

COMMENCING SATURDAY, OCTOBER 23rd, at 8 O'CLOCK

Speaker - Mrs. COOPER, of Nelson.

TUESDAY, OCTOBER 26th, at 7-30, Miss BONDFIELD, London.
THURSDAY, OCTOBER 28th at 7-30, Miss REDDISH, Button School for Mothers
SATURDAY, OCTOBER 30th, at 3, Mrs. LAWTON, of Hanley.

ADMISSION FREE.

The Guild became actively involved in the social policy debates of the early twentieth century, though it was particularly concerned to press for improved maternity and infant welfare facilities. The Central Committee orchestrated a series of determined, sophisticated and effective campaigns which made the Guild the chief protagonist of the welfare rights of working class expectant mothers and their infants.

Birthday parties were one of the most popular events organised by Guild branches. This was held at Tooting in the late 1940's.

In the 1920's and 1930's the Guild campaigned strenuously for loyalty to Co-operative productions with a designated range of CWS products being chosen for particular years.

reduced the Guild's effectiveness as a promoter of social change, while more complex central and local government administration altered the context in which new ideas could be applied. Yet the Guild's power as a pressure group was diminished by its own expanding range of interests. This problem was recognised by the Central Committee for in 1924 it issued a paper warning the branches and sections not to spread their efforts too thinly but rather to join with others in concentrating upon those issues which were strictly relevant to the Guild's objectives. Part of the problem was that branches were invited to lend their support to the work of a variety of other bodies. The Central Committee itself noted that it had been asked to participate in 'activities of all sorts from disarmament campaigns to a war on house-flies!'[8] The growth in membership also created difficulties of this type since new members frequently belonged to one or more other organisations, some of which had radically different interests from those of the Guild.

Guildswomen were reminded in 1937 that 'We must be very careful that we do not sink our identity in these other organisations nor must we allow our Co-operative ideas and outlooks to be overshadowed by temporary and less important issues.'[9] The increasing number and range of resolutions at Guild Congress also reflects the way in which members' energy was being dissipated across a wide area rather than, as in the past, focused upon particular concerns. This was one of the inevitable organisational problems which resulted from growth. It is noticeable that one of the Guild's most effective campaigns was unconcerned with social welfare policies, but concentrated specifically upon the peace issue.

The Guild Expands

Despite the difficulties which derived from the general circumstances of the interwar years and the Guild's involvement with a growing range of social and political causes, the period was one of considerable success, particularly in terms of the growth of membership. The First World War created special problems for the Guild as meeting halls were taken over by the military and an increasing number of women took up paid employment, so that membership declined and some branches closed. As normal conditions were resumed after 1918, membership picked up and the year ending May 1920 saw the largest ever increase of some 11,600 new members. Economic conditions deteriorated in the Spring of 1920 and with the consequent rise in unemployment membership stagnated and no further significant increase was recorded until circumstances improved again in the mid-'twenties. It was reported in 1923 that as unemployment came to affect the families of many guildswomen, and the retail societies suffered from declining incomes, several branches 'found difficulty in keeping up their membership, and some had to suffer reduced grant or loss of their meeting rooms.'[10] The impact of unemployment upon the branches naturally varied between one area and another, but it was said to have had a general restraining influence upon the Guild's campaign activities in the early 'twenties.

After 1925 membership grew steadily, punctuated by particular events, such as the general strike and further sharp upturns in unemployment, which had a depressing, though temporary, effect upon the overall trend. From May 1920 until May 1939 the number of branches more than doubled, from 784 to 1,819, while total membership increased from 44,539 to 87,246. It is noticeable, however, that the increase in membership was heavily concentrated in the Midlands and the South where the level of employment was high and the societies prospered. In the Yorkshire and Lancashire regions, where economic conditions were far less favourable, membership increased, but not by very much. One consequence of this was that the occupational characteristics of members and their husbands also changed, away from the traditional activities of the industrial North towards the science based industries of the Midlands and the South.

Administration

Growth of this magnitude inevitably placed considerable strain upon the Guild's administration. In September 1923, for example, the General Secretary, Miss Enfield, informed her executive that a widespread feeling had developed within the branches that they were out of touch with the Guild's central administration. This reflected the fact that it was becoming increasingly difficult for Guild officials to maintain personal contact with the branches, and also that the office staff had to struggle hard to cope with routine administration. In addition, as Congress agenda lengthened, it became more difficult to give each item the appropriate amount of attention. In 1924 an Inquiry Committee was appointed to review the Guild's structure and operation, the report of which led to the appointment of a chief clerk in place of the Assistant Secretary, and increased powers for the Standing Orders Committee in dealing with Congress business. Other methods used to improve the Guild's management efficiency included the sub-division of districts, the appointment of further clerical staff and the removal in 1936 from John Street, Bedford Row, to more spacious accommodation in Great Prescot Street.

One of the most significant management changes of the interwar period was a shift of influence from the General Secretary to the Central Committee. To some extent this was a natural response to the retirement of Miss Llewelyn Davies whose long service and national reputation had provided a special authority. In addition, Miss A. Honora Enfield, who succeeded Miss Llewelyn Davies, combined the secretaryship of both the International and English Guilds so that she was unable to devote as much time to domestic affairs as had her predecessor. There is, however, evidence that even before Miss Llewelyn Davies' retirement some members of the Central Committee were becoming irritated at the degree of personal independence which she and Lilian Harris appear to have enjoyed. In September 1920, for example, the Committee decided to propose that it should itself elect the General Secretary, thus removing responsibility from the branches. This suggestion was rejected by the 1921 Congress, though it was agreed that in future the Committee would furnish a short list of suitable candidates, the final selection being made by branches. It was also decided that the Secretary should be a full-time official, subject to dismissal by the Central Committee. There was some suggestion at the time that these decisions precipitated Miss Llewelyn Davies' retirement, though she herself denied that this was so. The change in management tone was reflected in a short paper on the Guild's history and organisation published on behalf of the Central Committee in 1932. Significantly, the General Secretary's role received only the briefest mention, responsibility for the implementation of Congress decisions, campaign work and relations with the sections and branches resting firmly with the Central Committee.

Mrs. Eleanor Barton, who succeeded Miss Enfield as General Secretary in 1925, was too strong a personality to adopt a subservient role. Mrs. Barton's administrative and judicial experience made her a formidable opponent in committee discussion and an effective advocate of the Guild's policies. She had served as a City Councillor in Sheffield and as a magistrate, while both she and her husband had been active supporters of the Co-operative and Independent Labour Parties. Perhaps her main contribution to the Guild was in helping to move it to a more political orientation. She is generally remembered by guildswomen as a very efficient but strict General Secretary, and Kathleen Kempton, who joined the Guild in 1935, thought that she could even be rather dictatorial.

Perhaps it was these personal characteristics which in 1937 led the Central Committee to assert its authority by declaring that 'The President should be the mouthpiece of the movement, and should accompany the General Secretary on all national and other important deputations'.[11] In addition, the General Secretary was henceforth required to furnish an explanation for all absences from the office. By 1939 an effective General Secretary was still crucial to the Guild's success, but, consistent with the Guild's democratic aims and structure, the position had lost the distinctive power and authority which it had possessed during Miss Llewelyn Davies' term of office. This was partly a question of personality, but was more particularly a natural response to the Guild's evolution from a relatively small body of women with limited horizons to an organisation of national reputation with a very large and politically sensitive membership.

The Guild at Branch Level

Branch work between the wars largely retained its pre-1914 pattern. Regular meetings were held to consider issues connected with the Movement, such as the price and quality of goods in the stores or the role of the Co-operative Party, while broader concerns, from health care to international politics, were also debated. Members engaged in a variety of fund raising activities in support of deserving causes, and shared in campaigns to press for improvements in local and national public services. Educational work remained an important and expanding feature of the Guild's activities, and by 1929 one of its main problems was 'how to keep up with the demand for knowledge shown by members throughout the country.'[12] In addition to sectional and district conferences, a growing number of day and week-end schools provided opportunities to assess domestic and international problems, as well as to acquire more knowledge of the Co-operative Movement itself. In 1930-31 the following topics were taken for discussion at branch, district and sectional levels.

Milk and Healthy Children
Modern Attacks on Co-operative Trade
Co-operative Societies and the Income Tax
Housing and Motherhood
Peace Training in Schools
Women's Work in International Life

As the 'thirties progressed, more time came to be devoted to the peace movement, both as a subject of discussion and source of campaign interest.

Problems at branch level were similar to those recounted earlier for the pre-1914 period. Although the general increase in membership helped to ensure good attendance at meetings, a few branches continued to fall by the wayside. This was partly because a more mobile population caused fluctuations of membership, but was mainly due to the difficulties associated with depression and unemployment. A larger membership, combined with improved public education, seems to have removed the problem of attracting suitable candidates to serve as officials at branch level and above. However, the more difficult academic topics which guildswomen were expected to discuss remained for some a formidable challenge. In September 1932 the members of the St. John's branch in Bristol were addressed on the topic of unemployment and land ownership, and the minutes record what must have been a widely shared experience.

Our speaker said the World produces everything we want, which has to be produced by labour, but there was a system by which some were very rich and some very poor. We were to understand the Land is the source from which wealth comes, as we have to pay to the people that own the Land. Mr. Brierley seems to know the history of the Land and how it was produced, but it takes a great deal of studying before we could thoroughly understand it.

Yet Guild meetings had their lighter moments for members arranged a variety of social activities, from sing-songs to cards, and followed the increasingly popular national pastime of charabanc trips to the coast and elsewhere. For example, in July 1932 the members of the St. John's branch enjoyed a day excursion to Exmouth.

> We started about 8.30 all feeling merry and every prospect of a nice warm day. It was beautiful riding through the Country, being blest with the sunshine all along the way, and all taking part in singing and enjoying a good laugh. We landed at Exmouth about 1.30 and after a meal, some made tracks for town and some for the sea, in which some of our members paddled.

Two months later the branch had a half day outing to Birdlip and Cheltenham. The minutes record that after tea at Birdlip:

> We then journeyed on through Cheltenham gliding through a heavy shower and mist, but when we got to Gloster it was nice and fine. We had a short look round, one being bound to notice the nice block of Co-op shops, which are not only a credit to our Society but to the Town. We left here just after seven, and our next stop was at Berkely, where all indulged in a little light refreshment. Of course, we all enjoyed a hearty laugh and sing song on the way. The leading turns being amusing speeches made regarding Guild officers (all in happy strain) and last but not least Oh. My. Hat.

Transport improvements and, for those whose husbands were in employment, higher real incomes, enabled guildswomen in the interwar period to enjoy more varied leisure pursuits than their sisters of an earlier generation. Guild officials eventually became concerned at 'the tendency to demand more social activities' and warned members that 'in the rush of present day problems some people do find it easier to live just on the surface and to go, as it were, with the tide, rather than face up to the more thought provoking factors which are so large a part of daily life.'[13]

A useful method of recapturing some of the flavour of Guild meetings is to follow the events of one year through the minutes of a particular branch. During the calendar year 1934 the Wesley Castle branch of the Guild in Birmingham normally met weekly with an attendance of between 40 and 50 members. Meetings were opened with the minutes of the previous session and closed with half an hour's social activity. Topics discussed during the year included:

Social Hygiene
Natural History
Rates and Social Service

Work of the Guild
Secondary and Special Education
Co-operative Politics (2 sessions)
Co-operative Butchery (2 sessions)
Co-operative Greengrocery
Dictatorship Versus Democracy

One talk given by the manager of a local Co-operative butchery department, which was also attended by a director of the Society, evokes memories of Mrs. Lawrenson's criticisms in the 1880s regarding the goods sold in her own store in Woolwich. It was reported that

> Mr. Lygo and Mr. Enon answered the questions fired at them very well and Mr. Lygo said several complaints he had heard would receive attention.

The pioneers would have been delighted at such a practical manifestation of basket power.

The Wesley Castle Guildswomen engaged in a number of charitable fund raising activities and participated in the Guild's national campaigns. Members canvassed in support of a petition to be presented to the Public Works Committee, though the most exciting event of the year was an anti-war demonstration which involved the preparation over many months of special dresses. The peace movement enjoyed considerable support from this branch and much of its members' time was consumed in discussing the relevant issues.

The Wesley Castle members experienced a varied diet of leisure activities, including:

Mystery night
Summer outing to Manchester (no children allowed)
Pantomime outing (no children allowed)
Singing
Raffle
Drama
Social and dance
Games
Whist Drive
Outing to Chepstow

In additon, perhaps from a sense of guilt at having excluded children from the pantomime excursion, members organised a party for the movement's younger elements. The social event of the year, however, centred around the branch's first anniversary in May when members gathered to enjoy a celebration evening.

> *After tea our President gave us all a hearty welcome and said she hoped we would have a jolly and happy time and forget our ages those who were nearing the 50 age. Our President then presented to her Guild a beautiful banner, which she herself has worked and on which many hours of patience have been given.*

The remainder of the evening was devoted to games and dancing. It was particularly noted that 'the balloon game was most laughable.' The occasion was clearly an unqualified success and after a farewell tune from the band all the participants 'went home tired but happy after a great day.' Not surprisingly perhaps, there was some competition to represent the members at the "birthday" parties of other branches.

The atmosphere generated at branch level may also be rekindled by the personal experiences of Guild members. Mrs. Olive Davies, who joined the Guild in 1928, informed the authors that it was principally the organisation's democratic structure which

> *won her admiration and provided the inspiration to play a part in helping to attain its Aims and Objects.*

On the same theme, Mrs. May Truscott reminds us that meetings

> *could be presided over by a factory worker, a teacher, an office worker or housewife. There was nothing, she adds, to prevent members from wearing the Presidential Chain. To enjoy a fellowship. To laugh, to build, to serve for truth and justice.*

A desire to support the Co-operative Movement within the company of likeminded women was clearly a major influence in the Guild's expansion and in shaping the pattern of branch life, but Mrs. Davies also highlights another important factor in the growth of membership.

> *I often wonder how many others joined the Guild for the reason of staying at home whilst their husbands were out attending their Union Meetings - local - district and so on, encouraged to join by them, and indeed continued to receive this encouragement. In 1928 this was happening to me, when I was longing for something more than home and its surroundings.*

Despite the popularity of "birthday" parties and day excursions, women joined the Guild and retained their membership throughout the years because they were committed to its fundamental principles, and it was this commitment which gave the branches their strength and vitality.

The Guild's campaigns were a major focus of interest for

many of its members. Mrs. Bristow explained that she joined the Guild in 1926 because she was so impressed by its surveillance of Co-operative store prices.

My first meeting I remember very vividly. I was welcomed by the Chairman who said "You can come as a visitor for two meetings after which you will pay your subscription 1s. 6d.

The members were up in arms because the 'Store' about a mile away was selling 1lb. tins of corned beef for 5½d. and our branch was charging 6d. for the same tins. That had to be investigated. I was so taken up with the way that was dealt with that I joined promptly the same afternoon.

It is no surprise perhaps, to hear Mrs. E.W. Mason recall that *a lot of the managers didn't like the Guild members too much, because they kept them on their toes.* But she added that, *I got on very well with them because I used to get a lot of Co-op members for them by explaining the good benefits.*

Mrs. Isobel Lee was born in 1892 and joined the Guild in 1918. She remembered another form of local campaign. During the course of a branch outing to Bury St. Edmunds, Mrs. Lee discovered that the public toilets were not only free but also contained washing facilities. She noted that

we had nothing like that in Chelmsford

and so initiated a campaign to rectify the situation. Mrs. Lee is proud to record that all the ladies' public toilets in Chelmsford are now free.

For Mrs. Olive Waterman, aged 30 when she joined the Guild in 1930, however, the national campaigns provided a great thrill and sense of occasion.

I can remember very large demonstrations marching to the House of Commons with the Guild banners. Many of them beautifully embroidered in silk, to lobby MPs on matters of special interest to women - women's suffrage (in the very early days with my mother who was a member), contraception, family allowance, and later on pensions, equality of opportunity in education, jobs, etc.

The particular character of individual branches must have varied considerably, though Mrs. Margaret Love's experiences were probably shared by very many guildswomen. Mrs. Love recalls joining the Guild in 1936 as 'a really shy young housewife.'

The officials at the table very correct and rule conscious, woe betide any woman who spoke out of place or didn't give a vote of thanks correctly. My first job in 1937 was making out reports for both our weekly local papers, any mistakes corrected at the next meeting. I remember how we all shopped at our own Co-operative branch, and I still do! making sure we bought Co-op brands.

The poor branch managers used to watch for guildswomen who made sure they were served with Co-operative makes. Letters were sent regularly to Parliament with suggestions, etc. The most important resolution sent to Congress year by year was for an increase in widows pension, many of our guildswomen being allowed only 10/- per week. This was not increased for many years.

Locally we requested policewomen for the town, also transport for the midwives to have for the gas in air machines, remember midwives then went by foot or by bicycle.

Another perspective on branch activities is provided by Mary Saran, who joined the Guild soon after she came to England in 1933.

Not only did this help me in becoming fluent in English; I also learned to understand the Cockney accent. Moreover, I was introduced to local women's activities which, I found, played a much more important part in public life in Britain than they had in Germany. I learned about problems as reflected at the local level, about methods and customs in the Labour Movement (of which the Co-operative Movement was an integral part, again different from Germany). I soon got over my astonishment at meetings being held in church halls and starting with a hymn. This was a far cry from the bitter struggle against the Church we had fought as German socialists.[14]

Full participation in branch life was a satisfying experience, but perhaps the final word should rest with Mrs. Davies who observed wisely:

being able to look back, and watch the campaigns of the Guild blossom into life - surely nothing could be so interesting and rewarding!

Guild Congress

The annual Congress remained the major event in the Guild calendar. A broad and growing range of resolutions was put before delegates to be debated and voted upon. In 1919 the Congress was held in Middlesbrough with 775 delegates in attendance, but twenty years later in Hull the corresponding event attracted more than double this figure. As we have already noticed, the escalating number of resolutions created serious problems for the conference organisers, while accommodating the expanding army of delegates also created difficulties. One of the many practical problems involved in conference management was the care of lost property. It was noted of one Congress that "The Guild Secretary has had to run a miniature lost property office to deal with the variety of articles mislaid daily by delegates. Every day articles have been spread out on the Chairman's table for delegates to claim. These have included gloves, brooches, umbrellas, notebooks, handbags, and even return tickets."[15]

Like other annual conferences, some Guild Congresses were doubtless rather dull, but most seem to have been occasions for serious and rewarding debate, interspersed with the occasional touch of humour. Delegates appear to have expressed their views in a blunt and uncomplicated manner. The "Daily Telegraph" correspondent remarked rather condescendingly of the 1929 Congress that: "The homely language used by delegates has been a feature of the conference. For example, one speaker, wishing to express disapproval of a resolution, said she was "dead nuts against it." Another invariably answered the chairman with "Right O!" All the speakers called the chairman "Mrs. Chairman," instead of the customary "Madam Chairman."[16]

To the accompaniment of roars of laughter, one delegate in 1929 suggested darkly that the introduction of female home helps might lead to attempts to "vamp" husbands. Amid loud cheers, Mrs. Lyhtfoot of the Central Committee retorted indignantly that

I trust my husband, and so do all Co-operative women.[17]

Congress could sometimes generate a high peak of excitement. One particularly remarkable example was that at Plymouth in 1928 when even the "Manchester Guardian" reporter was clearly astonished at the exuberance of Co-operative women. "By the time the morning session finished the members were in a state of wild excitement, and the fact that many took the wrong turning in coming out of the hall and went into another entrance instead, thereby encountering hundreds more coming out, nearly led to a free fight. Women struggled, pushed, and jostled each other aside with their elbows. Some of the frailer women got crushed against the wall, and one, at least, hurt her arm rather badly."[18]

Fortunately, most conferences were of a less raucous character so that delegates normally returned home sound in wind and limb.

Yet for pageant and drama the London Jubilee Congress of 1933 was the outstanding event of the interwar period. At the opening session on June 19 almost 3,000 women crowded into the Central Hall, Westminster, with the strongest national and international representation ever known. The meeting was dominated by two events of high emotion. One concerned the presentation of the First International Guild Banner by Frau Freundlich, the President of the International Guild. The banner was worked in the International Guild's colours of white, blue and green, while shining from the tricolour was a sun with 15 rays representing the national guilds, in the centre of which was a shopping basket symbolising women's powerful role as consumers. The second incident involved the platform appearance of Miss Llewelyn Davies and Miss Lilian Harris, both of whom received a rapturous ovation. The "Daily Herald" recorded that 'the delegates cheered Miss Llewelyn Davies again and again as she urged them not to be content with the triumphs and the progress of the past, but to go forward with faith and trust in the irresistible advance that is bringing the new civilisation.'[19]

Even the drama of this occasion was surpassed three days later when the Guild held its celebratory rally at the Crystal Palace. The "Daily Herald" again captured the magnificent atmosphere which enveloped the proceedings, and is worth quoting at length. "Fifteen thousand women sat massed in the Great Transept of the Crystal Palace last night with admiring eyes and intently listening ears. Outside the barriers hundreds more stood four deep.

"In the centre of the great stage, with nearly 5,000 listeners piled up in the tiers behind her, and the rest of the great multitude facing her, a very charming old lady delivered a speech.

"She had sat resting for half an hour during some soul-stirring preliminaries. Now and then she wiped her eyes as the great organ pealed forth the strains of grand old hymn tunes, and the 15,000 women almost sang their hearts out.

"But when Mrs. Eleanor Barton, the Secretary of the Women's Co-operative Guild, who was presiding over the great celebration that signalised the Jubilee of the Movement, called on the first speaker this remarkable Victorian tucked her handkerchief away, rose from her chair, walked to the microphone, and made a speech which everyone a quarter of her age ought to have envied and probably did.

"She was Mrs. Lawrenson, 83 years old, a grey-haired, comely figure dressed in black, but with the light of a lingering youth still in her eyes and a note of inspiration still in the voice that the microphone helped to ring through the glass-covered hall.

"Fifty years ago she helped to found the Women's Co-operative Guild. She was then one of seven. Tonight she was one of a 70,000 membership.

"And as she walked off the platform the cheers that almost engulfed her must have told her a strange and beautiful story of dreams come true. It was an amazing night.

"The 15,000 women sang their Guild songs and as they did so there was a procession up and down and round and about the aisles, such as even the Crystal Palace can never have seen before.

"It was a floral procession symbolically and beautifully carried out. First there were the marguerites for alertness, then poppies for courage, sunflowers for brightness, cornflowers for hope, clematis for perseverance, white roses for purity, honeysuckle for endeavour and pansies for harmony.

"The processionists, most of them mothers and some of them grandmothers, carrying their banners and wearing their colours proudly, represented the eight geographical sections of the Guild and represented them magnificently.

"The organ rolled on and on until the dignified march ended and the grouping was complete."[20]

For those guildswomen fortunate enough to be present, the beautiful and stirring events of that June evening must have been the occasion of a lifetime.

The Guild Fights On

The Guild's reaction to the political and social problems of the interwar period may be grouped under three headings - unemployment, social policy and the protection of the family, and the peace movement. Unemployment was viewed as symptomatic of the weaknesses of capitalist production and was a scourge which could only be finally resolved by the introduction of Co-operative economic principles. As the 1931 Congress explained, the 'way of facing the present difficulties is by the organisation of industry on a Co-operative basis, and by the extension of trade through International Co-operation'.[21] In the early post-war years the Guild continued to press the Union and the CWS on credit trading and the restriction of dividends, but the traditional issues soon came to attract less attention and much greater emphasis was placed upon promoting Co-operative production and trade.

In 1921 the Guild began a campaign to assist the stores through the depression and within a few months guildswomen representing 257 branches were taking part in canvassing and organising propaganda meetings, concerts, processions and exhibitions. Members also distributed 100,000 copies of a leaflet prepared by Mrs. Barton entitled, 'Co-operative Women, Support Your Own Stores.' In 1928 the Guild introduced a promotional drive for selected Co-operative products and in that year special attention was given to boots and brushes and corsets and clothing, while sales of CWS china were pushed in 1929. Thereafter the scheme lost its momentum until it was resurrected in 1935 when soap, jams, Keighley Wringers and Belmont garments were designated products of the year.

Perhaps the Guild's greatest promotional success, however, concerned Co-operative milk. This was particularly satisfying since it was the Guild which in 1925 was largely responsible for encouraging the Co-operative Union to promote this branch of trade. The Annual Report for 1934 noted proudly that 'the subsequent growth and development of Co-operative milk services throughout the country has more than justified the optimism and far-sightedness of the Guild.'

During the 1920s a number of methods were introduced to protect British industry from imported goods, but with the rise of unemployment a more general tariff structure was introduced in 1932 which brought to a final conclusion the free trade policies of the nineteenth century. The Guild's principal objection to the return of protection was that it hindered the flow of international trade, including that between the national Co-operative Movements, which, it was argued, was essential for economic recovery. The Guild's position was vindicated in the interwar period, particularly in the 1930s, when a general movement towards trade restrictions served to depress the international economy and keep world unemployment at an unusually high level.

The Guild's views on economic affairs were taken seriously

and in 1924, for example, it was invited to present evidence before the Government Committee on National Debt and Taxation. Perhaps the most distinctive feature of its economic policy was what would now be described as Keynsian economics. This involved the maintenance of a level of private and public demand sufficient for the achievement of full employment. Keynes' ideas were not particularly well received by interwar governments, all of which were concerned with moderating rather than expanding public expenditure. Certainly the National Government would not have been sympathetic to the Guild's suggestion in 1933 that the most practical way of reducing unemployment was through public expenditure on bridges and roads, water, sewerage and electrification schemes and a massive programme of council house building.

Apart from considerations of social justice and welfare, the Guild believed that a reasonably high and stable level of wages was fundamental to the maintenance of consumer demand and full employment. Particular concern was expressed at the plight of the low paid. Protests were made against attempts to restrict the operation of the Trade Boards, which regulated wages in low paid jobs, while the 1931 Congress suggested that legislation should be introduced to secure a national minimum wage of £4 per week. Moreover, it was argued that consumption could be encouraged by reducing taxes on essential produce, and that any loss of revenue could be recovered without harm to the economy by taxing land values and wealth. Industrial action by trade unions was also supported for a mixture of economic and social reasons. Good wages were said to promote both good health and the prosperity of industry and commerce. With the benefit of hindsight, the Guild's economic thinking may not appear to have been particularly radical. However, at the time it was well in advance of that of many elements within the working class movement, including the period's two Labour administrations!

The Guild advocated a number of other measures to restrict the severity of unemployment, including work sharing, raising of the school leaving age and better training facilities. Loud protests were also made against employers whose redundancy practices discriminated against women. Practical assistance was rendered to communities which suffered particular hardship. This mostly concerned the coal mining areas which

103

were badly affected by both the General Strike in 1926 and the decline in sales as other sources of energy became available, and as competition from foreign producers increased. At the end of the 1920s guildswomen raised £1,000 for distribution to miners and their families. Clothing was also sent and, in the other direction, children were given temporary refuge in members' homes. Special relationships were developed as Guild branches in the distressed areas were 'adopted' by their sisters in other more prosperous parts of the country. Support was also given to marches and demonstrations by the unemployed. Mrs. Isobel Lee recalled that:

> Several of our members helped when we welcomed the Jarrow marchers as they came through the town. I went round cadging stuff to make them some nice hot soup. Our Mayor of the town had butchers shops so I asked him for bones, etc. and we gave them a good meal when they arrived.

Improvements to the scale and conditions of benefit developed as a major aspect of the Guild's unemployment campaign strategy. It became especially concerned at the new arrangements for the maintenance of the unemployed introduced by the National Government in 1931, objecting in particular to the reduction of benefit and the general application of means testing. The means test, which was applied on a household basis and thus discriminated against families with children at work, was administered by the Public Assistance Committees, still associated in the public mind with the Poor Law Guardians whose responsibilities they had inherited in 1929. At their Congress in 1932 guildswomen objected strongly to 'the inquisitorial methods that are used,'[22] and to the fact that in some instances young people were being forced to leave home in order that their parents might qualify for benefit. Under the Unemployment Act of 1934, the payment of benefit was transferred from local to central government, an arrangement which the Guild regarded as undemocratic and which introduced 'a definite measure of Fascism.'[23] During the remainder of the 'thirties the Guild continued to campaign for a more flexible system of relief, including abolition of the waiting period before the payment of benefit, and assistance with travel expenses for claimants attending interviews with prospective employers. It was in the following decade, however, when the sacrifices of war produced thoughts of a more egalitarian society, that the pressure exerted in the 1930s by the Guild and other organisations produced a major overhaul of the machinery for the relief of the unemployed.

Maternity and Family Welfare

Throughout the interwar period the Guild retained a strong interest in maternal and infant welfare. In November 1919 the Central Committee issued a 'Memorandum on the National Care of Maternity under the Ministry of Health,' which recommended positive government involvement in the consolidation and extension of services, including home helps, maternity homes and welfare centres, midwifery services and milk supplies for nursing and expectant mothers. These issues remained at the centre of the Guild's health care campaign, though by 1929 Congress was demanding nothing less than a fully state controlled medical service incorporating hospitals, midwifery and general medical facilities. Important gains were made, though the pace of change was uneven. The Annual Report noted in 1920 that 'After five years of effort Shipley Branch has succeeded in getting a Municipal Maternity Centre opened, the Shipley Society providing the room and Guild members doing most of the work for the first three months.' By 1923, however, the Guild was switching its attention to the provision of local authority housing, an area where councils were more responsive to pressure since they had to meet certain statutory obligations. In the late 1920s the Government housing subsidies were reduced and the Guild's attention returned once again to health care. Special campaigns were mounted in 1928 and 1929 to encourage local health authorities to implement more fully their powers under the Maternity and Child Welfare Act, 1918. New initiatives were also demanded, including the provision of local authority ante- and post-natal clinics. The number of infant welfare clinics increased from just a handful at the beginning of the interwar period to 3,580 in 1938. Of course the Guild was not solely responsible for this dramatic progress, but its unique grassroots campaign experience was of outstanding importance in persuading local authorities to use the powers at their disposal. Yet at the end of the 'thirties Congress continued to lament the fact that maternal mortality remained high and that significant improvement was still required in the medical care of mothers and infants.

One of the Guild's most consistent demands during the

interwar period was for the provision of a suitably staffed and equipped midwifery service. The 1927 Congress resolved that all midwives and maternity nurses should be public servants controlled by the local authorities and distributed according to population density. The Guild was also concerned that midwives should be properly trained and provided with adequate opportunity to update their knowledge, while the 1928 Congress suggested that all country midwives should be supplied with motorcycles in order to attend to isolated maternity cases. Maternal mortality actually rose in the early 'thirties, and as a growing body of evidence came to demonstrate the inadequacies of self-employed midwives, the Government responded to the pressure exerted by the Guild and other organisations with the introduction of the Midwives Act of 1936, which obliged local authorities to provide properly trained personnel. Thereafter, the Guild's energies were devoted to securing a more generous local provision of qualified midwives. Although municipal health care by the end of the 'thirties left much to be desired, its progress during the decade contributed significantly to the overall decline in infant and maternal mortality. The Guild's share in this improvement was something of which it could be justly proud. Apart from local and national resolutions and deputations, the Guild exercised influence through its representation on the Ministry of Health's committee set up in 1929 to review the training and employment of midwives, the reports of which contributed significantly to the legislation of 1936.

The campaign for better maternity and infant care was a natural extension of its earlier concerns, but the interwar period also saw the Guild moving into new areas of family welfare. It became involved, for example, in the public debate on family limitation. This was an issue which captured public attention in the late nineteenth century, but to begin with it was principally the middle and upper classes who restricted family size through the use of contraceptive devices.

In March 1923 Marie Stopes, one of the pioneers in the establishment of family planning clinics, discussed her work with the Guild's Central Committee. Although the Committee initially resolved to promote Dr. Stopes' ideas, it was decided later in the same year not to make birth control a topic of special discussion. The decisive factor in this change of attitude appears to have been renewed pressure from the Salford

Catholic Federation. However, by 1926 the Guild was prepared to brave the wrath of the Catholic interest for in that year Congress took the view that the time had now arrived 'when birth control information should be given by fully qualified medical officers at Maternity and Child Welfare Centres, assisted out of public funds, to married women requesting such knowledge.'[24] The Guild had become convinced that more effective contraception was one important answer to the very high level of maternal mortality. It was said in 1928 that 'unscientific attempts at contraception are responsible for a great number of maternal deaths.'[25] The Guild's interest in birth control continued into the 1930s and its efforts were important in helping to establish the topic as a matter of public health rather than personal morality, though the main pressure for an improvement in local authority services came from other organisations, including the Family Planning Association, which was set up in 1930. In addition, as unemployment remained relatively high during the 1930s, the pressure on working class incomes encouraged the restriction of family size, and by the end of the decade concern was being expressed by demographers and others at the serious implications of a very low birth rate.

Abortion was also widely discussed in the 1930s as an adjunct to the debate on maternal welfare. The Guild Congress of 1934 overwhelmingly passed a resolution in favour of legalised abortion. As with contraception, the issue was perceived in part as one of female rights - whether women should be compelled to have a child they did not want - although the principal emphasis was again upon the high level of maternal mortality and the danger arising from 'back-street' abortionists. As one delegate argued:

> Being compelled to bear a child unwillingly is injurious to both mother and child.
> In advocating the legalisation of abortion, we emphatically claim to have that operation carried out by skilled members of the surgical profession. The high maternal death rate is largely reflected in the practices of quacks and by making it legal for a woman to have abortion, it would remove the dangers that arise through the employment of quacks.[26]

Congress also demanded an amnesty for women who were in prison for procuring an abortion. The Guild's stand enjoyed some public support, and it is possible that the formation in 1936 of the Abortion Law Reform Association owed something to its propaganda. However, it was not until the 1960s that there was a major swing of opinion in favour of legalised abortion. By that time the feminists identified abortion as related to women's rights rather than maternal mortality and thus returned to one of the issues which guildswomen had discussed thirty years before.

During the interwar period the Guild's welfare interests expanded greatly to include family allowances, pensions, housing and even civil protection. By the mid-'twenties the Guild was expressing its support for the principle of family allowances, though this issue was rather overshadowed by the maternal and infant welfare campaign and by the belief that workers ought to be paid a wage sufficient to meet their needs. The 1924 Congress advocated pensions for widows and for women whose husbands had deserted them or were incapacitated, while by the close of the interwar period old age pensions were recommended for all at 55 since it was argued that by that age many people had surpassed their productive working life. Early retirement was also seen as one method of combating unemployment. The provision of public housing was an important Guild topic in the 1920s when its propaganda machinery was used in support of an increased supply of good quality accommodation but at rents which working class people could afford. The housing subsidies of that period were in fact often used in support of more expensive dwellings well beyond the reach of low income families. Cheaper property was released by the massive growth of private house building in the 1930s, and, while the Guild continued to press for slum clearance and more council accommodation, its interest was at a lower pitch than in the previous decade.

Throughout the interwar period Congress passed a number of resolutions connected with law and order. It called for the abolition of capital punishment and of the birching of young offenders, the latter of which was described as a 'survival of barbarism'. A Home Office committee, which included Guild representation, reported in 1938 against the birching of juveniles, except for the protection of warders, a decision which brought great satisfaction to guildswomen. However, the Guild's principal concern in the area of public order was with the appointment of women police officers, which it regarded as essential to the protection of women and children. Delegates to the 1926 Congress also argued that in cases of offences against these two groups evidence should in the first instance be given in the presence of a policewoman or female magistrate or probation officer. As in matters of social policy, the Guild's approach to the maintenance of public order was liberal and enlightened, reflecting the practical experience of its members as wives and mothers.

The Guild's Peace Policy

Perhaps the most dominant feature of the Guild's activities in the 1930s relates to its involvement with the peace movement. In its early years the Guild was almost entirely concerned with domestic issues, but the onset of war in 1914 broadened its horizons and the Congress of that year declared its belief 'that civilised nations should never again resort to the terrible and ineffectual method of war for the settlement of international disputes.'[27] The Guild's anti-war feeling was again in evidence at the 1916 Congress, which carried a resolution urging 'the Government to seek the earliest opportunity of promoting negotiations with the object of securing a just and lasting peace, and protests against the adoption of Conscription by this country.'[28] The 1914-18 conflict brought home to guildswomen the fact that war could affect their lives even more profoundly than the domestic social concerns to which they devoted so much energy.

Throughout the 1920s and 1930s the Guild supported the League of Nations in its efforts to settle international disputes through negotiation rather than force and consistently supported moves towards disarmament. In 1932, for example, the Guild engaged upon a programme of meetings, demonstrations and conferences to rouse public opinion behind the League's Disarmament Conference of that year. In addition, hundreds of branches sent telegrams to Geneva to wish the delegates well. Conversely, the British Government's rearmament programme of the mid-'thirties received the Guild's condemnation. Following the announcement in March 1935 that weapons expenditure was to be increased, the Guild organised a number of public protest meetings, and Members of Parliament were bombarded with deputations and resolutions. The Guild's executive wrote to the Prime Minister informing him that as 'an organisation that is working vigorously for peace and disarmament it views this departure from the principles of arbitration and disarmament with profound regret, and it deplores that huge sums of money shall be spent on weapons of destruction when expenditure is so badly needed on Social Development and for the alleviation of suffering and poverty.'[29]

As part of a long term policy to promote its pacifist aims the Guild lobbied local education authorities to drop military activities in schools, especially training corps. The 1927 Congress urged that military training in schools and universities should be replaced by such activities as games, pageants and choral singing, while in the following year guildswomen demanded that peace studies should be included in the curriculum of both elementary and secondary schools and that special attention should be given to the work of the League of Nations. In the early 'thirties local authorities were also encouraged to set aside a special day in schools to be celebrated as Peace Day. The suggestion was first implemented in Sheffield, though by the Spring of 1935 five other authorities had adopted the scheme, including the mighty London County Council. In addition, the 1928 Congress condemned war films as harmful to children and urged its members to picket cinemas where such entertainment was offered. The Congress of 1933 also called upon Co-operative societies to refrain from the manufacture and sale of war-like toys. At Mrs. Barton's suggestion, the Guild introduced a Peace Pledge Card in 1933 which committed those who signed it to take no part in war or any preparations for war. The scheme proved moderately successful and Cards were signed by several thousand guildswomen and their friends.

Yet perhaps the most imaginative and successful propaganda initiative in the peace campaign was the wearing of white, in place of or in addition to red, poppies on Armistice Day. The idea originated in 1933 when a number of branches approached the Central Committee to request an emblem which could be worn by those guildswomen who wished publicly to dissociate themselves from the evils of war. The Committee adopted the suggestion and the wearing of a white poppy on Armistice Day was introduced as a focus for the peace movement in general. The CWS was unable to provide white poppies in time for use at Armistice Day in 1933, but members improvised with the wearing of white paper poppies and white ribbons. One member recalled that

*I had the first white poppies made in paper by a dear crippled
lady, Miss Miller, who managed a hardware shop in
Wellingborough Road, Finedon.*[30]

The idea attracted great attention and one London
clergyman was so impressed that he reserved seats at the
Armistice service for all those who wore white poppies. Despite
some opposition, the white poppy became a radical symbol of
peace, bravely worn by guildswomen and others. For Armistice
Day 1938, sales of white poppies reached a record 85,000.

As with other campaigns, demonstrations formed an
important part of the Guild's peace strategy, but they were
larger and received more publicity. For example, in June 1938
the "Manchester Guardian" reported that a Guild peace rally in
Southampton attracted well over 2,000 people, and was
probably the town's largest ever pacifist gathering. Armistice
Day in the same year was the occasion of another large
demonstration which attracted wide public attention and
deserves recognition as one of the outstanding events in the
Guild's history. The Annual Report recorded the day's
programme and captured some of its atmosphere. "A Pacifist
Service was held in Regent's Park, London, attended by 3,000
guildswomen, and conducted by Canon Stuart Morris of the
Peace Pledge Union. The many banners of guild branches and
peace societies made a wonderful background for the great
assembly in the open air, and the service and singing were
reverent and beautiful. The great procession walked through
the busy London streets to Baker Street station, where members
entrained for the Central Hall, Westminster, and a splendid public
meeting was held addressed by the Rt. Hon. George Lansbury,
Canon Stuart Morris, Mrs. Pavitt, and Miss Vera Brittain, with
the National President, Mrs. E. Williams, in the chair. The
National President and General Secretary afterwards laid a
White Poppy wreath on the Cenotaph at Whitehall."

To some extent the Guild's pacifism evolved naturally from
an organisation whose membership was dominated by wives
and mothers and for whom the loss in war of a loved-one was a
very real possibility. The letter below, which was written by a
London guildswoman in May 1939 and sent to Neville
Chamberlain, must have echoed the feelings of almost every
Guild mother with a young son.

*Please be notified that I have not nurtured a son for twenty years
in the principles of Christianity and good citizenship, training
him to become obedient to the law and a credit to his generation,*

111

*for you, or any other Government, to claim him now to be a cog
in the wheels of a military machine which threatens mankind
with annihilation or, by its colossal cost, with abject starvation.*

*When I gave birth to my son immediately after the Great War,
which I believed was to be the last war, I dedicated him to God
and to Peace, in the firm faith that prehuman history had
finished, and that human history was about to begin. In his
interest I took up a keen study of post-war political trends and
events, and have deplored the cunning deceits and intrigues of
the various statesmen of Europe, and I hold them responsible
for the situation which obtains in the world today. My son has
had no hand in it.*

*Since I am responsible for his being, I mean to see to it that he
shall have the life which I thrust upon him and not the living
death which you seek to offer him, nay to demand of him. So if
you choose to collect him, you will first have to collect me, and
behind me, I hope, for the sake of the freedom of England, all
the mothers of sons of twenty, and also the mothers of sons who
have already made the supreme sacrifice to show us that war is
not the way to transform the world.*[31]

The Guild's pacifism also drew support and inspiration from
the development of a wider anti-war sentiment which by 1935
was at its height. By the middle of 1936 the Peace Pledge Union,
which had been initiated by Canon 'Dick' Shephard in 1934,
had attracted some 100,000 members who had renounced war
and committed themselves to persuading others to do the same.
There was also a strong pacifist tradition within the Labour
Movement. Ramsay MacDonald, for example, had taken this
position during the First World War, while in the 1930s, George
Lansbury, the leader of the Labour Party from 1931-35, was a
staunch pacifist who gave great personal support and
encouragement to the Guild's activities. In the 1930s Lucy
Middleton came to London to work as organiser for the No
More War Movement. The warmest reception she received was
from Margaret Llewelyn Davies personally, and she talked at so
many Guild branch meetings that, she told the authors, she
sometimes felt that she was working solely for the Guild!

Yet the Guild's pacifism derived essentially from its belief in
the importance of a Co-operative Commonwealth which would
traverse national boundaries to bring a more just and
harmonious social fabric. Miss Llewelyn Davies summarised
this view when she argued that:

*the brotherhood of nations is the religion of Co-operators, and
under an International Co-operative system of trade and*

112

*industry the material interests of nations are no longer in
opposition, but the resources of the globe are pooled and
divided in the interests of all.*[32]

Miss Llewelyn Davies was perhaps the most ardent and
outspoken female pacifist of the 1920s. Soon after the First
World War she noted scathingly that new methods of warfare
were being developed which

*instead of filling men with such horror as to lead to their
suppression, are being calmly investigated and perfected.*[33]

She condemned war as a further example of capitalist
exploitation since it lined the pockets of the armaments
manufacturers at the expense of the common man and woman.
The Guild's anti-imperialist spirit and its stand on militarism in
schools also emanated directly from Miss Llewelyn Davies.

The International Co-operative Women's Guild

The Guild's internationalism was also promoted by its
international contacts. From 1889 the annual reports record a
growing interest by foreign co-operators in the work of the
Guild culminating in 1894 in the first foreign visitor, Frau
Schwerin from Germany, to the annual conference. Frau
Schwerin later reported that

*There was much emotion: my hands were shaken till there was
no feeling left in them; flowers were presented to me, and the
train carried me away.*[34]

The first overseas guild was established in Holland in 1899
and its example was soon followed in other countries. With the
growth of personal contact between guildswomen in different
countries the possibility emerged of an international guild.
Catherine Webb records how the foundations of the
international guild were laid at the International Co-operative
Congress at Basle in 1921. ''The representation of women at the
Basle Congress showed the keenness of Guildswomen for
international work. More than a third of the English and Dutch
delegations were women. This Congress constitutes a landmark
to co-operators, because it was there the foundations were laid
of the International Co-operative Women's Guild. It was a
thrilling occasion when the 40 women representing seven
nations met together. The largest number came from England,
Holland and Switzerland, and the other countries represented
were Austria, Czechoslovakia, Russia and the United States.

113

The enthusiasm showed on all sides gave promise that this little seed would grow into a mighty tree. 'You are making history,' said one of the men delegates who regretted he could not be admitted.''

The conference unanimously decided to form an International Women's Committee. Frau Emmy Freundlich of Austria was appointed President and Miss A. Honora Enfield was elected Honorary Secretary. The English Guild also provided accommodation at its own headquarters for the secretarial work. The foreign contacts which the Guild maintained in the interwar period were of great importance in promoting its ideal of international Co-operation and contributed significantly to its pacifist beliefs. The spirit of international Co-operation was brilliantly captured in 1933 by Evelyn Sharp.

During the Russian famine of 1921-22, I attended as a relief worker a committee meeting of the Co-operative store of a village in the Volga Valley, not far from the foothills of the Urals and fifty miles from the nearest railway station. The villagers, dressed in their sheepskins and high fur hats, the women carrying jars on their shoulders and all of them embarrassingly eager, on seeing the Quaker relief worker's badge, to prostrate themselves in the snow and kiss one's boots in token of gratitude, looked so Eastern and seemed so remote from Western civilisation that I did not think of connecting their Co-operative Movement with ours until I saw, on entering the committee-room, a bust of Robert Owen. Then I knew that in Co-operation we have another of those touches that make the whole world kin. And, indeed, our Guild celebrations of 1933 remind us that the British Women's Guild is the first to have a Jubilee, and, therefore, the first to be presented with an international banner by the President of the International Women's Co-operative Guild, which now has branches in fifteen countries and holds regular Congresses. That banner is a symbol of the Workers' Commonwealth for which every Guildswoman is working, consciously or unconsciously, in which all barriers of race and class will be swept away and the competitive spirit driven from trade and industry.

The Guild's pacifism generated wide support, both among its own members and the outside community. There was however, some opposition. The white poppy campaign, for example, attracted the wrath of a few local councils which arranged for the removal from their war memorials of wreaths containing the offending emblem. This type of opposition declined as the

Guild conducted a highly effective campaign which emphasised that the white poppy was not intended to lessen reverence for the fallen, many of whom were relatives of guildswomen, but to symbolise the evils of war and the virtue of peace.

Catherine Webb noted that during the hostilities of 1914-18 'there was much difference of opinion in the Guild as regards condemnation of the War.' Although throughout the interwar period as a whole the Guild's pacifism retained the overwhelming support of members, some guildswomen did express certain reservations. Delegates to the Congress of 1938 discussed the suggestion that the Guild's anti-war policy should be suspended in favour of the principle of collective security advocated by the Co-operative Party. According to the 'Manchester Guardian,' Mrs. Atkins of Watford argued that

> absolute pacifism was not wrong but was impracticable at the present time. The ideal of all Co-operators was a pacifist State, but they were a long way from that at the present time. There were two mad dogs running riot over Europe and it was essential that they should be restrained.[35]

The vote was 897 to 623 in favour of retaining the Guild's pacifist stand, but the victory was relatively narrow and shows the sensitivity of guildswomen to the rise of Nazi Germany. Guild members appreciated the benefits of peace, but they had also been taught to love democracy and its freedom, and in this respect their vision had been extended to incorporate other countries as well as their own. As war approached, the pacifist debate continued in the pages of the "Co-operative News" and reflected the genuine and touching dilemma which many guildswomen must have felt. Yet the issue was discussed without rancour and bitterness — a tribute to the maturity of the organisation and its members. In the event, guildswomen remained loyal to the beliefs and principles developed during the preceding twenty years. They marched with their banners flying and their heads held high, but for peace, not war.

By the close of the interwar period the Guild had survived two of the most traumatic decades in the nation's history. Problems of management and policy had manifested themselves but the essential structure and attitudes established before 1918 had proved resilient. Guild members had seized with enthusiasm the opportunity of personal development. They were perhaps the most outstanding group of liberal and well informed women of their day. By 1939 the Guild was in good shape to face the new challenges posed by the onset of the Second World War.

Notes to Chapter 4

1. These quotations are from the Guild's Annual Reports.
2. Annual Report, 1927.
3. *Daily Herald,* 22nd June 1927.
4. Annual Report, 1922.
5. *Evening Standard,* 14th June 1928.
6. *The Times,* 17th June 1939.
7. *Manchester Guardian,* 22nd April 1935.
8. Anon. The Relation of the Guild to Other Organisations (1924).
9. Annual Report, 1937.
10. Annual Report, 1923.
11. Minutes of the Central Committee of the Women's Co-operative Guild, 22nd/28th September 1927. University of Hull, Manuscript Collection.
12. Annual Report, 1929.
13. Annual Report, 1937.
14. M. Saran, Never Give Up (1976).
15. *Daily Telegraph,* 17th May 1929.
16. Ibid.
17. *Daily Telegraph,* 16th May 1929.
18. *Manchester Guardian,* 13th June 1928.
19. *Daily Herald,* 21st June 1933.
20. *Daily Herald,* 23rd June 1933.
21. Annual Report, 1932.
22. Annual Report, 1933.
23. Annual Report, 1936.
24. Annual Report, 1927.
25. Annual Report, 1929.
26. *Daily Herald,* 8th June 1934.
27. WCG, The Guild in War and Peace (undated).
28. Ibid.
29. Annual Report, 1935.
30. *Co-operative News,* 25th March 1981.
31. *The Guildswoman,* May 1939.
32. M.L. Davies, Death or Life (undated).
33. Ibid.
34. C. Webb, The Woman with the Basket (Manchester 1927).
35. *Manchester Guardian,* 22nd June 1938.

CHAPTER 5

THE GUILD AND THE SECOND WORLD WAR: 1939-1945

Introduction

The war dealt the Guild a blow from which it never recovered. It started the war with a membership of 87,246 in 1805 branches and finished it in 1946 with a membership of 57,153 in 1714 branches. Declining membership meant declining income. This vicious circle was to remain central to the problems of the Guild during the war and also from 1952 onwards. The reasons why the membership dropped and branches closed were unique to the war situation: first came evacuation. The blackout discouraged evening meetings, and meeting rooms were taken over for war work. Later, mass bombing and the increasing numbers of women who went out to work were important factors.

Yet the spirit of the Guild remained high. The monthly Bulletins and the Annual Reports of those years show an organisation constructed to last. It showed an organisation which whilst continuing to argue clearly for pacifist solutions and for the safeguarding of civil liberties, was deeply involved in practical welfare work. Before looking at the issues taken up by the Guild during these years, it is important to realise the extent to which, despite their abhorrence of war, the Guild immediately recognised the needs of those involved in it. If their pacifist convictions show in their work for conscientious objectors, their recognition of other needs, and a practical determination to meet them, shines through the reports of branch activities that appeared regularly in the Head Office Monthly Bulletin.

The war also sees the Guild improvising: Mrs. Margaret Love of the Fairfield Branch, Warrington, wrote how during the war the branch carried on in a corridor during the blackout, knitting and sending parcels for "our lads" and needy people. Mrs. Hilda Foulkes of the same branch wrote that they helped organise salvage and went to Liverpool with the Fire Service during the Blitz. Mrs. Doris Fisher (later Baroness Fisher) joined the Guild in 1941 and remembers war-time meetings because of the constant clicking of needles when branches had a speaker - knitting socks for the navy and balaclava helmets. After the war she went to officials' classes and was firmly told members should not bring their knitting as this was discourteous to speakers!

The war also saw the Guild working more closely with both local and national government. They were increasingly consulted and were represented on a growing number of national and local official committees as the war progressed. In 1941, some of the proceedings of the Annual Conference were broadcast on the BBC Overseas Service.

War on the Horizon

As the success and bravery of their White Poppy Campaign showed, pacifism was a central part of the philosophy of the Co-operative Women's Guild. Despite some controversy in the letter columns of the "Co-operative News" in the late 1930s, it was a policy accepted by most of the membership - and the Guild leadership was always united on this issue. The rise of Hitler and Facism in Italy and Spain was of course of tremendous concern to Guild leaders, but their conviction that only peace could lead to a world without competition did not waver. Guildswomen supported a wide range of anti-war activities and were, in the mid-'thirties, opposed to participating in preparations for war - such as gas mask drills.

Yet at the same time, Guild members had a practical approach to the realities of war. The April 1939 edition of "The Guildswoman" contains a form for branch secretaries, headed 'Child Evacuation in War.' It asks for details of members of the branch who would be willing to exchange or accept children of Guild members in case of war or crisis.

In addition, it was recognised that Guild members could, and indeed would, join services like the ARP (Air Raid Precautions) should war come. It was agreed by the leadership that such members joined as individuals: Guild policy was pacifism and they would not be representing the Guild in any way.

In terms of the Head Office, 1939 saw a move to Shrewsbury in order that Guild work could continue uninterrupted and the safety of Guild records would be assured, although the Guild Office at 17 Prescot Street, E.1. was not bombed until September 1940. Due to the problems of running the Guild from

118

Shrewsbury, the office moved back to London in July 1940, but the air raids in September damaged Prescot Street and it could no longer be used. The Guild office staff worked for two months in the CWS London Branch at Leman Street, but further bombing made another move essential. Leicester Co-operative Society offered suitable accommodation and the Guild was established in Leicester by October 1940, moving back to London again only in 1944.

In 1937 the General Secretary was Miss Rose Simpson. She had won a hotly contested ballot, against Cecily Cook among others. Like all the Guild's General Secretaries from the first, she was a committed pacifist. Rather more unusual, she was the niece of her predecessor Mrs. Eleanor Barton. A handsome young woman of strong views, she argued for a new monthly Guild Publication - it was the "Guildswoman", published monthly from February 1939 until October of that year. It did not last long enough to ascertain whether the fears of those who opposed it were justified. Those fears were that any new publication would be harmful to the sales of the longstanding publication by the Co-operative Press - "Woman's Outlook".

It was not just the "Guildswoman" that failed to last long. Rose Simpson resigned in 1939, and in April 1940 elections for a new General Secretary were held, but with Rose Simpson's name on the ballot paper! The Central Committee then decided that the background to Miss Simpson's resignation had to be made public, and sent a circular to all Guild branches headed "Election of General Secretary - Central Committee statement re Miss Rose Simpson."

The six-page circular begins by regretting some branches had nominated Miss Simpson and 'that she should have allowed her name to go forward in view of the unhappy events of the past few months.' Her resignation had been accepted unanimously by the democratically elected Central Committee - and they stress that she *did* resign although Miss Simpson had appeared to suggest that she was dismissed.

Rose Simpson had criticised Guild staff openly and made accusations against Central Committee members - but the main problems seem to hinge round "The Guildswoman." It began to lose money; investigation by the Guild auditors revealed a 'most unsatisfactory financial position.' Even more crucial, Rose Simpson had engaged two *men* without the knowledge of the Central Committee, 'when women amongst the Guild

119

membership would have been well able to carry out the duties allotted to them.' Significantly, one of the men was Miss Simpson's brother and the second was a friend.

Although it had been suggested that an independent Co-operative tribunal investigate this issue, Miss Simpson -through the National Union of Co-operative Officials and their lawyers -had threatened to sue the Guild for breach of contract. (In fact by January 1941 we know that the case brought by Rose Simpson was dismissed, 'for want of prosecution.')

Having accepted Miss Simpson's resignation as in the best interests of the Guild, Central Committee stresses that it would be 'most distressing for the whole Guild organisation if any attempt were made to return Miss Simpson as General Secretary.' The election was won by Mrs. Cecily Cook. She was to be General Secretary from 1940-1953, so for the years under review in this chapter, the Guild was mostly in her competent hands. Kathleen Kempton describes her as a very able woman, who was a marvellous and moving speaker - if rather high voiced; the more emotional she became the higher up the scale went her voice. She also wrote well. Kathleen Kempton who observed her closely as she was working at Head Office with her by 1944 described her as 'manipulative' - giving as an example that Central Committee usually elected as National President the woman Cecily Cook favoured. Baroness Fisher's interpretation was that she was a real intellectual, who had a good eye for women with potential and encouraged them to become leaders.

The monthly publication "The Guildswoman" was replaced in November 1939 with Head Office Monthly Bulletins, published free as opposed to the one penny charged for the "Guildswoman." The front cover of the very first issue advertised the Armistice Day Meeting in the Central Hall, Westminster for 11th November, 1939. It carried one advertisement from the CWS, later issues were to carry several pages of CWS advertising.

The first issue of the Head Office Bulletin finds the Guild at the start of the war. Problems of meeting places were just starting, and this was recognised in the development of correspondence courses. They had been prepared by the Co-operative Union and covered three main topics: Consumer Co-operation; The Wage System and the Co-operative Way Out, and War and the Woman Co-operator. Yet this November 1939

*Mrs. E. Williams (national president) and
Rose Simpson (general secretary) leading
the Women's Guild section in the great
protest march against conscription in
London, on May 4th, 1939.*

Perhaps the most dominant feature of the Guild's activities in the 1930's relates to its involvement with the peace movement. The most imaginative and successful propaganda initiative in the peace campaign was the wearing of white, in place of or in addition to red, poppies on Armistice Day. Here, Falconwood Branch are at the Cenotaph in Whitehall on Armistice Day 1937.

Bulletin, which recommends these courses, contains nearly three full pages of news from Branches - these short reports on the activities of just 68 of the Guild's Branches show the Guild in action at its peak of success.

Several branches reported remarkably high attendances: Rusholme, Manchester - 150 members present out of a membership of 260; Earlsfield, 130; Peckham, 146; and Morden in Surrey holding two meetings each week because of large attendances. Most of the branches reported attendances between 20 and 50. The wide range of activities showed some involvement with war work. Stockport branch had some new members: 30 evacuated children and four mothers. Members were involved with Red Cross work, the ARP, St. John's Ambulance and canteen work, with older members sick-nursing or staying with patients whilst householders went shopping. Other branches reported knitting, outings, classes on modern problems, increasing sales of "Woman's Outlook," and a variety of lectures and socials. As the war went on, involvement with practical war-time work grew.

War Welfare Work

Guild members worked in feeding centres and in the supply of hot meals to those bombed out. They helped find new homes for guildswomen after the Blitz. They were involved in mending and making clothes for those in need. As the Annual Report for 1940 pointed out, the work in the public interest for the public good extended knowledge of the Women's Co-operative Guild beyond the Co-operative Movement.

Members served on a wide range of local and national committees set up during the war - on Food Control Committees, Salvage Committees and they became increasingly involved in welfare work. Hospitality to overseas troops, for example, or providing baths for forces in camps without such facilities. This personal service was obviously a very satisfying activity for those taking part.

In replying to the questionnaire sent to Guild members asking for their help in compiling this history, many mentioned these war activities. Mrs. Mary Newman of Wallsend wrote:

We were entertaining the soldiers from a Newcastle Hospital at least once a month for about a year. We would give them tea and have a dance afterwards and before they left they were given a

*packet of cigarettes, a box of matches and 2/6d. in the old
money. That was a lot in those days.*

Mary Tromans of Stockton-on-Tees, still a Guild member at
the age of 89, said:

*We entertained the wounded soldiers from World War Two to
an afternoon tea. It was very interesting and enjoyed by all that
afternoon with jokes and songs.*

Guild members were involved in several national schemes, as
reflected in the Head Office Monthly Bulletins. One of these
involved a scheme for knitting for the Forces. The scheme was
worked out whereby members of the Guild were registered, and
vouchers would be available for them to purchase, without
coupons, a limited quantity of knitting wool in service colours.
The scheme was intended by the Board of Trade to apply only to
members of specified organisations. Contravention of the
conditions meant the knitter would be struck off the register.
Particulars of persons knitted for had to be recorded and
evidence of final delivery of garments had to be available. It was
noted, in the September 1941 Bulletin which outlined the
scheme, that the Guild was recognised as a national
organisation and the scheme would operate from Guild Office,
through the branches. 'Once more,' the Bulletin records, 'we
are demonstrating the value of the WCG in the daily life of the
community, and in view of the letters which have been received
at Head Office, it appears evident that guildswomen will
appreciate the step which has been taken in this connection.' By
March 1942 the Bulletin records that 100,000 vouchers had been
sent from Head Office and that 'in many cases Guildswomen
are working for the scheme in close co-operation with the local
Co-operative Society, and the Guild is being brought more to
the notice of store members than has been previously the case.'

Another link with the local Co-operative Society lay in the
Guild's efforts in publicising and participating in the Board of
Trade's "Make Do and Mend" circles. Branches were urged to
use Co-operative premises as both "Make Do and Mend" and
"Food Advice" centres.

The Guild was also active in negotiations with the Ministry of
Food over the use of surplus soft fruit for housewives who had
saved their sugar ration for use for jam. From 1941 onwards, the
Guild was involved with the Ministry of Food for a scheme to
ensure that surplus fruit was made into jam for communal not
private consumption. One condition for participation was that
non-members must be allowed to take part and must be given

full share of responsibility. In urban areas, representatives of many organisations formed a Food Preservation Committee and Guild branches were urged to become involved.

One of the most exciting stories of all to emerge from our research into the Guild during the Second World War concerns London's deep shelters.

Catering in London's Deep Shelters

One major involvement was with the catering in London's Deep Shelters. Freda Whittaker put the story of this amazing enterprise into a Guild Pamphlet called, 'Meeting War Emergency.'[1] The story is outlined in her first paragraph:

How would you like to cater for 10,000 people at a time? It sounds an impossible task, yet it was actually done by a small group of London guildswomen during the war, and they were none of them professional caterers or experts in large-scale feeding. The story of their marvellous achievement.... shows the value of the spirit underlying the Women's Co-operative Guild -the spirit of service for humanity. Here you will read only of ordinary working women with homes to run and the rigours of war to face. Yet they found time to undertake voluntary work of a strenuous nature and demonstrated the great effectiveness of co-operative effort. They are typical of the many guildswomen up and down the country who sought, in the hard and dangerous war years, an outlet for the constructive work and ideas that were a mental salvation in a world devoted so relentlessly to wholesale destruction.

The story begins with Mr. Wadlow, manager of the Balham Branch of Royal Arsenal Co-operative Society writing to Mrs. Kempton, then Secretary of the South Metropolitan District, asking if guildswomen would undertake voluntary canteen work in the newly constructed deep shelter at Clapham South - some of the deep air-raid shelters were to be used as transit dormitories for servicemen passing through the capital. The deep shelter committee had made this suggestion based on guildswomen's reputation for running successful tea parties. The job was to cater for service personnel each weekend, and for a thousand people a night if the shelter was needed for the general public.

And what a job it was! Not just preparing and serving the food - the women were to be responsible for buying provisions, handling the money, paying the bills and dealing with Food

Office returns.

Whilst enthusiastic, Cecily Cook had to say that district funds could not be used for the initial outlay on food. The South Metropolitan District Committee held a meeting, inviting two members from each of the 46 branches and from the Management and Education Committees of the RACS. Mrs. Kempton wrote later:

> Everyone present thought it was a real humanitarian job and agreed then and there to accept the responsibility. I often wonder if we would have made such a decision if we had known at the time that it would not be one thousand people but many thousands, and not one shelter but four. Representatives promised to go back to their guilds and appeal for help, as we had no fund to start with.

An appeal led to £15 in donations and about 50 volunteers - with Mrs. Kempton as organiser. Following a slow start, when most of the catering was for light refreshments for visitors, including the Press, came December 1942. One thousand men from the Forces were due in Clapham South - a mountain of pies, buns and bread were prepared but only 250 men turned up. Freda Whittaker wrote:

> So the curtain went up - rather humorously - on work that was now to be uninterrupted. The gap between supplies and customers did not occur again. For the next year the 50 guildswomen were taking their turn at looking after servicemen every weekend. They might get to bed - for a rest rather than a sleep - about 3.30 a.m. on Sunday morning and would be up again at 6.30 a.m. to attend to breakfast. Then the final clearing up, and off to their homes and their own work, not getting back sometimes till about 11 a.m.

As one shelter was soon inadequate for the thousands of men of all nationalities passing through London, the Stockwell, Clapham North and Clapham Common deep shelters were opened too and the guildswomen took on this increased responsibility. The shelters had an international and co-operative spirit, and the work went beyond catering: sewing on buttons, for example. Over 200,000 men were fed between December 1942 and December 1943, and from January to April 1944 between 500 and 1,000 American soldiers nightly stayed and ate in the shelters.

Although the women lived in areas of London being bombed, there was a steady stream of helpers, many elderly, many with homes of their own damaged in the blitz. Although the catering did not aim to make a profit, surplus money did accrue, and was used on welfare and Co-operative work such as the Guild Convalescent Fund, as well as to help guildswomen who were bombed out.

In July 1944 came the day everyone had hoped not to see: the shelters had to be opened to the general public. On the first public night, Sunday, July 9th, 3,000 came to the Stockwell deep shelter. The following Wednesday Clapham North shelter opened and the week after Clapham Common. In more than four months, as London was bombarded by V1s and V2s, the guildswomen were feeding ten thousand people nightly. Until the end of the war, the women kept on working. Canteen Supervisor, Mrs. Kempton, whose job took her from shelter to shelter canteen missed only eight nights in that final two months.

The Co-operative involvement was wider than the catering by the guildswomen. The RACS Education Committee was responsible for film shows, discussions, lectures and a library — education for all age groups in fact. Indeed, Freda Whittaker points out that some of the Co-operative Youth Clubs (Playway and Pathfinder) operating within the RACS areas in the 1940s, sprang from the work in the shelter. Co-operative publications including "Woman's Outlook" were circulated in the shelters, and all the catering provisions came from the RACS branch store in Balham.

The task was enormous. In July 1944, 190,000 hot drinks, 1,070 main meals, 72,300 subsidiary meals and 50,000 tea meals were served in just one shelter in four weeks. In the last year of the work, £15,000 was handled by the shelter caterers - over £12,000 of which was spent at the Balham Store. And all this work was undertaken by just 50 volunteers! Even on Christmas Day 1944 some of the women went to the shelter, where 50 or so homeless people were staying, to serve them tea - taking their husbands with them!

Involvement from outside the Guild came when Cecily Cook took a choir of the Free German Movement to the shelter - songs were sung in five languages, and Freda Whittaker noted that from an initial grudging reception, one of those in the shelter said 'If all Germans were like this lot, we wouldn't be killing each other now.' This action was typical of the Guild's concern for peace and reconstruction, a conviction of the value of international friendship that had roots early in the Guild's history and continues to flower.

The years of work were rounded off at a celebration lunch in September 1945, when the 50 Guildswomen, the Guild's General Secretary, the Balham Branch manager, as well as other RACS co-operators, heard a tribute from Sir George Wilkins, late Lord Mayor of London and Chairman of the Deep Shelter Committee, and Mr. Copement, Manager of the Deep Shelters who expressed appreciation of this work. As Mrs. Kempton's final report said:

> Our fifty-odd members deserve all the praise and appreciation it is possible to show them, especially knowing the sacrifice that they have made.

Pressures for Reform

At the same time as co-operating with the Government in this way, the Guild continued its radical pressure for change in other directions. The February 1942 Bulletin discussed the National Campaign that was being organised to press Guild policy. Sectional Rallies were planned, and it was hoped that Districts would also organise rallies. Although not the only issues the Guild were pressing for, it was felt that they were the essential ones to concentrate on if public opinion was to be roused and improvement secured.

The Campaign issues were:
1. Treatment of civilian injured.
2. Compensation for Property Allowances.
3. Conditions of women in Uniformed Services and Industry.
4. Education Facilities, Child Labour and Delinquency.
5. War time Nurseries.

The Treatment of Civilian Injured is a good example of the Guild's concern to press the case for equal treatment of women; for why should women who were not working be treated worse than women who were working, when they were all injured in bombing raids?

A resolution at the 1940 Congress was the start of a campaign, eventually successful, against the Personal Injuries (Emergency Provisions) Act 1939. The resolution made the point that the Congress, representing 70,000 housewives, was dismayed at the refusal of the Government to grant compensation to housewives, unless they were gainfully employed, when injured through or by aerial bombardment.

The May 1941 Bulletin reports that whilst the Minister of Pensions' concessions for war injured women are not as high as the Guild had wanted, they represent the result of Guild work and pressure. The Minister of Pensions decided that women not gainfully employed should in fact receive more adequate compensation under the Personal Injuries (Civilians) Scheme — up to 16s. 4d. from 14s. per week when not in hospital, and up from 7s. to 9s. 4d. when in hospital. The concession affected housewives and single women with household obligations, and at the same time the Minister announced that widows with households to support would be dealt with on the same lines as the 'gainfully employed man.'

The February 1942 Bulletin repeats the plea made so often in earlier years, and to recur, that it is a mistake to "assume that all effort can be made from the centre or even that the most effective use of Guild strength comes from Head Office. Guild policy is decided by the membership and it is for the members in the branches up and down the country to press it home through the individual branch.... But it is the big mass of membership of thousands of women citizens which has the power to influence events, and national and local authorities will pay more attention to a widespread agitation than to a single representation, even though its importance is recognised when it comes from a big national body."

The example given to back up the argument is the Guild's campaign for women in the Police Force, recalled by Mrs. Hilda Foulkes of Warrington as one of the most effective campaigns waged during her 48 years of Guild membership. She joined in 1934 at the age of 35. The national demand was followed by local action including resolutions and deputations to Local Authorities and where local authorities were in fact appointing women to the police, this was often because of effective local pressure.

The April 1943 Bulletin reported that 839 policewomen were now attested but that not all of them were being well used. The Guild wanted policewomen to supplement the work of policemen in regard to the public well being, not be put on special work such as finger printing. Branches were therefore urged to campaign locally to ensure that policewomen carried out policeman's work, that they were paid the correct police rate and that they were given promotion opportunities. This was still an issue a year later, when the April 1944 Bulletin reported that

Central Committee had been represented at a London conference to demand that more policewomen were appointed; once again local action was urged.

In 1940 a Guild Maintenance Fund was set up, with £495 donated by the end of 1941. Branch problems multiplied. Recognising the difficulties of getting speakers, one Bulletin advised speakers to use Co-operative publications as the basis of discussion. A mock International Peace Conference was another suggestion. "As members begin to work, membership must fall." Readers were reminded that many women were troubled with tragedies like bereavement and homelessness, and that the support of fellow guildswomen was of inestimable value at such times. Finding meeting rooms remained a problem, with a reluctance to meet in members' homes as they are less businesslike - although of course homes were used.

The first Congress held during the war, at Great Yarmouth in May 1940, shows the Guild discussing the usual wide range of resolutions. Guildswomen were pledged, ... as housewives with purchasing power .... to do everything possible to increase Co-operative trading operations. There were as usual many resolutions concerning the unequal treatment of women. One of these, which deplored the fact that the War Bonus supplementing the wages of employees was less for women than for men, went on to say that where women replaced men in industry, these women should be asked to relinquish the employment at the end of the war so that men returning to civilian life could find work.

The way in which war adversely affected the poor as well as women came over time and time again from the work and campaigns and resolutions of the Guild during these years of war: more clothing coupons for expectant mothers, price controls, higher soap ration, communal feeding facilities, extension of the cheap milk scheme to widows and old age pensioners. Another basic issue was the fact that coupons were not needed for made-up sheets, curtains or towels, but were needed for the cheaper alternative of the poor - to buy material. and make your own. This theme governed the constant call for rationing and price controls.

The resolutions and campaigns throughout the war also mirrored wider perspectives: concern for the women of Asia, for the persecution of the Jews, for the health of those in occupied countries like Greece and by November 1942 branches were being urged to lobby their MPs to ease the plight of Greek children by sending adequate supplies of milk and baby food. Concern for those worse off in society was always to be found on Congress Agendas - on 99 to be precise - and this first year of war was to be no exception: abolition of the means test and higher grants for old age pensioners appeared, together with arguments for increased Public Assistance and improved allowances to men of the Forces and their wives.

Four resolutions on Peace were passed, one calling for a World Peace Conference and another for a Ministry of Peace to be set up, with 50% women members. One resolution showed the extent to which the Guild stuck to its principles, however unpopular with the Co-operative Movement. The resolution viewed with alarm "a tendency which is apparent on the part of some sections of the working class and Co-operative Societies to urge their fellow members not to work with conscientious objectors. This Congress is of the opinion that since legislation has provided for persons recognised by the appropriate tribunals as conscientious objectors to exercise their freedom, it is not desirable that trade unionists should override the law by taking action of the character here condemned, and it also requests all Co-operative women to abstain from victimising conscientious objectors with whom they may come in contact in the course of shopping."

The concern for the plight of the Conscientious Objectors was constant throughout the war and they were always ready to take up individual cases of C.O.s felt to have been badly treated at the time of their Tribunal, whilst waiting for it or after recognition as conscientious objectors. As the July 1941 Bulletin explains "this is part of the Guild's firm stand for freedom of opinion and liberty of conscience."

Growing resentment of conscientious objectors is reported in the September 1941 Bulletin, which says the temper of Tribunals was hardening and that there was less consideration for the unpopular views of the conscientious objectors - "Members of the Women's Co-operative Guild have a very grave responsibility in this matter. For years we took the completely pacifist stand, we taught our sons to hate war, we must not let down those who learned - only too well for their own comfort - the lesson we gave. It is those who stand against war when war seems to so many a righteous thing who make the bravest fight. Many sons of Guildswomen are standing in this

129

way.... They need a "prisoner's friend." The Guild is endeavouring to do this, but money is needed for fares and other expenses..... There will be many things of which the Guild, as an organisation, will be proud when history tells of the present conflict, but there will be nothing of which we shall have more right to be proud than the fact that we remembered the stand we had taken for peace and we stood by those who turned our policy into practice."

The "Co-operative News" carried a letter from five Guildswomen casting doubt on the unanimous support for the pacifist stand reflected in resolutions passed at Congress and in the pages of the Monthly Bulletin and Annual Reports.[2]

Five guildswomen wrote hoping that the Guild would reconsider policy on pacifism saying it was necessary to recognise that if it was not for those in the Forces, the Guild would not be free to hold its Congress at all. They say that if the Guild does not believe in this war, then "we should have the courage to say 'Let the Fascists in.' ....Let them torture and kill more men, women and children. For this is what we shall mean if we reaffirm our Peace Policy at Congress."

Ever practical, the 1940 Congress also urged railway companies to install conveniences clearly marked "Ladies" and "Gentlemen" on all trains and railway stations without any increased cost to passengers. It also passed an emergency resolution arguing that, in view of the degradation to the women concerned, in any country with licensed brothels the "Houses" should be declared out of bounds to every member of the British Forces.

Another 1940 Resolution expressed alarm at the increasing number of deaths, accidents and attacks on women due to the blackout and demanded that a reasonable amount of street lighting and light for shopping should be made compulsory.

1940 was a year when Co-operative principles were firm, as shown in campaigns for Co-operative loyalty through registration for food rationing and the space given once more in the December 1940 Bulletin to the "Co-operative News" campaign of trying to find Co-operative hosts for evacuated children from Co-operative homes or for homeless guildswomen.

The Guild was co-operating with the Government and being taken seriously. Correspondence in the August 1940 Bulletin with Lord Woolton, Minister of Food, was about the importance of tea - because of its cheapness - to the poorest section of the community, as well as its value in keeping up the spirit and morale of the working class home. Lord Woolton's reply said that whilst bearing in mind the need for rationing 'we should greatly appreciate it if the Central Committee of the Women's Co-operative Guild could use its influence with its enormous membership in educating women in the use of alternative drinks. For example, cocoa, of which the Co-operative Movement itself produces an excellent brand, is probably a better bedtime drink both from the point of view of food value and as a sedative to the nerves than tea.' The Guild was asked, through talks to its members, or through publicity in its excellent journal "Woman's Outlook" to give simple instructions for the making of coffee. In its reply, Central Committee pointed out the difference in price between a good cup of coffee and a good cup of tea!

The pattern of activity, the mixture of co-operation with Government and criticism of Government policy and a wide range of Congress resolutions remained throughout the war. As it became more and more difficult to organise meetings, and to travel, declining membership and reduced finance dominated much of the time of officials and guildswomen at all levels - Central Committee, Section, District and Branch.

Nevertheless, the morale of the Guild remained high. One example of the wide range of Guild activities appears in the September 1941 Bulletin, when a district secretary writes:

> Branch activities have been many and concentrated on the humanitarian side of the war and in raising funds for same. Members report on knitting comforts for all forces and our own "Pals Away" scheme, work for evacuees, Guild Office War Victims Fund, Mary MacArthur Holiday Home, distribution of milk for schools during holidays, making shirts for prisoners of war. Three branches are in charge of the Rest Centres and Communal Feeding. Members are connected with the WVS in several ways, in shelter work, billeting and first aid. Members report on representation to all Guild and Co-operative Conferences and branches have taken up courses of lectures on Co-operation, Citizenship, Industrial History and the work of the Co-operative Union.

It must be remembered that as younger women increasingly began to work, much of this activity was arranged by older members.

Guild leaders took up all the issues raised by branches so that

131

the May 1944 Bulletin gives the CWS response to the many complaints received about the quality of corsets. It seemed the problem was the labour shortage though the Bulletin reports the manager of the relevant CWS factory saying "the quality has now improved and corsets are now virtually comparable with the pre-war standard."

The war-time resolutions passed at Congress were in essence concerned with looking at war-time life with the practical eyes of the working class woman. A typical campaign was that concerning coupons for household linens, curtains and other textile goods. The Guild was concerned that household linens had to be bought using clothing coupons because, they argued, women would ensure their children and menfolk were adequately clothed and the family had sufficient towels before they began to think of clothes for themselves. Only coupons specially designated for household textiles could prevent this inequality within the family. As reported in March 1943 Bulletin, the Board of Trade replied that 'families should budget for towels and teacloths when planning the spending of their coupons, and each member of the family should take his or her turn to contribute a coupon when necessary. In this way each person, including the housewife, will still have his or her fair share of coupons to spend on clothes.'

Not just equality within the family but also equality of treatment for both rich and poor concerned the Guild. At the 1945 Annual Congress for example, an Emergency Resolution was passed which began: "In view of the cuts in rations which will press with particular hardship upon the working class, this Congress of the Women's Co-operative Guild calls for the adoption of a points scheme for restaurant meals. We have yet to hear of the wholesale dismissal of chefs employed by the upper classes, whose duty it will now be to cook one shillingsworth of meat, and two pennyworth of corned beef with one ounce of cooking fat per person. We realise that people with money and influence go short of nothing, as there is still unrationed food such as poultry and game, and meals can be obtained in hotels and restaurants. We also protest at the hypocritical propaganda of the BBC and the Press in trying to make us believe that everyone is on the same rations."

Guildswomen were involved in day to day matters like rationing and blackout. They were also busy using their practical skills - initially on campaigns like "Make Do and

Mend," later knitting for the Forces and, towards the end of the War, knitting for children — the tragic victims of Nazi occupation. But practical work had to be complementary to the routine work on each Guild branch. In a section headed "Factors to be observed in connection with the Relief Work Scheme," the September 1944 Bulletin gives the first factor as 'Guild normal business must be carried on in the usual way and Guild meetings must not be turned into knitting parties.'

It is clear that Head Office was sometimes disappointed by the lack of Branch involvement in campaigns. The March 1943 Bulletin replied to complaints that the Guild was not making its contribution to national affairs - "Such criticisms are really an indictment of those who make them. The Guild is a national organisation - consisting of 1,700 Branches, ... some branches do not even read the Bulletin .... a recent enquiry on behalf of the Co-operative Union sent to all branches was answered by only 162 .... public affairs consist of a multitude of small issues and not in a few big events .... we shall only make our mark as an organisation in the national field insofar as we are working vigorously in each branch by means of a live membership which is pressing Guild policy in its own area."

There is no doubt about the vast amount of welfare, practical and fund-raising work undertaken by the vast majority of branches and their members during the war years, although one major disappointment was the branch response to the issue of married women's property.

In 1943 the Guild was involved with the need for legislation following the High Court Case of Mrs. D. A. Blackwell. This had shown a married woman's savings were vulnerable. The December 1943 Bulletin said that the Married Women's Association's response to this High Court Case was to argue for a change in the Married Women's Property Act but the Guild thought this was not enough. Instead, the Guild launched a Petition which emphasised the injustice of the Blackwell case, and called for legislation 'which would secure to every married woman the right to an equal share with her husband in the home, its income and any savings which may accrue from home administration.'

Co-operative MPs were approached and the 1943-44 Annual Report said the Guild Petition would give them the necessary backing to press for this long overdue reform. The March 1944 Bulletin reports branch involvement in this petition, including house to house canvassing, public meetings and reports in the local press. However, the Annual Report for 1944-45 was to say that the petition did not receive sufficient support from branches to justify it being sent forward, but that a resolution on the issue was proposed by the Guild and passed at the Co-operative Party Conference. The Guild's views on reform were therefore now Co-operative Party policy. Given the pressures of life in war-time perhaps it is understandable that insufficient signatures were collected, although on an issue of such fundamental importance to women, branches might have been expected to show greater interest.

That the Guild was thinking of reconstruction was clear in that very Bulletin. The detailed plans of one branch, presented to their local Maternity and Child Welfare Committee with suggestions for post-war improvement and expansion of the services is printed. It included purpose-built welfare centres, transport facilities, a library, and health education with provision of some child care facilities. Attendance at pre-natal and child welfare clinics was to be compulsory, maternity homes, day nurseries and the home-help service for families where the mother was unable to cope with domestic work were recommended, as were nursery schools and special facilities for mentally defective and physically malformed children. Put forward in 1944 it provides a detailed picture of facilities not yet achieved even now in Centenary Year! Another positive and constructive suggestion was to fail when the Co-operative Union Congress voted it down. This was the idea that the Co-operative Union should form and finance a Co-operative Personal Service Unit able to give co-operators the chance to work voluntarily overseas.

Members were still heavily involved with knitting for those in need overseas. The July 1944 Bulletin describes the knitting scheme worked out by the Minister of Supply where the Guild became one of the organisations acting as principals (the others were the Central Hospital Supply Service, Women's Institute and the WVS). Knitting groups were to be organised, committees set up locally and the task of knitting half-a-million garments for children under two began — for children living in the newly liberated countries.

And the maternity issue, one of the Guild's most significant early campaigns, was not forgotten. Congress in 1945 passed a resolution on making gas and air available to mothers having babies at home or in hospital, 'thus doing away with the mental and physical suffering associated with childbirth.'

The Beveridge Report on Social Insurance and Allied Services

The Guild submitted a memorandum on the position of women to this Committee chaired by William Beveridge, in which equality of treatment of women with other workers in regard to sickness, disability and pension was urged. Beveridge himself replied, saying he was circulating the letter to the Inter-Departmental Committee and that he hoped the Report would give full weight to the claims of women. And once the Beveridge Report was published the Guild argued and pressed for its full implementation.

Perhaps one of the most important 1943 Congress Resolutions concerned the Beveridge Report.[3] Having welcomed the report, which proposed a unified social insurance system and fairer treatment of women, the resolution urged that the scheme be introduced without delay, and called for the establishment of a Ministry of Social Security with a woman assistant unless the Minister should be a woman. Guild views on this vital issue were so strong that the Resolution was immediately taken to the House of Commons for presentation to Co-operative MPs.

When the Central Committee went on their deputation to the House of Commons with this resolution, they urged that apart from pressing the Government to implement the proposals, a widespread campaign should be organised, to include a petition. This would go to all Co-operative Societies and branches were urged to help, in the October 1943 Bulletin. Members were asked to keep in mind Sir William Beveridge's statement that 'what action the Government will take depends upon what the people effectively demand.' The same Bulletin announced the publication of a 52-page booklet called 'The Beveridge Plan Explained to Co-operators.' The November 1944 Bulletin reports on the Government's response to Beveridge, and asks branches to study the scheme so that pressure 'can be put on the Government when the legislation is under discussion.' Of special interest to the Guild, says the Bulletin, is the fact that 'single men and women will receive equal benefits for sickness and unemployment.' The Guild also wanted to see equal treatment for married women. It also urged that children's allowances were inadequate, and that there were many anomalies in the proposals for widows. In addition, payment to the mother of the children's allowance was demanded - and eventually won.

1944 was the one year in the war when no Congress could be held, although the 1944 Bulletins are full of campaigns and activities, and the Guild members were also turning their attention to new legislation. All Councils Meeting in 1944 discussed the Education Bill, arguing against the retention of public schools and fee paying pupils in secondary schools.

Retaining the Guild's Integrity

Whilst the war years saw an increasing amount of co-operation by the Guild with other bodies, this brought its own problems. The April 1942 Bulletin carried an article on 'The Guild and other Organisations' which hinged on the fact that local Women's Parliaments were being set up and some branches had asked what action to take about invitations to co-operate for the purpose of pressing forward demands on social and industrial matters. The Bulletin pointed out that the programmes sponsored by these Women's Parliaments were identical all over the country and were clearly in line with Guild policy. It continues - "It is claimed that through unification the utmost strength and power of the workers can be mobilised to support them. It is because the arguments put forward by the promoters of Women's Parliament have so much truth that we need to examine the position carefully, and it becomes necessary to lay down a clear policy for guidance in regard to our association with this and all other organisations. IT MUST BE EMPHASISED THAT THE GUILD CAN ONLY CO-OPERATE WITH OTHER BODIES AS AN ORGANISATION AND IT CANNOT BECOME PART OF ANY OTHER BODY That is to say, a Guild branch can be represented on a Joint Committee set up to further policy which is in agreement with Guild policy ... such a Joint Committee may be set up under a public authority ... other organisation or even group of individuals." A national example given was the Standing Joint Committee of Working Women's Organisations made up of representatives of women from Co-operative, Labour and Trade Union bodies. The Guild should secure representation on committees set up to deal with public affairs in order to put forward the Co-operative point of view and press for Guild policy, but the work should not be undertaken by the Guild under the auspices of any other organisation, such as Women's Parliament or Housewives' Union. (This was a theme also discussed in Chapter 4, and returned to in later years).

' The article pointed out that the Women's Parliament was the child of the People's Convention which was largely under the control of Communists and whilst branches were advised that they could convene a local committee on which the Communist Party could be invited to co-operate, if other participating bodies were willing, Guild members needed to preserve the integrity of the Guild and press for Guild policy.

The article is specific on the problem of working with Communists: "…. experience has shown that the Communist Party does not work on immediate problems except for a given end, that end is dictatorship of the proletariat. The object of the Women's Co-operative Guild is a Co-operative Commonwealth. We are co-operators and not Communists. We are ready to carry our fight for Co-operation into all camps, but we can do so only under the banner of the Women's Co-operative Guild."

Despite this attitude, and the ban on Communists from holding office in the Guild, one of the major successful financial achievements of the Guild during the World War was the Aid to Russia Fund.

Aid to Russia Fund

Whilst Guild funds such as the War Victims Fund and the Maintenance Fund collected hundreds of pounds each year, the money collected for the Aid to Russia Fund was an astounding £5,000. This contrast between support for the Guild - whether for special funds or reflected in a willingness to raise membership subscription - was marked before, during and after the war. Year after year Guild projects concerning outside charities attracted more money than the Guild's own funds. To return to the Aid for Russia Scheme, Guild branches raised £5,000 for medical aid for Russia through the National Council of Labour, and it was then agreed the Guild should raise money for a specific project. It was decided, after consultation with Madame Maisky, wife of a former USSR Ambassador, that an

137

ambulance should be purchased, at a total cost of just over £1,000 (the CWS arranged to purchase this at cost price). It was presented to Madame Maisky on August 12th, 1943 (and reported in the November 1943 Bulletin). The cream ambulance had green lettering in English and Russian saying 'A Gift from the Co-operative Guildswomen of England and Wales.' In presenting it, Mrs. Webb, then National President, said that Co-operative Guildswomen looked forward to the time when the two countries should exchange not the accessories of war but the products of peace and visit fraternally without restraint of any kind.

The Diamond Jubilee

A major event that occurred during the war was the Diamond Jubilee of the Guild. A Diamond Jubilee Demonstration was held in the Albert Hall on Sunday, 27th June 1943, the eve of the 1943 London Congress. Speakers included Mrs. C.S. Ganley, J.P., President of the London Co-operative Society, Alderman Mrs. L'Estrange Malone, of the LCC, Chairman of the Standing Joint Committee of the Working Women's Organisations and Dame Anne Loughlin, DBE, Chairman of the Trades Union Congress. Alan Bush conducted the Co-operative Choirs with the organ and the London String Orchestra.

The Annual Report described the Albert Hall assembly, the proceedings of which were recorded for broadcast by the BBC Overseas Service. The highlight of the afternoon was 'a magnificent ceremonial of greeting' which was arranged and presented by the President and Secretary of the International Guild, Frau Freundlich and Mrs. Naftel. "Groups of women in national costume, representing 18 different nations, passed in colourful cavalcade down the centre of the hall to the platform where they turned to face the audience and - in their own language gave greeting to the English Guild. They were followed by women from British organisations and by young co-operators from different sections of the Movement. It was a scene to make history and can never fade from the memory of anyone who was present."

Apart from the two Cabinet Ministers present, the Rt. Hon. A.V. Alexander, First Lord of the Admiralty, and Ernest Bevin, Minister of Labour, Sir William Bradshaw, President of the CWS Board and Richard Coppock, Chairman of the LCC greeted the Opening Session of Congress.

An editorial in the "Co-operative News"[4] said that Diamond Jubilee Year had fittingly seen Mrs. Caroline Ganley, J.P., succeed to the Presidency of the largest retail Society and Mrs. M.L. Lidington take her seat as the first woman on the Co-operative Union Executive Committee - its most important committee. "An organisation which can train ordinary working class housewives for such positions deserves much more than empty flattery and good-humoured tolerance. It deserves recognition as a very important, useful and responsible member of the Co-operative organism and should be consulted as such."

What was so impressive about the Guild Diamond Jubilee, taking place as it did in such adverse circumstances, for the organisation, its members, and the Co-operative Movement, was the fact that the publication issued to mark the Jubilee was forward-looking - called significantly WOMAN OF TOMORROW.

Woman of Tomorrow

The booklet, well-illustrated, was rooted in the present: ending with some of the resolutions passed at the 1943 Congress.[5] It begins by restating the great ideal of the Women's Co-operative Guild: "A world in which men and women shall work side by side in creating a democratic way of life, a new order in which all may share freely and equitably the abundance of the earth; an international structure of society founded on the basic principles of consumer Co-operation, eliminating for ever the causes of poverty, racial antagonism, and war; thus may be summarised the idealistic aims of this nation-wide community of working women."

The booklet also says "whilst it is tempting to look back along the difficult and tortuous road the Guild has travelled... we are living in fateful days, when the demands of stern reality claim our attention, in preference to the happier but less useful contemplation of the past ... In the comparatively brief span of sixty years, against the background of the Guild, women have emerged from the obscurity of the kitchen to the front rank of the consumers' movement.... In the social services of the nation feminine opinion and influence have become a force which no

139

politician can afford to ignore. The part played by the WCG in this transformation can never be too fully appreciated ... of the two catastrophic world wars, women could do nothing to prevent them .... Civilised woman is, instinctively, a pacifist .... No enlightened woman would have agreed that any circumstances justified the colossal slaughter of husbands, sons and brothers which is inevitable in modern war.''

Female employment is another aspect of post war industrial organisation discussed in the Jubilee Booklet. Fear is expressed that the increased number of women in industry will adversely affect male wages and conditions of work after the war. Readers are reminded that even the urgent demands of wartime production have not resulted in equal pay for men and women.

Of the women who will be released from the services, the authors ask if the Guild can secure their allegiance. It goes on to say that "many thousands of women have acquired new independence and a broader outlook from work in the Forces, factories, offices and shops; many have become more enlightened regarding their rights and responsibilities as citizens. Young women must be made to see in the Guild unlimited scope for service, and opportunities for leadership. The Guild has taken an interest in all social reforms affecting motherhood and family life and is concerned with the effect on today's youth of the disturbance of family ties due to the war. Attracting young women to the Guild's ranks is seen as the prime concern, and this is linked with the need to make sure, through the British Federation of Young Co-operators, that there is a way of affecting a transition of girls from Co-operative Youth Clubs to the Guild.''

The Guild it said would continue to press for more comprehensive Co-operative education, and had responsibilities in regard to education about the position of women in the national political and social system. The section on education concludes that 'as an efficient, virile community of earnest women, the Guild has a vital part to play in arousing feminine interest and influence in the creation of a new and better world.'

On their role within the Co-operative Movement, it had already been proposed by the Guild that a Women's Advisory Committee should be set up to advise on questions of consumer demand. The Guild leadership and members were working women who knew the importance of the ordinary needs of home and family, thus representing a guide to domestic requirements that could help extend the national appeal of Co-operative products and trading services. Turning to the future, it is argued that continued success depends on the Guild's ability to adapt to the new social era and meet the demands of the more sophisticated and critical consumer whose vision now extends beyond the four walls of home. 'The Women's Co-operative Guild must attract to its ranks the intelligent, worldly wise and mentally alert woman of tomorrow.'

This theme, of how to attract younger women, was to become a central concern of the Guild in the 40 years between the Diamond Jubilee and the Centenary, and a satisfactory answer has yet to be found. But the Jubilee Congress was a triumph: 1460 delegates gathered in London during war-time to survey the achievements of 1943 (a year that included the donation of the ambulance to Russia), to discuss 43 resolutions covering the usual wide range: from vegetable prices to famine relief. As the Central Committee's Report to the Diamond Jubilee Congress said, 'There is still a tendency to regard the history of a nation as a record of wars and tabulations of Kings, Queens or other rulers.... history is the life and growth of common people manifest in their conditions and through their activities.'

Co-operative Links at the End of the War

Stress on loyalty to Co-operative trade and principles continued during the War. Experience in local shops, such as inability to purchase Co-operatively produced goods, led to resolutions at Congress. Guildswomen were to be found (albeit in small numbers in relation to their membership) at most levels of Co-operative management.

The 1944 Annual Report announced the election of Mrs. C.S. Ganley, J.P., as President of London Co-operative Society, the largest retail co-operative society in the world. Another 520 guildswomen were on management committees of societies throughout the country, other members were reported as serving on other Co-operative Committees and Boards. In the same Annual Report we learn that Mrs. Edith Williams was a member of the Board of the Co-operative Press and that the Guild had members on Sectional Boards and the National Education Council. We also learn that despite a Guild request for inclusion, the 1944 Co-operative Delegation to Russia was all male. Representation on the Co-operative Party Executive was direct. At the beginning of the War, the Party refused Central Committee's nominations for the Parliamentary Panel due to disagreement over Peace Policy. By 1944 Mrs. Hutchinson and Mrs. Mabel Ridealgh had been accepted (with other Guildswomen nominated by local constituency parties), on the Panel.

Topics for Guild discussion during the year always included Co-operative issues. For example, the Sectional Schools in 1944 covered:

Private Monopolies and People's Co-operation
Improved conditions for the Housewife
Post-war Employment

and in the same year Spring and Autumn conferences, held in all Sections and addressed by visiting Central Committee members were on:-

Co-operative Trade and the Menace of the Combines, and
Foundations for a Permanent Peace.

The International Co-operative Women's Guild and the Second World War

Each year the September Monthly Bulletin was devoted to news of the International Co-operative Women's Guild (ICWG), by then working from London. This reflected the keen interest Guild members took in women co-operators abroad, as well as their view that only a replacement of international competition with international Co-operation could lead to peace. The September 1944 Bulletin reviews ICWG experience during the war, based on the ICWG pamphlet, 'The Guild Movement in Peace & War.'[6]

The ICWG had grown steadily from 1921 until the International Conference in Paris in 1937. Frau Emmy Freundlich who had played such a key role in creating the ICWG and who was its President, came to England early in 1939 to try to keep the ICWG alive and at work.

The main wartime tasks were listed as keeping existing national Guilds united in a common international purpose, to retain and extend contacts, and to maintain ICWG prestige and influence in international circles. The London office sent out

500 copies of an International Information Bulletin. Mrs. Theo Naftel, Secretary of the ICWG, had been involved in helping refugees. Most had been co-operators, and they were put in touch with British Co-operative organisations.

From 1943, questions of relief and reconstruction in occupied countries became the major concern. A practical plan was drawn up, covering not merely the services that would be needed in the countries, but role of governments and of women at home. (The plan was reported in full in the September 1943 Bulletin).

The difference between the ICWG and other women's organisations is outlined - showing clearly the involvement of WCG pioneers in the setting up of its international sister. The ICWG is described as operating within the framework of the International Co-operative Movement believing that the interests of housewives and mothers and the interests of the Movement are inseparable.

It sought to 'anchor women to Co-operation and also show Co-operative organisations how much their development depends on women's collaboration and loyalty.' The task was defined as 'to increase Co-operative influence and deal with all current world problems from the Co-operative angle.'

ICWG detailed proposals for post-war relief and reconstruction were published in their pamphlet of that name, also written by Frau Freundlich and Mrs. B. Naftel.[7]

In 1941 the WCG became a member of the Liaison Committee of Women's International Organisations, formed to ensure closer collaboration and better representation of women on the League of Nations and the ILO. Contact was maintained with a wide range of other international organisations as well as with the International sub-committees of the Standing Joint Committee of Working Women's Organisations.

On the Brink of Peace

With the end of the war in sight Congress resolved that the Guild Office should return to London, and the March 1944 Bulletin was published from an office in Leman Street, London, E.1. rented from the CWS. As the first Bulletin printed in London said: "The return of the Guild Head Office to London will have deep significance for Guild branches all over the country. It marks clearly the point at which our attention turns definitely and decisively to the things of the future. The war is not over. There is still a hard and difficult path to tread but we do now feel a conviction that the end will come and will bring with it an opportunity greater than we have ever known for establishing a finer and better way of life.... As one of the great women's organisations the Guild can do much to mould public opinion both within and outside the Movement."

The Guild ended the war aware of their setbacks and the struggle ahead. Membership down from 87,246 (1939) to 57,153 (1946) and branches down from 1805 to 1714 in the same period.

The spirit of weariness is caught in the January 1945 Bulletin, where the editorial says: "Peace still lies ahead. Just around the corner we hope! But the noise of battle is ringing in our ears, and we are spiritually sick with longing for the corner to be turned. War is not only demoralising but it takes away vitality and weakens the will to strive for better things. Total war is so overwhelming that the main desire of all is to escape from the strain it imposes, and there is a tendency to avoid effort and to shrink from action. But if we are to play our part in establishing that better world which is our objective and for which we have steadfastly striven for over 60 years. We cannot afford to slacken, however tired and discouraged we may be.... The new world we want will not grow, it will be built, and we must be the builders. We must plan and shape if the structure is to be to our requirements."

In June 1945 the Bulletin welcomed the end of the War in Europe but recognised the difficulties ahead. The editorial said: "We have almost ridden out the storm but the task of clearing up is appalling in its magnitude.... The cry of the children which went up from the factories in Britain in the early part of the nineteenth century roused the conscience of the nation. The cry of the children which is going up from war-ridden countries today should rouse the conscience of the world. Not only is it necessary to see to present material need, but it is also essential to provide conditions in which the future citizens of every country can grow up without feelings of bitterness and resentment ... which sow so inevitably the seeds of future War. As Co-operative guildswomen let us mark our thankfulness for part deliverance by dedicating ourselves anew to our high purpose - the establishment of a co-operative and war free world. ... We were compelled to sacrifice comfort for war. Let us now come forward and volunteer what further sacrifice may

144

be needed to build a secure and lasting Peace''.

It is to how the Guild took up this challenge, sent out as World War II nears its end, that we now turn.

Notes to Chapter 5

1. F. Whittaker, Service in London's Deep Shelters. (The Guild in War and Peace, No. 2, Meeting War Emergency, undated).
2. *Co-operative News,* 26th June 1943.
3. Sound Insurance and Allied Services, Report 6404, 1942.
4. *Co-operative News,* 3rd July 1943.
5. WCG. Woman of Tomorrow. The Women's Co-operative Guild 1883-1943 Manchester 1943.
6. International Co-operative Women's Guild, The Guild Movement in War and Peace (1944).
7. ICWG, Post-war Relief and Reconstruction (undated).

CHAPTER 6

THE GUILD FIGHTS BACK:
1945-1951

The Drive for New Members

In 1945 Guild membership stood at 51,392 in 1,671 branches. This was the lowest membership recorded since 1923, and recruitment became the immediate major priority of the Central Committee. It was in fact to remain a major priority. Although membership rose in the period discussed in this chapter, reaching 61,037 in 1951, this was to be the peak post war membership figure.

Life for women was never to be the same. As Laurie Pavitt, MP said, 'the war took women out of the kitchen.' The opportunities to remain at least partially outside were to continue and indeed grow. The need for change was recognised by the Guild leadership, who argued that the key to attracting new members was to be a new approach to branch activity and therefore a new approach to education which was to remain the centre of branch life. Education here meant learning how to administer an efficient branch, as well as relating to a deeper knowledge of Co-operation, and public affairs generally.

Formal education for women was already a possibility. After the 1902 Education Act the newly created Local Education Authorities had established secondary schools, but if girls did benefit, they were predominantly from the middle classes. Working class girls were more likely to be found in elementary schools. The 1944 Act, strongly supported by the WCG, was to mean (in theory at least) equality of opportunity for all irrespective of social class or sex. Guild concern for education is found in resolution after resolution on Congress Agenda as well as Guild participation in the work of the Council for Educational Advance.

But the major triumph of the WCG educational work had been its pioneering role in educating women to stand up in public and say something - to educate women both to be public speakers and to educate them in terms of giving them a thorough understanding of the issues they were to talk about.

"Woman's Outlook"[1] had an editorial headed 'Wanted — Youth and Vigour' which expressed admiration for the efforts of ordinary working class women to supplement the inadequate education most of them have received: "It takes a high degree of courage and determination for a woman to tackle the duties imposed by home and family and also to fit in the time for mental concentration needed for studious pursuits.... Somehow I feel that the Guild is at a turning point in its history. Most strongly do I feel that its future progress depends upon the rate at which new and vigorous young women can be recruited into its ranks. And not only recruited - but given an opportunity to take office and responsibility. During the war years, older members have done - and still do - untiring work. They have battled against physical, and mental weariness and kept the Guild alive. But their places must gradually be taken by younger women trained in the way to speak and conduct meetings, and in knowledge of the Movement they have joined. This latter point is perhaps the most important of all. So it seems to me that, with the proposed new education which Guild leaders envisage, must go serious encouragement of young people and a tolerance of the hot-head, who can, remember, be schooled by wise guidance... So often resentment is shown towards a better-educated woman. It is founded, perhaps, upon a certain awe which a less well-educated person often feels in the presence of such a one. Sometimes the resentment is created by the unconscious arrogance which a certain type of educated person displays. The process of smoothing away arrogance on the one hand and resentment on the other is painful and sometimes disastrous but it must be faced courageously by the wise Guildswoman wherever she may find it."

Mrs. A.L. Kennedy, Secretary of Osidge and Old Southgate branch, wrote in the same issue that although:

the modern young Guildswoman has poise, I feel the conscientious sensitive woman would be far more willing to undertake official duties if there was adequate tuition beforehand. Lessons on Committee procedure are useful for all members, for an ignorant branch is an indifferent one... no Guildswoman can be an intelligent worker without a mental background of Co-operative history and international Co-operation... in the coming new social epoch, Guildswomen cannot afford to 'muddle through'; they must be trained and fit to do their share in Co-operative work and the larger sphere of local and national government.

Talking about Northfield branch in Birmingham, which she joined in 1941 at the age of 22, Baroness Fisher said that recruitment of women in her age group was quite easy after the war - mainly by personal contact (recruitment was not a problem until the early 1960s).She recalled one new recruit after the war who left the meeting early, at 9.10pm (the branch had met in the afternoon during the war but returned to evening meetings once it had ended). The following week she left at 9.30 and all the members left together. The new member's husband was standing on the opposite side of the street. The next week he did not meet her, having been convinced she really was going to a women's meeting. Baroness Fisher felt recruitment was good after the war because factory and other war time experiences had involved women in more "do gooding" and joining the Guild was perhaps a sign of wanting to stay involved in the community.

This debate was to lead to an extension of Guild educational provision outlined in the pamphlet, Education for Service.[2]

Education for Service

This publication suggested that the new and younger women the WCG needs to attract have been 'taught to move to a quicker measure than was customary in pre-war years: and old ways which have served in the past will not, in many cases, be ways which they will approve or be ready to adopt.'

The pamphlet is a report of a sub-committee set up by Central Committee to survey the whole structure of Guild education. The survey is followed by recommendations, which incorporate changes made when the proposals were discussed at All Councils Meeting in Derby in February 1946.

The purpose of Guild education is given as "to fit the ordinary housewife to take her full place in the Co-operative Movement and in the State by training through the branch, the district, the section and the national sphere; ...the purpose of the Guild is to make the ordinary housewife a democratic co-operator and an informed citizen. The Guild provides education for its ordinary membership, but makes special provision for training Guild officials, as the Guild has always taken pride in its competence to manage its own affairs, and the good Guild official 'must be able to express herself clearly and convincingly, and be competent to give a lead to others'." The pamphlet goes on to say that Guild officials must understand the rules and support the policy of the Guild.

The pamphlet then makes the point that the structure then operating was developed in the early days of the Guild when general education was at a low level. Future guildswomen would have better opportunities, so the machinery would have to be adjusted to take this factor into account.

What could not, of course, be taken into account in 1946 was the explosion of leisure opportunities (inside and outside the home) combined with greater affluence, which were in fact to make it increasingly difficult to attract into the Guild the younger women being sought.

And what, in 1946, did the education provision consist of? Officials' classes were intended as training for branch officials, taken by Sectional Secretaries (or a member of Central Committee) they covered topics such as preparing minutes, agenda and keeping accounts as well as conducting meetings, the meaning and importance of rules; and how Guild policy is controlled through Congress decisions. Many of those who wrote to us mentioned enjoying such classes, and Mabel Ridealgh talked about enjoying them as a student and later as one of the teachers. Proposals for change included that, in future, training should be at residential schools, where possible, with separate sessions for secretaries, presidents and treasurers, with a Sectional Secretary or Central Committee member teaching. The classes should remain at District level.

Training for District Officials was by means of District Committee School and covered instruction in:-

(a) the meaning and purpose of Guild organisation;

(b) the methods by which Guild members can be educated in Co-operation and citizenship;

(c) the Guild's relations, as a Co-operative organisation, with other progressive bodies;

(d) the Guild's place in politics as an autonomous political unit associated through the Co-operative Party with the Labour Party.

The new recommendation was for people to come from a wider area, and to be residential. It was considered 'especially necessary that District Secretaries understand the rules which govern the Guild.'

Discussion group methods, just begun, should continue, with those attending thinking about the subjects beforehand and coming prepared to contribute. Speakers should prepare their own notes and not rely on notes issued from Head Office which were intended as a guide to shape of speech and the main arguments. Those best fitted should speak, includng women now out of office, and it was proposed that a panel of lecturers be prepared, 'particular consideration being given to those whom the Guild has trained and who have specialised in some particular line.' Working in a period where there was keen competition to hold office in the Guild, the authors could say that those taking up District Committee work were expected to give time to it, and that attendance at District Schools was essential.

The pamphlet then turned to the training of speakers, which included the issue of notes from Head Office on 'How to prepare and deliver an address.' It was considered so important that how to prepare and deliver an address should be thoroughly understood by speakers at the beginning of their training that 'it is felt to be very inadvisable that this important item should be taken on by Sectional Secretaries. The best assistance available should be used to train speakers.'

Where Joint Guild Councils, i.e. covering one Society's area, existed it was suggested public speaking lessons be run with the help of society education committees, 'who would in all probability be ready to pay expenses and provide teachers. All aspirants for office should use the facilities which are offered, and qualifications thus gained should be borne in mind when elections are taking place.'

The extent to which subjects available for speakers was controlled is shown in the section on "subjects and notes." Subjects are decided by the Central Committee and notes prepared by Head Office. Matters such as housing, health or Co-operative organisation are studied with a view to taking action and achieving an objective. Baroness Fisher explained how topics discussed thoroughly at all levels of the Movement led to informed debate at Congress, and good resolutions too.

Only District Secretaries should interpret Rules but all District speakers should be competent to speak on them. District Secretaries who wished to talk on a subject in addition to Rules were free to do so, but it was pointed out that duties of District and Sectional Secretaries were mainly organisational, District speakers in the first year should take only two subjects, and not those taken by sectional members.

'The predominant interest of the Guild should be the principles of Co-operation and their application through our

151

own Movement as well as through citizenship' says the pamphlet stressing the importance of keeping guildswomen fully informed of the structure of the Co-operative Movement. 'All Guild speakers should adhere to Guild policy as laid down by Congress, ... but all Guild branches were to have Guild speakers on Guild subjects before asking for outside subjects or speakers.'

The topics for speakers laid down by Central Committee were wider after publication of this Report than before it. So in 1947, District speakers spoke on:

1. The New Education Act.
2. The New Health Proposals.
3. Consumer Co-operation and the Socialist State.
4. Social Insurance.
5. What do we do - a Year's Review.

Sectional Schools considered three new subjects:

1. From River to Tap.
2. Modern Design and Co-operative Production.
3. The Multilateral School.

and Spring and Autumn Sectional Conferences took "Consumer Responsibility" and "The Free Trade Position and the Co-operative Housewife."

Kathleen Kempton recalls her year as a District member. She had to talk on Co-operation in China, but says that her favourite topic was "From River to Tap," and said members got notes from the Training Courses and were then 'let loose on branches.' Some did little homework and just read from the notes. Kathleen Kempton considered that the subjects got more and more complicated whilst members' own knowledge was improving. As a member of staff from 1944 and, from 1963, General Secretary, she was particularly well-placed to observe these changes.

The 1946 Annual Report was able to say that many of the recommendations in Education for Service were being carried out and others would be when finance allowed, whilst the formation of new branches with a preponderance of young members showed an encouraging response to the new approach.

Education for Service marked the start of an attempt by the Guild to modernise its educational provisions - both in terms of method and of content. It was a process that was to continue. The Annual Report of 1949 shows a move away from the original educational provisions, and says: "We are learning each year that the post-war demand in women's organisations is for recreational and cultural activities. Serious education has to be the pill which is well camouflaged with a great deal of jam. Social conditions which were the vital educational factor for the Guild in earlier days have no significance for the young housewife today, even if she is a member of a Co-operative society.

A New Approach to Guild Education

1949 saw the publication of a circular to Co-operative societies entitled a 'New Approach to Guild Education.'[3] This circular whilst concerned with education was a response to Guild fears that societies were offering help to non-Co-operative women's organisations. The circular pointed out that home conditions were changing and that whilst Central Committee appreciated the appeal of classes in topics such as handicrafts and cookery, they believed the aim of adult education should be to make self-reliant and socially conscious citizens and that co-operators should aim for a well-informed membership able to apply Co-operative principles to wider civic problems as well as to trade. A list of subjects was given, and the Education or Publicity Committees of Co-operative societies were asked to help fund speakers. Subjects listed include Developments in Medicine, Drama, Child Care, Needlecraft, Labour-saving Devices, Bee-keeping and Archaeology.

The Central Committee reassured societies that there was no fear that these additional activities would affect the serious side of the Guild work. The new approach was seen as a way of attracting young women into the orbit of Co-operative education - and to continue to educate them in Co-operation and citizenship for the common good, thus increasing Guild membership and extending Co-operative trade. The 1949 Annual Report says the circular was well-received, and many offers of assistance were received.

Recognition of the need for a balanced programme was of course not new. One of our oldest correspondents is Mrs. Mary Tromans of Stockton-on-Tees, who was born in 1893 and joined the Guild in 1930. Looking back at nine years as assistant secretary and 26 as secretary - she is still on the branch committee - she writes

*during my period of office I was always getting a good
programme for 12 months at a time consisting of speakers,
entertainment and guild debates.*

The 1949 Report also discusses the link between education
and politics, saying that careful study and widespread
discussion developed a strong sense of citizenship and that
before Co-operative politics became a practical issue,
guildswomen were associated with the progressive thought that
gave rise to the Labour Party. The Guild, the Report says, has
functioned as an educational rather than a political force -
guildswomen 'desired satisfactory homes where self-reliant
men and women could rear happy children for future citizens in
a prosperous peaceful world. They learned that only the right
kind of government could bring their desires to fulfilment.
Their politics are the outcome of that education.'

The changes in educational provision outlined here resulted
from the rise of other women's organisations, and the challenge
of women who were better-educated and had more
opportunities for work and leisure, in a rapidly changing
society.

The change brought a new approach to recruitment, with a
leaflet showing a woman with handbag rather than basket.
Called 'The Woman of Today Steps Out' it stresses factors like
'new ideas and new ways of life,' and says the WCG is 'desirous
that Co-operative women shall touch upon many other things
than the political and social matters that have hitherto been
almost the sole activities of bodies that work for the
advancement of women.' Instead, new topics for talks, visits
and film shows are listed.

The extent to which this new approach did attract more
members is difficult to assess. In the next chapter we discuss the
declining membership that was to concern the Guild from 1951
onwards. The reasons for declining membership were complex,
so that the changes in educational style and content, in
themselves radical, impressive and welcome, could not alone
stem that decline.

The educational context of the Guild was obviously enjoyed
by Guild members. Asked what aspect of Guild work she
enjoyed most, Mrs. Annie Rickards from Clapham, South
London, singled out WEA lectures. She joined the Guild in
1936 when aged 34, and says she remembers an elderly Guild
member telling her that this was the only place where you could
hear ordinary working class women discussing their lives.

Education was more usually remembered alongside other aspects of guild work, and from the questionnaires received from members there is also no doubt about the pleasure given by participating in social activities, visits and Guild competitions.

Nevertheless it is important to see the changes in educational approach, at least partially, as a reaction to the success of other women's organisations. The "Manchester Guardian"[4] reported Cecily Cook's speech to the 1946 Congress when the issue was discussed. The Guild faced the problem of how to attract young women, eager to take advantage of cultural facilities, to an organisation which concentrates mainly on education for citizenship. Mrs. Cook is quoted as saying 'we have never attracted people by offering them "jam" — but admits the need to be realistic about the problem as it seems likely that potential Guild members are drifting into the Townswomen's Guild. However, as the report points out, members will not get "jam" all the time — only at one meeting in four.

Despite the concern with new approaches to education, and the need to recruit younger women, the period of this chapter is a positive one in the Guild's history, not least because they were at long last working with a government putting into effect so many Guild policies.

The Guild, the Labour Government and Guildswomen in the House of Commons

The June 1946 Bulletin said: "This year is unique ... it will be the first Congress in the whole of our history where our debates will be conducted not with an eye on an antagonistic authority sitting in the seats of government at Westminster, but with the knowledge that the Government of the country is in the hands of those whose programme is in the main directed along lines that we ourselves approve. This fact will give us a feeling of satisfaction and inspiration. But it must also be realised that if heads are high in air, feet must be kept firmly on the ground ... Two things therefore must be watched and carefully guarded against:-

1) A complacent satisfaction that having elected a people's Government, it is their job to legislate us into Utopia without delay;

2) A too-critical attitude, which is impatient of the necessary process of bringing about those improvements which have

155

been laid down as policy so often and so long.

For these reasons Congress deliberations this year must be well-considered and carefully weighed.

The 1946 Annual Report made the point that one Guild task was to make sure that those in power know 'the things we want.' Equally important, ordinary people need to understand the work that is being done. So guildswomen must watch government's activities and help to interpret them, but as Mrs. Mason, a member of Worcester Park Branch from 1935-1963, when the branch closed, wrote

Since about the early 1950s everything has disappeared. There were classes to take to help the housewife to understand the government.

The 1946 Annual Report went on to say: "Sixty years of work have laid some foundation for the new order but the building has not yet begun to arise. Its beauty, its utility for our purpose, is yet dependent upon our effort. It is our post-war task to go forward with courage and determination.... Co-operative Guildswomen ... must also play a very vital part in translating Society from individualism to the practice of Co-operation.

Not only was the government sympathetic to Guild policy — three guildswomen were elected to Parliament in 1945:

Mrs. Mabel Ridealgh, MP for Ilford North

Mrs. Caroline Ganley, MP for Battersea South

Mrs. Edith Wills, MP for Duddeston.

The August 1945 Bulletin described this news as encouraging and described the three guildswomen MPs as 'our standard bearers,' going on to say 'we are proud to have helped in the victory they have won.' It is interesting to note the maiden speeches of these three guildswomen MPs — Mrs. Ridealgh on the Insurance Bill, Mrs. Wills on Furnished Houses (Rent Control) and Mrs. Ganley on the National Health Service.[5]

The Annual Reports for 1945, 1946, 1947, 1948 all talk warmly of the help and advice received from those three guildswomen MPs. Regular contact with them was established, and the 1946 Annual Report says it is 'impossible to detail the work done but it is continuing and important.' The 1948 report does pick out specific issues and mentions the help given by Mrs. Ridealgh in connection with a deputation to the Foreign Secretary, by Mrs. Ganley in connection with the visits of German women, and by Mrs. Wills in connection with BBC publicity.

Guildswomen are also reminded in several Bulletins (e.g.

December 1945) that the guildswomen MPs are busy, and must give priority to constituency work, so all approaches on WCG matters should be channelled through the General Secretary who met the three MPs regularly.

Sadly, the 1950 election brought defeat to Mrs. Ridealgh and Mrs. Wills, leaving Mrs. Ganley as the only guildswoman MP. She in turn was defeated in 1951.

In 1947 General Secretary, Cecily Cook, was awarded an OBE. This honour was accepted with great modesty — the article in the February 1947 Bulletin referring to the matter could only have been written by her. The article says that the spate of letters that poured into Guild office during the early days of January showed that 'alertness and sensibility to public affairs operates in the majority of Guild branches.' The article refers to the Guild song quoted at the 1947 Annual Congress by the National President:

Then sister, you I call;
Be next to me, keep the line;
And hold me out a comrade's hand
To pledge your soul with mine.

and ends: "Every Guildswoman from the General Secretary downwards has to make that appeal to her fellow members. Only by standing next to one another and keeping the line shall we win not small honours, which are pleasant fruits to pick by the wayside, but that world of our dreams, the world of Co-operation and Peace".

Recordings of the 1948 Congress at Great Yarmouth were included in a Woman's Hour programme for the first time and it is difficult not to see this as an example of the way the Guild was taken more seriously in the period of the first post-war Labour Government.

Further, and more concrete, evidence comes when we look at the larger role played by guildswomen on official committees. For example, the 1948 Report shows guildswomen represented on the Women's Advisory Council on Solid Fuel, Fuel Economy Committee, Ministry of Health Rent Tribunals, National House Builders Registration Council, and the Cabinet Economic Unit Women's Committee. These are in addition to a wide range of other bodies with which the Guild was represented or associated. The 1947 Annual Report stresses yet again, that the Guild "cannot affiliate to an over-riding body but can only work with other bodies on equal terms." These included the

Nuffield Women's Advisory Committee on Hospitals and Healthy Nation Provisional Committee (Child Guidance), National Peace Council, National Council for Civil Liberties, Mary MacArthur Holiday Homes, British Soviet Friendship Society, No Conscription Council, Central Board for Conscientious Objectors, and the Women's Committee of the United Nations Association. These organisations reflect the causes and concerns of interest to the Guild in the post-war period. How the Labour Government responded, and the issues that were pursued, is now discussed.

Campaigns and Concerns at Home and Abroad

The campaigns and concerns of the WCG, as reflected in the pages of the monthly Bulletin as well as in Annual Congress Resolutions and Annual Reports reflect the domestic and international interests of the Guild. And as usual there is a mixture of the practical and the idealist in the Guild's approaches. It is impossible, in a book of this length, to deal with all the issues of concern to the Guild, but no-one who looks in detail at the meticulous way issues were followed through and resolutions framed can fail to be impressed by the quality of Guild leadership and members — itself a tribute to the education provided by the Guild. Not all members and branches are equally diligent. Monthly Bulletin and Annual Reports often reflect frustration with the branches for failing to work locally on issues pursued vigorously at national level.

For example, a major international concern in the post-war years was famine and shortages in recently occupied countries. The August 1945 Bulletin tells of a letter from a young co-operator, who was unable to go to Guild meetings because of caring for young babies, and had used all her current soap coupons in order to respond to the Guild appeal for soap to be sent to Yugoslavia. Her letter to the local Guild Secretary was unanswered. As the Bulletin article points out, 'The mothers of young children today are our best members in a few years' time,' and urges branches to be on the lookout for offers of assistance.

The same Bulletin describes Guild involvement in the Co-operative Overseas Clothing Relief Scheme based on collecting used garments, organised by the Co-operative Union, with individual Co-operative societies acting as collecting points. Auxiliaries set up combined committees to deal with collecting, mending, sorting and bundling and the CWS provided central depots for baling and despatch. Finally, shipping and distribution was to be arranged jointly by the CWS and the International Co-operative Alliance. The 1946 Annual Report reported that clothing was being sent to Holland, Poland, Yugoslavia, China, Germany and Austria and the 1947 Report tells how this scheme continued, together with food parcels being sent by individual guildswomen to families in Europe.

By 1948 the Annual Report is recording 124 parcels being sent from the Co-operative League of the USA — they came from farmers in Iowa to the Co-operative Union for distribution by the Guild to its needy members!

Peace Policy

Alongside the practical efforts on relief come strong resolutions on peace. The implications of the atomic bombs dropped on Nagasaki and Hiroshima were immediately obvious to the Guild, as Congress resolutions show. It was perhaps on the issue of peace that the Guild was most at variance with the Labour Government of this period.

The pamphlet entitled the 'Road to Peace' outlines Guild policy on peace, which may vary as circumstances change but is based on the firm, fundamental principle that the settlement of differences should be by conciliation and mutual adjustment.[6] The other factor important to Guild peace policy is that it is a woman's organisation and the authors say most guildswomen are mothers, 'and motherhood everywhere carries with it an urge for the preservation of life. This urge combined with Co-operative principles has inspired the policy on Peace which has been so great a part of Guild work over the last 30 to 40 years.'

After a historical survey of Guild peace policy, the pamphlet reminds it readers that during the war, members had been free to act according to their convictions, but the organisation had refused to take an official part in the war effort, although involved in the relief of suffering. It is acknowledged that attempts were made to change the Guild attitude, and Congress resolutions urging full support for the war effort were narrowly defeated on more than one occasion.

The Guild wrote to the Prime Minister after the war,

expressing dismay at the slowing down of demobilisation and at the establishment of peace time conscription, and calling for a new kind of army — one trained 'to help backward or conquered peoples' or 'those visited by war or the calamity of natural catastrophe to progress towards equality in status and opportunity with the most forward of civilised nations.'

The pamphlet concludes by setting out the Guild resolution on Peace, passed unanimously at the Guild Congress in Sheffield in 1950. There had of course been other resolutions since the war. They included resolutions against conscription in 1945 and 1946; against arms manufacture and sale in 1947, together with one deploring the absence of women in the Peace Treaty negotiations. The debate on this latter resolution, as reported in the "Daily Herald" reports Mrs. K. Davies of Bolton as saying

Women can never get the world into a bigger mess than men have got it.

In 1948, three resolutions out of the total of 14 passed concerned peace.

The 1949 Congress resolution on Peace called for reduced arms expenditure; formulation of a policy on the peaceful use of atomic energy and destruction of atomic weapons; refusal to use Britain for stationing foreign troops, withdrawal of manpower from Greece, Malaya and other countries, and called for trading agreements with the countries of Eastern Europe and the Soviet Union.

The resolution passed at the 1950 Congress in Sheffield and featured in the Guild pamphlet 'The Road to Peace' was similar to the one passed in 1949, with emphasis given to the need for scientists to divert scientific discovery from methods of destruction to ways and means of industrial development and creation of substantial additions to fuel supplies. The resolution goes on 'we believe it is the duty of a Labour Government to refuse to accept war as an inevitable outcome of international difficulty but to work for peace not only by being unprovocative, but by refusal to be provoked'. British policy should be reduced arms expenditure, abandonment of conscription, improved international relations by abstention from adverse comment on other countries on press, or radio, and the promotion of better East/West understanding by friendly co-operation with both and by partisanship for neither.

The pamphlet, after quoting the 1950 Guild Resolution,

concludes with three tasks for Guild branches: first, to protest in regard to actions or statements likely to lead to international misunderstanding; second, to use its influence to maintain and strengthen a Labour and Co-operative government and third to continue activities at home and through the International Co-operative Women's Guild which will lead to the abandonment of force as a method of avoiding disputes.

Domestic Campaigns and Concerns

Whilst resolutions on Peace and International Relations appeared regularly on Congress Agenda in the post-war years, domestic concerns were very varied. Some Guild campaigns were successful. The April 1945 Bulletin records Guild protest against the coalition government proposals that Family Allowances, when introduced, would be the property of the father. Central Committee interviewed representatives of Co-operative MPs at the House of Commons, and Head Office asked District Secretaries to contact local branches. In some branches, the Monthly Bulletin records, all members sent postcards to their MPs. The Guild also argued for Family Allowances to be tax free (passed at 1945 Congress); and the 1946 Annual Report is able to say that original proposals on reducing its value to families on Public Assistance were modified.

Congress in 1946 passed a resolution urging that children's allowances should be payable to the first child but at the 1949 Congress at Margate, the "Daily Herald" tells us, 'complete satisfaction with the government's family allowances was expressed' when Congress rejected a call for tax-free allowances for all children including those over 16 still at school.[8] A resolution calling for increased family allowances was also defeated in 1951.

Housing Policy

The Guild in this period was also very concerned about housing following years of destruction by war-time bombing. The 1945 Congress resolution on housing was long and detailed, calling for at least four million new dwellings in the first five years of peace, with a range of subsidiary demands including release of 500,000 builders from the Forces, compulsory purchase of land needed for building, more attractive Council estates, and rent controls. The 1946 Congress at Torquay resolved that regulations should ensure a house is deemed unfit for human habitation within five years if it lacks inside water, bathroom, hot water, separate lavatory for each family, facilities for keeping food cool and either gas or electricity. An additional resolution passed in 1946 called for electric washing machines to be provided for all new houses built for family occupation, the cost of this to be included in the rent.

The July 1946 Bulletin discusses local advisory committees on housing, often initiated by Guild Branches and described in the February 1946 Bulletin in relation to the advisory housing councils being set up under the authority of the Central Women's Advisory Housing Committee with which the Guild was associated nationally. The problem at local level was to ensure that the Guild was involved along with other women's organisations. As the Bulletin pointed out, 'because of the lead which the Guild has given in the past, it is well that it should be inside the bodies which are picking up the work it has done. Otherwise, these bodies may do the work alone, and take credit which rightly comes in great measure to the Women's Co-operative Guild.'

The 1948 Housing resolution was concerned with high prices of houses for sale as well as the premium charged by private landlords. Congress in 1950 passed four resolutions on housing and demands included nationalisation of the building industry, direct labour and control of private lettings. Protests against increased council house rents were recorded, and a demand for better accommodation for homeless families was linked to opposition to the practice of splitting up members of homeless families.

The resolutions on Housing have been explored in detail as they reflect the Guild's attention to the detail as well as the major directions of housing needs and policies. Also, these resolutions remind us that some of these radical suggestions are far from being implemented 40 years on. Apart from formulating housing policy the Guild was often consulted on domestic issues related to housing. For example, the 1950 Annual Report details participation on enquiries into household routines in prefabricated houses and suburban houses conducted by the Sub-Committee on Scientific Management in the Home of the Women's Group on Public

Welfare (under the auspices of the National Council of Social Service) on which the Guild was represented nationally. Links with the Council of Industrial Design and representation on the Women's Advisory Committee of the British Standards Institution were also relevant.

The other topic selected for examination in this section dealing with domestic concerns between 1945-51 is health.

Guild Policy on Health

Guild policy on matters relating to health, during the period when the National Health Service was being set up, reflects a wide range of concerns. 1945 Congress covered resolutions on the extension of mass radiography, and the creation of a separate National Maternity Service, with more Maternity Homes and Maternity and Child Welfare Clinics to be set up everywhere. Removal of purchase tax from drugs, free artificial limbs, gas and air to be made available to all mothers whether having babies at home or in hospital, and rest homes for women on the borderline of mental sickness, were other demands.

1946 resolutions show concern for the poor facilities available to adults with nervous diseases and to mentally defective children. Child Guidance clinics for every area are asked for, as well as better sanitary arrangements in prisons. A demand for analgesia in childbirth, and training of midwives to use it, occurs in 1947 together with resolutions on making VD a notifiable disease, X-rays for blood donors, the provision of mobile foot clinics and the employment of full-time salaried doctors in the new NHS.

The 1950 Congress objected strongly to cuts in expenditure on health, as well as wanting to install chemical toilets on trains to combat polio, and to include sex-education in schools (sexes to be segregated, with women doctors as tutors for the girls and a male doctor for the boys). Facilities for washing hands in all public toilets, together with the abolition of turnstiles, were demanded.

By 1951, the health service was in trouble, and at the 1951 Congress in Southend a resolution opposing charges for spectacles and dentures was passed — a resolution which ended by saying 'It feels that a very ironical position is created by saving on the health service in order that the money so saved can be spent on armaments'. The "Daily Herald" reported the debate on this resolution during which one delegate, Mrs. Clark, said that whilst not wishing to embarrass the government she insisted on preserving pride in the free health service.[9] Mrs. Mabel Ridealgh, former Co-operative and Labour MP (and later Guild General Secretary), had a rough reception when she argued against this resolution on the grounds that costs had gone up by millions, and that extending hospitals was more important than glasses and teeth. (Other health concerns in 1951 included pets in food shops and uncovered food on display).

Here we see the Guild sticking to its policies, irrespective of the difficulties faced by the government, although on other domestic issues the difficulties of the government are understood, and consequent policies defended.

In the "Daily Herald" report of the 1948 Congress at Great Yarmouth the support of government's food policy is mentioned — the government were urged not to capitulate to Tory agitation to reduce or abolish food subsidies or remove price control.[10]

This survey has not considered whole areas of Guild concern — for illegitimate children, spinsters, the elderly, children, human rights, prices, or their continued and detailed concern over educational policy, and issues remaining from the war years such as separate coupons for household linens.

Although the years under review mark the only period of membership growth in the post-war period, internal Guild matters were as important to guildswomen as campaigns being waged and policies being formulated.

Guild Organisation, Funds and Internal Issues

The earlier examination of Guild reappraisal of its educational content and approaches, showed it responding to the major challenge of membership losses during the war and a changing social pattern for women after the war. Yet there were other problems that had to be faced, above all the relationship between declining membership and finance.

In 1944 Kathleen Kempton was President of South Metropolitan District Committee (when she stood for election there had been 30 candidates for the seven places). Cecily Cook had come to speak to Southern Section and one topic raised was the need for staff when the Guild office returned to Leman

Street. 'Perhaps I can help you' said Kathleen — who could type — not realising this was to mean a desk at Guild Head Office from 1944 to 1983. Starting as a volunteer, she became a part-time, later full-time member of staff, although she did take some time off in 1948 when her son was born.

The Leman Street, London, E.1 office, which the Guild rented from the CWS, was hardly ideal. It had been an old greengrocer's shop; initially they had problems of mice and rats. The steep and narrow stairs on three floors meant it was a difficult working environment. Financial problems hindered efforts to find new premises and the Guild's bombed offices in Prescot Street were still the subject of a War Damage claim. The Guild was therefore relieved to be able to move. The December 1951 Monthly Bulletin was the first to be published from the new modern offices at Pioneer House, 348 Gray's Inn Road, the home of "Reynolds' News," rented from the Political Committee of the London Co-operative Society, for five years initially.

Staff in this period usually came from a Co-operative background. For example, the November 1947 Bulletin contained an advertisement for a junior clerk, saying the job should particularly appeal to the daughters of guildswomen and members of Co-operative junior and youth organisations. True to their principles, the salary scale offered was to be at the Union of Shop, Distributive and Allied Workers, (USDAW) rate (men's scale). Staff turnover was to be a problem in later years, but loyalty to the Guild is shown in the 1949 Report announcing the retirement of Mrs. Pidgeon after 33 years on Head Office staff; she received a gold watch as a token of thanks and appreciation. Her replacement was a guildswoman's daughter.

Financial problems faced the Guild throughout the post-war years, and are linked with problems of recruitment. The situation was set out in a Guild pamphlet entitled 'Guild Finance.'[11] It made the dramatic point that losing 44% of membership from 1939-1943 meant a loss of nearly half the Guild's income. This lower income came in a period of heavily rising costs and the imposition of Purchase Tax. Expenditure also increased due to organisational changes, as Sections went up from eight to 10, meaning two additional Sectional Secretaries and two additional Central Committee members. The recruitment of additional members since the war did not offset the problems of higher costs, and membership at 59,666 on January 1st 1950 was well below the 1939 figure of 87,246.

The Maintenance Fund set up during the war to help the Guild survive the losses to Central Fund had reached £2,000 by 1945, and in 1946 income and expenditure had roughly balanced. But improved Guild education services, urgent if new members were to be attracted, proved expensive. For example, District Committee Schools cost £546 in 1946, £811 in 1948 and £879 in 1949. Cost of postage, stationery and printing had also risen — from £951 in 1946 to £1,635 in 1949.

Steps were taken to make the Sales Department more profitable and sales of £2,323 were reached in 1949. Grants in 1949 are reported as £500 from the Co-operative Union, £750 from CWS and 25 guineas from the Co-operative Productive Federation. Income and expenditure accounts for 1949 show a deficit of £137. The Report for 1950 reveals a small balance (£34 on a turnover of £9,805), but says "considerable retrenchment is inevitable if the financial situation does not improve."

The importance of the Sales Department's potential contribution to funds was stressed, and unsold diaries at a value of £600 were said to be a considerable drain on funds. Head Office expenditure had been kept to a minimum explained the 1950 Annual Report and the 1951 Report threatened that without a substantial rise in membership, expenditure would have to be reduced or Branch subscriptions raised.

The Monthly Bulletin for December 1951 said that removal to the new office will 'intensify the financial stringency which has been a feature of Guild circumstances in recent years.'

The need for increased membership was entangled with the financial problems of the Guild. The 1950 Report records that the formation of new Branches is frequently balanced by the closing of an old one; sometimes one that was very old, with declining membership due to death, increasing age or infirmity. 'There is a considerable danger in an organisation like the Guild,' said the 1950 Report. '...that older members will set a standard in regard to Guild meetings and Guild work which is not so much unacceptable to the younger generation as it is unintelligible.' The Report goes on to talk of the need to make the Guild as attractive as the meetings of other women's organisations. The Report pointed out that 'No Branch should be content to plod along in the same old way with the same old ideas and a fitting contribution to the Festival of Britain would be a critical examination of Branch activities by Branch members themselves.' The 1951 Annual Report continues this theme, pointing out that developments in radio, cinema and magazines make women critical of "Prosy" gatherings.

Did branches make new members welcome? The constant references to companionship and fellowship suggest this was so, but we are sure Joan Baker's experiences were not unique. She joined the Guild in 1943, at the age of 23, and in her early thirties belonged to a Guild branch where the Secretary was always saying that if they could get another secretary she would retire. Mrs. Baker agreed to stand. But there had to be a vote as the "retiring" secretary stood as well! 'The vote was equal' writes Mrs. Baker, 'and the Chairman gave her vote to the then secretary, who when asked if she would stand down said "No, the Guild voted for me."' Although she stood down the following year, Mrs. Baker wrote that

this highlights the attitude of some Guild members to younger members. It has been one of the Guild problems over the years.

Internal Politics

If we recall the large amounts of money collected for Russia during the war and the stress on better East-West relations in Congress resolutions, we see the Guild concerned for maintaining a constructive relationship with Communist regimes. Yet the attitude to individual Communists within the Guild provides a contrast. The January 1946 Bulletin explains the interpretation that was made following the defeat at the 1945 Congress of an amendment that Communists could not hold office in the Guild. The rule to be followed was that 'Only those who are prepared to support the Co-operative Party and work and support Co-operative and Labour candidates at both Parliamentary and Municipal elections are eligible to hold office and act as delegates to Congress.' Any Guild member who supports or works for a candidate standing against a Labour or Co-operative candidate would not be eligible to hold office or be a delegate to Congress. Bulletin points out that 'Branches must accept responsibility for electing persons to office who will stand by Guild policy, and work to serve Guild and Co-operative interests rather than the interests of other bodies.'

Rule 21 said while persons of any political persuasion are welcomed as members of the Guild ('subject to the approval of the Branch' was added in 1948), any person who is a member of a political party other than the Co-operative and Labour Parties will not be eligible to hold office and act as delegate to Congress.

The "Co-operative News" reported the resignation in 1946 of 33 out of 44 of the members of Monkton Branch over the rule that only those belonging to the Co-operative Party or Labour Party could hold office in the Guild.[12] Those who left had joined the National Guild of Co-operators, (the mixed Co-operative Auxiliary). The editorial in the 'Mainly for Women' pages said the fact that branches must close down where officers are of other Parties must be faced, but in the long run 'a new spirit will enter the Guild that will be worth all the intervening unpleasantness.'

The Annual Report for 1950 refers to the Sheffield decision that only individual members of the Labour and Co-operative Parties could be eligible for office. It said that as this would prevent branches opening unless officials were available who were Labour or Co-operative Party members, this Congress resolution was suspended.

An article in "Reynolds' News" headlined 'Co-op. women lift ban — a little' said the rule was now to welcome women of any political persuasion as members of the WCG but any who belong to another Party will not be eligible to hold office.[13]

Linked to this debate is the Guild's relationship with the British Soviet Friendship Society, discussed in the January 1948 Bulletin. Guild branches may work with the British Soviet Society on matters which both organisations were in agreement — friendship with the USSR. But this did not mean affiliation by the Guild and branches were reminded that they were organised for Co-operative and citizen work in accordance with Guild Congress decisions. No branch should be used to further the work of other organisations, the article concluded. And were women of other political beliefs interested in the Guild? Baroness Fisher recalls that of 40 members of the Guild Branch she joined in the 1940s, one was a Conservative, the rest were involved in Co-operative politics. 'But the Conservative was a marvellous guildswoman' said Lady Fisher!

This survey of the immediate post-war years closes with a brief look at two other issues: Guild relations with the wider Co-operative Movement, and international concerns, and then gives some idea of what it meant to be a guildswoman in those post-war years.

The Guild within the Co-operative Movement

Although not given much space in this chapter, the Guild's aim to extend their links and representation on other Co-operative bodies and to further Co-operative activities dominate Congress Agenda, the pages of Bulletins, and Annual Reports. Space is often given to expressions of regret: for example, regret that the auxiliaries played no part in the national Co-operative Exhibition which formed part of the Festival of Britain in 1951, although a record of activities was to appear in the educational exhibition (and details of the Guild and its work were included in the official leaflet on Women's Organisations). Regret of a different kind is expressed in the March 1946 Bulletin which reports rejection of the Guild suggestion that Mrs. C. Ganley, JP, MP, should preside over the first Co-operative Congress since the war. Margaret Llewelyn Davies in 1922 had been the first and only woman to preside over Congress and the Bulletin argues that it was up to the women of the Movement to exert their influence, as 'The matter is definitely linked with the prestige of women and their general position.' The Bulletin goes on to point out that there was no woman on the CWS Board, and that whilst the Co-operative Movement membership was overwhelmingly female, representation of women was far behind men — 'the only remedy which can be found is for the women of the Co-operative Movement to assert their rights and secure equal representation with the men.'

Yet these justifiable and often repeated complaints in no way affect Guilds' loyalty to the Co-operative Movement. The December 1950 Bulletin, for example, prints a letter from the editor of "Reynolds' News" answering the large number of letters received protesting against the whole page advertisement for a non-Co-operative soap powder that was published.

Let us look at Co-operative links in the last year being dealt with in this section: 1951. Four relevant resolutions were passed: that the CWS should co-operate with the Council of Industrial Design in order that Co-operatively produced goods may lead the way in design as well as quality: that Co-operative societies should be fairly allocated shops on new estates, that the International Co-operative Movement should give support to all countries for the development of Co-operative principles, and that a scheme for training Co-operative salesmen should be implemented.

Good relations are recorded with the CWS and Co-operative Union, and Guild representation on Sectional Education Associations is mentioned. Resolutions for Co-operative Party Conference (against German re-armament, for foreign language teaching and for a publicity campaign by the Co-operative, Labour and Trade Union Movements to be initiated by the Co-operative Party) are also recorded. Close contact with the Co-operative Press is established, with a representative calling weekly for news items. A Director of the Co-operative Press met the Central Committee to discuss "Woman's Outlook," the Women's Pages in "Co-operative News" and "Reynolds' News." (Support for these publications was often urged in the Bulletin.) Good relations with the Co-operative Productive Federation, Co-operative College, and National Co-operative Men's Guild are mentioned. The work of the National Co-operative Joint Auxiliaries Council is also discussed - it enabled auxiliaries to discuss common problems, and allowed youth and adult bodies to meet.

The overriding feeling one has, however, is the Guild's commitment in terms of loyalty to Co-operative trade and production, and their work in spreading knowledge of Co-operative ideas and principles is never fully recognised by those controlling the Co-operative Movement - men!

International Work

The post-war years marked a steady increase in international contacts, with visitors from abroad visiting the Guild office and attending Congress, visits to other countries and participation in the work of the International Co-operative Women's Guild as its work revived after the end of the war. Each year, the September Bulletin was given over to the ICWG.

The Guild Exchange Fund was used to pay for guildswomen from abroad to attend Congress and stay with a guildswoman, as well as to send guild members abroad. The May 1947 Bulletin, for example, records the visit of the National President and General Secretary to Germany.

1951 was a crucial year in the history of the Guild's relationship with the post-war ICWG. Over 100 British women attended the Congress in Copenhagen — many paying their own expenses - and Cecily Cook was elected President of the ICWG for three years, having been nominated by several countries.

Other international work in 1951, recorded in the Annual Report, included sending a number of letters and telegrams on the Korean war to the Prime Minister and Foreign Secretary, and a letter sent jointly by the Guild, the Peace Pledge Union and the Women's International League arguing the case against German rearmament and asking for it to be conveyed by the British Foreign Minister to the Four-Power Conference of Foreign Ministers in Paris. An interesting exchange of letters with the Czech Government is quoted in the 1951 Bulletin, with the Guild defending British foreign policy against general criticism as well as against the Czech protest that they were excluded from the Sheffield Peace Congress.

This episode shows the Guild defending the British Government but asking the Czechs to continue to work with the Guild 'in order that through the application of Co-operative principles we may establish world peace with freedom and prosperity for common people everywhere.'

Experience at Branch Level

Some Guild members interviewed as the book was written did in fact feel that one major drawback over the years has been the Guild's reluctance to publicise its achievements, although Monthly Bulletins often contain exhortations to branches to try to get more publicity for local activities, whilst the significance for publicity for the national Guild of the demise of the "Daily Herald" is clear when the press cuttings on the Guild held at the Fawcett Library are examined.

The need for branches to watch public affairs and pick up issues is stressed in the November 1946 Bulletin which says 'the opinion is far too common that Head Office should be responsible for voicing protests and making known Guild demands.' When Guild branches *do* pick up issues then 'the Guild voice becomes not one but many' says the editorial. The advantage is seen to be not merely results achieved or increasing Guild influence and prestige but in making Co-operative ideas more widely known, which would be 'helpful in attracting the attention of younger women and drawing them into membership of the Co-operative Movement and the Women's Co-operative Guild.' And those women who were "drawn in"

171

certainly enjoyed and benefited from the experience offered to them. It is important to realise, as we read about the Guild in these post-war years - of difficulties overcome, campaigns fought (some won and some lost) - just how important membership was to tens of thousands of women throughout the country.

The Guild stressed loyalty to Co-operative trade and Co-operative ideals. In turn, the Guild and its leaders inspired loyalty and affection among its members. Before turning to look at the Guild in the more difficult period that began in 1952, let us listen to the voice of some of those who were active in the Guild in the post-war years.

Mrs. Josephine (Vinnie) Walker joined the Guild in 1950 at the age of 42. She has since been Branch Secretary of Central Guild, Leeds, Treasurer of Yorkshire District and is still an active member of her Branch.

> *She particularly enjoyed spring and autumn sectional conferences as they gave her a chance to meet members of other branches. And she enjoyed week-end schools 'with good speakers and debates keeping people up-to-date with current events, MPs able to explain things that sometimes we find puzzling.' She says how the Guild helped her when she lost her husband and she was left with three young children, 'they helped to give me confidence to face up to a difficult life'... and she ended by writing 'I feel I owe so much for the companionship of my Guild, and interest in many subjects I would never have known about otherwise.'*

Mrs. McCallum of Dagenham, Essex, also joined in 1950 when she was 46. Through Guild membership she was elected to the Gray's Co-operative Society Education Committee

> *where she 'learnt how to organise and was able to meet people.' She had been branch secretary for 28 years now, and she says 'My service to the Guild has been to help people.'*

Mrs. Frances Stabeler writing from Ashton-in-Makerfield branch in Wigan, talked to some of the branch members. Two of them said to her that they would die for the Guild - they adored Guild meetings and they could never repay the debt they owe it.

It was this loyalty and commitment that enabled the Guild to build up again after the war and helped it through the difficult decade that it faced.

Notes to Chapter 6

1. *Woman's Outlook*, 20th October 1945.
2. WCG, Education for Service: The Guild in War and Peace, No. 1 (Manchester undated).
3. WCG. A New Approach to Guild Education (undated).
4. *Manchester Guardian*, 9th May 1947.
5. Mrs. C.S. Ganley, Unpublished Manuscript loaned by Women's Co-operative Guild (copy in Hull University Library).
6. WCG. The Road to Peace. The Guild in War and Peace, No. 3 (Manchester undated).
7. *Daily Herald*, 25th June 1947.
8. *Daily Herald*, 19th May 1949.
9. *Daily Herald*, 28th May 1951.
10. *Daily Herald*, 28th May 1948.
11. WCG, Guild Finance (Manchester undated).
12. *Co-operative News*, 19th March 1946.
13. *Reynolds' News*, 23rd May 1951.

CHAPTER 7

FROM WOMEN'S CO-OPERATIVE GUILD TO CO-OPERATIVE WOMEN'S GUILD: 1952-1963

Introduction

The years discussed in this chapter were years of challenge and reappraisal for the Guild. Membership was 61,037 in January 1951 - and had declined by a massive 23,000 to reach 38,380 in January 1963. 1958 saw a gain of 1,000 members, lost again by 1959.

These were years when the Guild was working against successive Conservative governments on virtually every issue that concerned guildswomen. They were governments that by fostering competitive and materialistic attitudes were directly opposed to Guild principles and to Guild policies.

The problems that had their roots in war and social changes after the war accelerated. More women worked so could not attend afternoon meetings. Increased leisure opportunities, especially the growth of television and the more home-centred family life that developed with men and women doing more together, hampered Guild recruitment. Increased educational opportunities for women made the educational activities of the Guild less unique. The average age of guildswomen was high.

The Guild was concerned with Co-operation and the role women could play by participating in Co-operative affairs. Retail trade was changing and the reduction in the number of retail Co-operative societies and number of shops had a direct effect on the ability of the Guild to recruit from its natural potential pool of members - those who joined their local Co-operative society and shopped there regularly. When Mabel Ridealgh was interviewed, she felt that the closing of shops was an important aspect of the Guild's decline in membership.

Retailing was changing with increased mobility and the growth of larger self-service stores. The higher standard of living and the growth of credit made the dividend less important. Norah Willis, Chairman of London Region C.R.S., who joined the Guild in the 1940s told us how her mother and her generation would walk miles to the nearest Co-operative store, and would use the dividend for school shoes. Mrs. Phyllis Hawker of Plymouth, a Guild member from 1936 until her Bristol branch closed due to the war, stressed the saving element of Co-operation, and the way the dividend was the only way for a woman to save.

These were years of achievement too - the cost of living rally in 1956, and influential evidence to the Royal Commission on Marriage and Divorce in 1952, for example, as well as the election of the second-ever woman CWS Director in 1959. It was a period of reappraisal - the Guild's own Committee of Enquiry in 1955, and responding to the Groombridge Report.[1] Even more crucial was the 1962 resolution at Congress to set up the Modernisation Commission, whose report was published as 'Movement for Moderns'[2] and led to the change in name from the Women's Co-operative Guild to the Co-operative Women's Guild (CWG), and to other fundamental changes discussed later in this chapter.

The printed Monthly Bulletin, which replaced the short-lived 'Guildswoman' was supported by pages of advertising of CWS and other Co-operative products. Headed 'Please keep this Bulletin for reference after reading it aloud and discussing it in your Branch,' it gives a detailed picture of the Guild: national and branch work is reflected in its pages. Important issues such as the role of the Guild in relation to other organisations were discussed, and details of the organisation of Congress found a place in its pages, which varied from eight to 12. It was published by the Co-operative Press. The loss of the printed Monthly Bulletin for financial reasons and the change of Guild name mark the end of the period discussed in this chapter: a period of increasing financial problems. Yet during these years constructive action was taken over a wide range of issues, the calibre of the leadership remained high, and the friendship so many members found within the Guild was as strong as ever. The enthusiasm and dedication of guildswomen remained impressive.

When our chapter opens Cecily Cook, OBE, is still General Secretary. She retired, to be replaced by former National President and former Labour MP, Mrs. Mabel Ridealgh in 1953. It ends in 1963 with a new General Secretary — Kathleen Kempton.

International Co-operative Women's Day

A new development in this period was the establishment of International Co-operative Women's Day, following a resolution passed at the 1951 Congress at Southend. The March 1952 Bulletin quoted from a letter sent to the Secretary of the Women's Day Committee saying that in the opinion of the Guild: "our efforts will be strengthened and international goodwill likely to be advantaged by our decision to organise every year an International Co-operative Women's Day... whilst we do not wish to hamper your efforts in any way, we should be unwise to diffuse our own energies."

The Bulletin article reminded readers that International Women's Day was organised to press for the 'International Woman's Charter.' which demands 'equality for women as workers and citizens and security for women as mothers.' It was noted that 'this is work which the Guild has continuously done over a long period of years.... such effort is best made by national organisations acting through their various groups and branches.'

International Co-operative Women's Day was to be held in October, (International Women's Day in March). The May 1952 Bulletin returns to the issue of ending the Guild's association with the International Women's Day Committee (IWD). Originally, the IWD Committee was a co-ordinating body linking various national organisations but recently the IWD Committee had become active in national affairs of interest to the Guild, and had now launched a national organisation to be known as the National Assembly of Women. The WCG Bulletin explains that the IWD Committee was setting up Assembly Groups and suggesting that sixpenny quarterly membership stamps could be purchased and 'stuck on ration cards, Co-operative Guild cards, etc. bringing together all women but in no way taking the place of one's own particular organisation.'

The Guild Bulletin sharply pointed out that Guild members had a loyalty to their own organisation and it was important to note that the Guild was the only organisation mentioned indicating that its support was being looked for, and whilst wishing the National Assembly of Women well, it should seek members among the millions of women belonging to no organisations at all, rather than appeal to the Guild which was 'fully competent to further our own policy.'

The Guild's determination to guard its integrity is not unique to this issue. The Guild was fighting to keep and gain members in a changing world, where the role and interests of women were changing, and where there were a growing number of organisations competing for 'unattached' women. And, because of the high reputation of the Guild, its past record of success in numerous campaigns and its high level of member education and branch organisation, existing Guild members were attractive potential members to any new organisation.

As for International Co-operative Women's Day, it grew both in range of activities and popularity amongst branches in the period covered by this chapter. Activities reported include meetings, rallies, pageants, peace playlets, tableaux and speakers from overseas.

The 1955 Annual Report says that 'joint meetings are increasingly popular, whether organised by District Committees or Joint Guild Councils.' Funds were often collected, for example for UNICEF in 1957, the World Refugee Fund in International Refugee Year in 1960, and the Freedom from Hunger Campaign in 1962. Meetings were usually well supported and open; by the late 1950s many of the activities were associated with Joint Auxiliaries Council Weeks.

International Co-operative Women's Guild

The Guild continued its support of ICWG, and one Monthly Bulletin a year was still devoted to its work. Fifteen countries were represented on the Central Committee of ICWG, with Mabel Ridealgh representing Britain. It met in 1956 to plan the 1957 Congress in Stockholm - 54 Guild members went (the largest delegation). Resolutions passed included opposing the testing of atomic bombs; and one saying that the International Co-operative Alliance and the ICWG should have more contact in order to seek maximum participation of women in Co-operative activities in every country.

The 1960 Congress of the ICWG was held in Lausanne, and the British delegation was 70 strong. However, the 1957-59 Report of the ICWG, published from the London Head Office, said the question of collaboration with the ICA was already being discussed and that a split was already indicated: - some wanted ICWG to remain independent - others felt financial and other help from the International Co-operative Alliance could only be expected if the ICA had some control of the ICWG especially in regard to policy.

The 1962 Annual Report shows concern for the ICWG, whose President, Cecily Cook, died before the Central Committee met in Helsinki.

The 1963 Annual Report reported on the ICWG's 1963 - and last - Congress. The British Guild Congress resolution welcomed closer collaboration with the ICA but argued that the appointment of a women's officer to the ICA could not replace the ICWG, whose objects included visiting Co-operative women of all lands, to raise the status of women, and promoting education for women co-operators to make them fit for practical tasks side by side with men.

This resolution was defeated - despite strong arguments put forward by Mabel Ridealgh. Mrs. Muriel Russell, who was ICA Women's Officer from 1965-1978, told the authors that the ICWG was out of money, was working from one room in Leman Street and had to face the problem that there was no growth in Women's Guilds, and indeed few countries had Women's Guilds on the British model. The ICA suggested a Women's Department with a Secretary and an Advisory Committee. This was accepted by the ICWG Secretariat, with the suggestion that the International Guild be suspended for three years, a suspension that signalled its end.

And so ended a brave initiative in international Co-operation, initiated by the English Guild led by A. Honora Enfield in 1921 and defended at its death by another formidable Guild General Secretary, Mabel Ridealgh. However, this defeat had no effect on the Guild's international links nor its concern for international issues.

International Links

In a period before foreign travel was cheap or commonly undertaken, guildswomen travelled extensively as well as receiving large numbers of foreign visitors, both as fraternal delegates to Congress and more informally. Mrs. Gwendoline Teather of Hornchurch who joined the Guild in 1958 wrote

> it led me to travel, to India, Russia, North Africa and the Arctic Circle.

178

1953 saw a visit to the USSR of five representatives, democratically chosen by Central Committee from 435 names submitted. Expenses were paid for by the USSR from Prague onwards, and branches subscribed nearly £200 towards the cost. Poland and Czechoslovakia were also visited. The 1953 report says 'In the USSR many wonderful achievements were seen in the social, economic and cultural aspects of Soviet Life and the delegation was amazed at the great progress made.'

We may be more aware now than these five travellers were of the darker side of Russian life under Stalin, but the extent to which the Guild visited and encouraged visits so extensively is a tribute to the strength of the Guild's commitment to the principle that international friendship would lead to peace.

1954 saw visits to Romania and Hungary as well as a trip by 64 guildswomen to Sweden and a visit by General Secretary Mabel Ridealgh to China.

At the Guild's Newcastle Congress there were fraternal delegates from the ICWG, Belgium, USSR, Ireland, Germany, Poland, China, Czechoslovakia, Scotland, Israel and New Zealand.

In 1957 visits were made to USSR, Hungary and Poland and 50 guildswomen went on a Study Tour of Norway. Such visits did not cloud the Guild's judgement on international affairs. In 1958 a letter was sent to the Ambassadors of Hungary and the USSR expressing admiration of the Hungarian leaders and sorrow at the judicial murder of President Imre Nagy and other Hungarians.

In 1960 UNESCO financed a 1,000 mile study tour of Germany and Holland led by Mrs. Doris Fisher of the Central Committee and Kathleen Kempton. A Study Tour/Holiday led by the indefatigable Mrs. Mabel Ewan (ex National President) went to Finland.

The international links went beyond visitors and visiting. Help to Co-operatives in countries such as Zambia and British Guyana is recorded in the years under review, and money and material aid was sent to countries in need. For example, donations in 1956 to help refugees from Hungary and Egypt, 1958 donations to the Defence Fund to help South African prisoners, 1960 to aid victims of the earthquake in Agidir, and in 1963 the earthquake victims of Skopje, Yugoslavia.

In addition a collection from branches enabled 350 rose bushes bearing the name of the Women's Co-operative Guild to be planted in the rebuilt village of Lidice.

Two further practical examples of international help were reported in the 1955 Report, with Guild members offering hospitality to overseas students, and the selling of various items produced by Ceylon Handicraft Co-operatives.

International Concerns

The years under review show resolutions and protests to the government over a wide range of international issues: Korea, Hungary, Cyprus, Suez, Formosa, Trieste, conditions in the colonies, Kenya, South Africa, Nyasaland, West Indies, the Common Market - were all discussed.

But the major concern remained peace. The banning of the H-bomb tests, hostility to German re-armament and to foreign bases and to arms expenditure appear regularly on Congress agenda. Three major Guild efforts were the 1955 and 1956 peace rallies and the 1958 Women's Caravan for Peace, in which the Guild took part.

The 1955 Rally was the Guild's first peace demonstration for many years. The May 1955 Bulletin said that peace was likely to be a big issue in the 1955 General Election and the meeting would show the new government 'the determination of Co-operative women to make an end of war and the manufacture of weapons of destruction.'

Nearly 3,000 guildswomen from all over England attended the Central Hall Westminster demonstration, which was addressed by the Rev. Donald Soper and Mrs. Cecily Cook, and was followed by a mass lobby of MPs.

The "Daily Herald" reported the 1956 Peace Rally of 2,500 guildswomen, again at Central Hall Westminster, under the headline 'Co-operative Women stage protest for Peace.'[3] Addressed by Shirley Summerskill, and followed by a lobby of Parliament, the resolution that was passed condemned British action in Suez, demanded withdrawal of British, French and Israeli troops from Suez and expressed support for the United Nations Organisation (UNO). Dismay at events in Hungary was expressed and the Soviet government was asked to cease from violating another country. The December Monthly Bulletin concluded its report of the 'splendid demonstration' which was called at short notice by saying 'we must not let this enthusiasm be lost. The international situation is still such that extreme

180

vigilance is necessary if we are to ward off world war three.'

Guild support for CND and publicity for its marches was given in the Bulletin and signatures for a petition based on the Guild's peace policy were collected (this supported CND but also recognised the need for total disarmament). Letters protesting against nuclear testing were sent to the Soviet Women's Guild, and American Women's Guild as well as to the French government.

A petition expressing concern at the continued manufacture and testing of nuclear weapons and drawing attention to the genetic effects was signed by 11,000 guildswomen and presented to the Minister. The petition was followed by the imaginative gesture of sending pictures of healthy children to the Ministry of Health with a letter asking him to do all he could to end manufacture and testing of nuclear weapons so that the children could grow up to be healthy.

The March 1958 Bulletin announced that 12 women would be spending three months travelling through East and West Europe in 'a pilgrimage of women in the cause of peace and friendship with other nations.' A Central Committee member, Mrs. Hilda Lettice, represented the Guild. Meetings at Blackpool and a Dedication Service at St. Paul's Cathedral provided a good send off, and there was publicity in "Reynolds' News" and on BBC TV. The October 1958 Bulletin records Mrs. Lettice's return, and her opinion that the caravan had been 'worthwhile' and the fact that she had been inundated with invitations to speak.

From the excitement of this major peace initiative we now turn to look at domestic concerns of the Guild in this period.

Campaigns and Concerns

In a period of Conservative government, the Guild maintained its tradition of campaigning for the rights of deprived groups. Congress resolutions covered the usual wide range of topics: against racial discrimination (1952); for higher old age pensions (1952); for Family Allowances for the first child (1955); for facilities for those suffering from senile dementia (1953) and the chronic sick (1955); better provision for the homeless (1962), and for increased unemployment benefit (1963).

Demands for better services incorporated protests against health and social services charges and cuts. Improvements demanded included more sheltered housing, better school dental health services, rehabilitation for parents who ill-treat their children, and unrestricted visiting of children in hospital.

Issues of particular concern to women, including equal pay, free contraception, abortion, and more representation, were debated as strongly in the 1950s as in the early years of the Guild. Issues like better facilities for childbirth were mixed with demands for radical solutions to rising unemployment, for safer toys, improved road safety, and for home safety. They were consulted on basic issues like jelly moulds, helping via a BSI questionnaire to establish the most efficient type and size so a standard could be fixed. They campaigned for stockings that did not ladder to be manufactured by the CWS. They wanted clean, covered and dated food - demands made in the early fifties for standards we now take for granted.

Education was also much discussed in this period, with strong support for comprehensive education and expansion of nursery education urged. The 1959 Congress saw a discussion expressing concern about posters, films and plays exploiting sex. Equally important was the Guild's evidence to the Royal Commission on Divorce. Guild evidence was given orally by Mrs. W. Barnes, SE representative on the Central Committee who had wide experience of Marriage Guidance. The April 1952 Bulletin says most of the points made had been Guild policy for many years, and announced that Divorce Law Reform was to be a subject for Guild study in 1952/3. According to the "Daily Herald," in a story headlined 'The ordinary woman has her say for two hours on divorce,' Mrs. Barnes was congratulated for the way she stood up to the questioning of judges, magistrates, barristers and doctors.[4] Guild policy included divorce by consent after three years of separation, abolition of claims for divorce damages, raising the age of marriage to 18, the right of a husband to sue a wife who leaves him with dependant children, divorce for incompatibility (e.g. refusal of intercourse, drunkenness), and family courts to deal with matrimonial cases and to try to effect reconciliation.

However, the major domestic effort was the cost of living campaign and it is this issue that is singled out for discussion in this chapter.

Cost of Living Campaign

Resolutions showing concern with the rising cost of living appeared on the Congress Agenda in 1952 soon after the election of the Conservative government.

A 1953 resolution deplored the budget that decontrolled essential foodstuffs and asked Central Committee to organise a mass demonstration on this issue. The 1953 Report said that two and three quarter million signatures had been collected, although the "Manchester Guardian" report said it contained 1,500,000 signatures,[5] and described how 3,000 guildswomen 'had a happy time listening to one speaker after another lambasting the government.' After the Central Hall Westminster meeting, said the "Guardian", several hundred women queued to enter the House of Commons to present the petition to their MPs. Speakers at the meeting included Doris Fisher, Harriet Slater, MP, and Jean Mann, MP, as well as a Darlington old age pensioner.

The January 1954 Bulletin urged branches to write to their local MP asking for a deputation to be received, and to let the local press know if the request was accepted or rejected. By February, the Monthly Bulletin could start with Mabel Ridealgh saying 'Our cost of living campaign appears to have brought a new spirit of enthusiasm into our Guild branches according to the many letters we have received. They tell us the campaigns have been like a breath of fresh air in their Guild rooms, so that members are taking greater interest and new members are being made.'

Yet branch activity seemed to decline, although the Central Committee protested to the government about food prices later in 1954, and the 1955 Congress carried another strong resolution urging Guild action.

The 1955 Report referred to the 1955 autumn Budget as an election budget, bringing forward 'further blatant class-biased measures giving further concessions to the better off, but laying heavier burdens on the poorer section of the community in increased purchase tax.' A cost of living demonstration called at short notice brought 3,000 women and a few men to the Central Hall, where speakers included Hugh Gaitskell, MP, Harriet Slater, MP and Mrs. Eva Dodds.

The final meeting of the cost of living campaign was fixed for May 1956, and in the June Bulletin Mabel Ridealgh recorded her disappointment that barely half a million signatures had been collected and the meeting was attended by 2,000, rather than the 3,000 expected, even though Aneurin Bevan was the principal speaker. Despite Guild disappointment, the protest rally was well reported in the "Daily Herald" under the heading 'Indignant Wives in High-Price Protest.'[6]

The declining enthusiasm for the campaign between 1952 and 1955 was perhaps symptomatic of the problems faced by the Guild in a period of ageing and declining membership. This chapter now looks at the way the Guild attempted to solve its fundamental problems, and how both the problems and the solutions are related to the Guild's relationship with, and the problems of, the Co-operative Movement.

The Guild as Seen by Other Parts of the Co-operative Movement

Congress resolutions, subjects for Guild discussion, factory outings, and demonstrations at branch level show a dedication to improving prices and products at Co-operative shops, to participation and representation at local and national level in all Co-operative agencies and a remarkable loyalty to Co-operative principles and trade. Was this support and loyalty appreciated? Even the change of name in 1963, from Women's Co-operative Guild to Co-operative Women's Guild was a statement of the Guild's dedication to Co-operation.

Jack Bailey, National Secretary of the Co-operative Party wrote a book[7] which described the Guilds (women's, men's, and mixed) as the Movement's conscience. Acknowledging the success of many of its campaigns, Bailey says the Women's Guild came to see itself not merely as an advanced guard of the Co-operative Movement, but an ally of other progressive movements. The Guild is seen as paying the penalty for its success, as many of their earlier aims had been achieved. He says that of 168 places on the main committees of the Co-operative Union, only 22 were held by women although approximately 60% of members of Co-operative societies were women. He gives four reasons for this inequality of representation:
   a) insufficient number of women stand as candidates;
   b) women do not vote at elections in the same proportions as men;
   c) women prefer to vote for men;
   d) women do not consider women candidates are as good as men.

The Guilds were training grounds for official committees and the slow progress emphasised the need for improved training. 'They will gain their places,' says Bailey, 'not by asserting the claims of their sex but by realising this is an obvious irrelevance in the choice of competent leaders, local and national.'

Bailey was writing at a time of problems for the Co-operative Movement, not just the WCG. "The Times" reported that the Co-operative Union faced a heavy deficit.[8] An article in "Woman's Outlook" (September 1961) discussed a survey which showed women averaging 61-70% membership of societies but holding 20% not the expected 65% of places on management committees. No wonder the Annual Reports of the Guild record disappointment about women failing to be elected to top Co-operative jobs!

Eva Dodds, standing for election as a CWS Director, was defeated (but only at the third ballot in 1957). Hannen Swaffer wrote an admiring article about her abilities in the "Daily Herald" asking why the Co-operative Movement remained hidebound and reactionary.[9] He says the WCG wanted to play a greater part in the largest trading concern in the world and to recharge it with more of Robert Owen's almost unexampled idealism. He quotes only one argument against a woman on the CWS Board - lack of a ladies' toilet in the boardroom suite. Eva Dodds was, however, elected in 1958.

Yet taking 1956 as an example of the years under review in this chapter, we find guildswomen serving as follows:

NATIONAL BODIES
Harriet Slater and Joyce Butler in Parliament
Miss C. Barker, OBE and Mrs. Cask, OBE on the Domestic Coal Consumers Council.
Mrs. E. Webb on the Milk Marketing Board
Mrs. Cook on the National Institute of Houseworkers' Advisory Council
Mrs. Mabel Ridealgh a member of the Women's Organisations Committee of the Cabinet Economic Unit

LOCAL BODIES
Mrs. O'Connor (already on the Board of the London Co-operative Society) on the London Transport Union Consultative Committee

Other guildswomen are listed as Chairman of a Rent Tribunal, Members of Gas and Electricity Consultative

Committees, Hospital Boards, and National Insurance Local Committees.

11 guildswomen were mayors, 14 were mayoresses, 49 were Chairmen of local authorities, 54 were aldermen, 355 were councillors, 219 were Justices of the Peace, 1,691 were co-opted on to local public committees.

REPRESENTATION ON CO-OPERATIVE COMMITTEES:

Sectional Boards of Co-operative Union	7
Management Committees	593
Education Committees	919

At least 15 members were Presidents or Vice Presidents of societies.

All this is additional to the Guild working on equal terms with a large number of organisations:-
Women's Group of Public Welfare
Women's Advisory Council on Solid Fuel
National Association for Mental Health
National Peace Council
United Nations Association
Central Board for Conscientious Objectors
No Conscription Council
National Council for Civil Liberties
British Standards Institution
Mary McArthur Holiday Home Committee
Women's Council on India and Pakistan
Standing Conference on the Economic and Social Work of United Nations
UK Committee for UNICEF

General Secretary Mabel Ridealgh was Vice President of the National Joint Committee of Working Women's Organisations. All this shows greater success in public life than in the Co-operative Movement, reflecting the way the Guild was involved with an ever-widening range of non-Co-operative organisations.

This same Annual Report also includes, as does each Annual Report, a section on Co-operative work. On CWS, the grant of £900 was gratefully acknowledged. The CWS had also supplied speakers notes, and organised displays of CWS goods, demonstrations, lectures and factory visits 'to counteract the offers of demonstrations and factory visits from private

186

enterprise.' A meeting with CWS directors 'to discuss Co-operative trade, production and other matters in which the Guild can play its part' was recorded.

Help and advice from the Co-operative Union covered several matters. Apart from the £660 grant, legal advice was given and speakers for Sectional conferences and district residential schools as well as providing speakers notes for officials. The Research Department scrutineered Guild elections, two representatives were invited to Co-operative Union Congress, and the Guild was represented on Sectional Education Associations.

Co-operation with the Co-operative Party was described as close, with advice given to help Guild protests and activities. The Guild felt there was prejudice against accepting women onto the Parliamentary Panel of Candidates, but were told otherwise when the Co-operative Party Executive met a deputation from the Guild's Central Committee.

The Co-operative Press was described as especially helpful with good coverage in "Reynolds' News." The Editor of the Women's Page in the "Co-operative News" (Mrs. Nicholson) attended Central Committee meetings.

Sales of 'Woman's Outlook' were said to be causing concern to the Co-operative Press, and support from branches was urged, including ensuring its sales at local self-service shops. The magazine was described as 'Our OWN MAGAZINE.' It carried stories, features, patterns, question pages - all the features of women's magazines - as well as Guild news and publicity for Guild competitions. Worry about its circulation is also shown in the columns of Monthly Bulletins.

These links are outlined in detail for this one year. They show a good relationship but as Guild Reports repeatedly said, as Bailey[10] wrote in 1955 and as Groombridge was to say in the 1960 report to be discussed later in this chapter, women remained under-represented on the key decision making organs of the Co-operative Movement.

Organisation and Financial Problems for the Guild

The major problem was the effect on Guild finances of lower membership. Constant appeals for money were made, although it was agreed in 1955 that an annual levy of 6d. a member was

187

preferable to lots of appeals. With the continued reluctance of Congress to increase membership subscriptions, a 1962 resolution was passed introducing a compulsory levy of 1s. per member, to be raised as branches chose.

One worrying element in the financial problems facing the Guild during this period, apart from the surprising reluctance of the members to raise subscriptions, was the use of funds collected for other purposes to meet the deficit (e.g. £500 from the Guild Office Fund was used in 1963).

The Guild's approach to the difficulties brought about by falling membership was a positive and constructive one looking critically at programmes and attitudes in the branches.

The 1952 Report points out that loyalty to the Guild was not enough - speakers must be experts in their topic. Topics listed for discussion by branches in 1952 included divorce law reform, World Co-operation, Co-operative membership and trade, modern design and Co-operative production. The general lessening of restrictions on speakers and topics continued during the years under review.

Olive Davies, formerly from Harrow Weald but now 'retired' to Sussex, told how she was sorry when District Committee members were no longer obliged to speak at branches.

> I know it was scrapped because it was said you could not get members to do the job, she told us, but I feel there is no such word as "can't."

Not everyone approved of the Guild. The "Co-operative News"[12] reports Nancy Astor speaking at Plymouth saying the Townswomen's Guild had made more progress than the WCG because politics were precluded; politicis should not be brought into social life, she had concluded.

Would the Guild have benefited at this stage from becoming more political? It was eventually to lose out to the radical feminist groups not yet on the horizon, whilst failing to attract the kind of women who did enjoy the mainly social aspects of organisations like the Townswomen's Guild. The 1952 Annual Report in dealing with the problem of membership listed alternative attractions available to the better educated young women of today: paid work, cinema, television, and many other women's organisations. The 1953 Report urged publicity for branch activities, leaflets for prospective members and more varied programmes. The District role was to create new branches, this Annual Report pointed out, and they needed to be first on new housing estates or in new towns - not letting other organisations get there before them.

By 1954 a Membership Trophy was introduced, to go to the section with the highest increase of paid membership in any year - sadly not presented in its first year as recruitment had been so disappointing.

In 1956, talking of closing branches and saying this was no credit to Districts, the Annual Report pointed out that whilst other interests are open to women, the Guild was the only women's organisation with a consumer interest and it was therefore of interest to all housewives. South Northumberland District Secretary, Mrs. Brown, was praised for showing it could be done - seven new branches had been opened in 1956.

1958 was the year of the last really successful membership campaign the Guild organised. It proved, said the Annual Report, that the Guild could attract lively young people by its comradeship, kindly interest in welfare and happiness of all. The need to hold and enthuse new members was stressed.

The 1959 Report expressed disappointment — the steady progress hoped for had not been maintained. Pointing to the 'Never had it so good' and 'I'm all right Jack' attitudes so prevalent, it said pioneer members who sacrificed so much would be shocked. The Report urged each member to recruit a new member, so more could understand the principles and potential power of Co-operation; give loyalty to Co-operative trade and production and persuade others of the goodness and purpose of the Movement. The same report criticised some branches for becoming small groups of elderly members — the 1960 Report suggested that whilst some branches were doing well, in others older people were not prepared to welcome younger members.

By 1960 the need for a full-time organiser to fight off the competition of other women's organisations and gain members was recognised. 1960 also saw a Congress resolution on the need to introduce up-to-date topics for branch discussion. Unable to find a full-time worker, three part-time field workers were appointed in 1963 (local societies often helping financially). This development was linked to the need to plan modern programmes — the Co-operative Union Education Department had in fact produced a film strip on programme planning by then.

189

The Guild was becoming more publicity conscious, and 1959 saw the formation of a Press and Publicity Committee which included two women directors of the Co-operative Press, the Editor of "Woman's Outlook" and of the women's pages of "Co-operative News," as well as Merry Archard, woman columnist of "Reynolds' News."

The Guild and its Administration

The key change in this period relates to the change in General Secretary. Guild rules meant that the General Secretary had to be nominated and balloted for by the branches. Candidates were required to have been members of the Guild for three years. The competition for this prestigious office had declined over the years. When Rose Simpson defeated Cecily Cook in 1937 and in 1940 when Cecily Cook was elected competition was strong. When Mabel Ridealgh won the election in 1953 she had seven opponents, and Kathleen Kempton won a ballot with even fewer candidates in 1963.

Ironically the rules have had to be changed to allow a non-member to replace Kathleen Kempton. Meanwhile, she had broken the rule regarding retirement at 65 — the Guild would probably have collapsed had she not done so!

In 1955, the lease on Pioneer House was re-negotiated for a further seven years at a rent recognised at below market level, for which the Guild was grateful to the London Co-operative Society. Although £2,426 was received from the War Damage Commission for the Prescot Street Office, the Central Committee realised a replacement Guild Office was out of reach financially.

In 1956 when four members of staff left, only two were replaced because of financial problems. Volunteer helpers were needed and appeared at Head Office, but the late 1950s were difficult in terms of recruitment and retention of staff. Through the Bulletin, attempts were made to recruit guildswomen who were more likely to have an interest in the work and so stay at Guild Head Office. Peak tasks at Head Office related to the mailing of the Bulletin and the knitting competition as well as distribution of clothing to refugees. 1960 saw the retirement of Mary Yuill, the Guild cashier, who had worked for 42 years in the Guild office.

But it was 1962 which saw the biggest change when the printed Monthly Bulletin was replaced by a duplicated monthly circular

190

— meaning less expense but more work in the office. 1959 Bulletin had recorded with pleasure the fact that an experienced guildswoman, Mrs. Douglas, then secretary of Southern Section, had joined the staff but the 1962 Annual Report said she had been given notice of termination of employment, so as to save money, and the Sales Department closed.

By 1963, the Annual Report was paying tribute to Mabel Ridealgh, 'chief official in the years of apathy and disillusionment that have characterised the affluent society.' The report paid tribute to the way she had kept the true spirit of the Guild alive whilst building an up-to-date organisation 'able to meet the challenge of a new and more difficult age' — a challenge to be taken up by Kathleen Kempton who succeeded Mabel Ridealgh after 11 years as Assistant Secretary. Mabel Ridealgh herself told the authors that when she took up the post of Guild General Secretary in 1953 she had plenty of experience of political and public life, but none of office administration. It was Kathleen Kempton who taught her that side of the job, and it was Mabel Ridealgh who encouraged Kathleen Kempton to allow her name to go forward in 1963.

In 1952 the accounts show a balance of £530 of income over expenditure in a total of £10,732 income and expenditure account. In 1962, balance of expenditure over income was £94 out of a total income and expenditure of £15,237, an improvement on the £1,488 deficit of 1960. One difference in these ten years is the fact that membership subscriptions to Central Fund were £4,409 of the total of £10,732 in 1952, but only provided £5,555 to the total of £15,235 ten years later. That the Guild survived the drop in membership, and the members' reluctance to raise subscriptions, is due to increased grants. Some grants were made by local societies (first approached in 1957).

Grants received by CWG	1952	1962
CWS	750	900
Co-operative Union	500	760
Co-operative Productive Federation	21	—
Co-operative Societies	—	232

1955 Committee of Enquiry into Guild Organisation

1954 Congress passed a resolution asking for a Committee of Enquiry to be set up, to be made up of five members elected by postal ballot. The cost of the procedure was brought home to members in the August 1954 Bulletin which said branches had passed the resolution and had to find the money: between £200 and £400. Six guineas was received by September! As only £76 was received by October, the Central Committee decided a postal ballot could not go ahead. Members were encouraged to start setting down their ideas and to send comments related to the terms of reference, published in the January 1955 Bulletin, and to send them to Sectional Secretary. The re-organisation and rule changes stemming from the Enquiry were thoroughly discussed at every level of the Movement, but they are not discussed in detail here, because they seem overshadowed by the Groombridge Report[13] and A Movement for Moderns.[14]

The Future of the Auxiliaries

In February 1958 the National Joint Auxiliaries Council (NJAC) held a weekend conference to discuss the future of the auxiliary organisations. It decided to establish a working party charged with formulating detailed proposals to ensure the continuance of auxiliary activity within the Co-operative Movement.[15] Representatives came from the Central Executive and the Education Executive of the Co-operative Union, CWS, NJAC, National Guild of Co-operators, National Co-operative Men's Guild, British Federation of Young Co-operators and the Woodcraft Folk. The two representatives of the WCG were Mrs. A. Lake and Mrs. Mabel Ridealgh, who became Chairman. Five meetings were planned but a detailed investigation into organisation and membership of the auxiliaries could not be undertaken, and it was agreed, given a donation from the NJAC, that the Education Executive of the Co-operative Union should use research scholarship funds to undertake this investigation. The research worker appointed was Brian Groombridge, MA, and his terms of reference and report are discussed later in this chapter.

The NJAC Working Party was set up in 1958 and before turning to their Report it is interesting to look at how the capitalist press saw the Guild in 1958 - the year before Eva

Dodds was elected to the CWS Board. The "Daily Telegraph" carried a column 'Co-op alarm at feminist campaigns.'[16] It starts off 'Chief Officials of the Co-operative Movement are seriously disturbed by the growth of intensive campaigns among feminist and politically minded pressure groups.' It goes on, after looking at the need for modernising and rationalising Co-operative trade on strictly business lines, to quote an official 'If we are not careful, political and women's pressures will determine questions of management and trading ...A fierce feminist campaign throughout the Movement is developing almost into a sex war. Once, women were elected to Co-operative boards and committees purely on the grounds of their capabilities. Now it seems a section has adopted the slogan "women at any price".' The article ends ominously "... in forthcoming elections in 1,000 local societies with an annual trade of nearly £11,000 million, pressure groups of women will be at work."

The key paragraphs in the NJAC Report[17] were in Section 7, the Role of the Auxiliaries in Present Day Circumstances, which started 'The function of the auxiliary organisations is to demonstrate the Co-operative Movement as a social force of meaning and potentiality within modern society and to contribute to the vitality of Co-operative democracy.' Two features of the present social climate were seen to make that task more difficult. 'People today are not concerned so much with changing society as the ability to live comfortably within it' and secondly, 'that the Movement has changed considerably, and has become more managerial in structure and outlook.'

A merger between the NGC, NCMG and BFYC was recommended. The WCG expressed the view that it was essential to maintain a women's Co-operative organisation clearly and principally devoted to the interests of women, although the Guild would consider a federation which did not involve the loss of a separate identity.

Women working was seen as a problem by many. Mrs. Ella Pamplin, joined the Guild in 1923 aged 24, and wrote to say
her Guild closed about 1962 when she was President, as it was 'losing so many members — women going out to work.'
Improvement in programmes was also seen to be important. The WCG was already thinking along these lines. The 1959

Annual Report showed programme topics becoming more varied, and a Speakers' Panel being formed. Central Committee members talked on Children in Care — and CWS Directors spoke on Co-operative Trade and Production. District Conferences examined the bakery trade, and the Ministry of Agriculture had supplied notes on 'The Starving World.' Policy statements were being prepared on Co-operative Trade and on Mental Health.

Groombridge Report

The terms of reference for the Groombridge Report on the Co-operative Auxiliaries[18] were as follows:-

To investigate how the purpose, organisation and programmes of the adult auxiliary organisations in England and Wales can be adapted to increase their strength and service to the Co-operative Movement in modern conditions.

The auxiliaries to be discussed were the Women's Co-operative Guild (WCG), National Guild of Co-operators (NGC), the National Men's Guild (NMG), and the British Federation of Young Co-operators (BYFC).

Brian Groombridge added to the terms of reference two more fundamental questions — not just how can the auxiliaries be adapted but *can* they? — And *ought* they to be? Some people in the Movement believe that the Guilds have had their day and they are frankly not sorry. It is important and relevant to bring this attitude into the open, partly because it can summon a lot of evidence in its favour, partly because I do not think that all the problems of the auxiliaries can be solved by the auxiliaries alone. They will need the support and goodwill of other sections of the Movement, and if this goodwill does not exist in all circles, it is important to find out why not, so that matters can be put right.

The Groombridge Report is an impressive document — a substantial pamphlet of over 80 pages, it takes a perceptive and sympathetic look at the work of the auxiliaries, and whilst often critical, it is full of constructive suggestions.

Brian Groombridge used questionnaires (sent to 1,547 WCG branches and returned by 956) and observation in order to refute some common myths. For example, declining membership was to be found in branches with good programmes, yet some branches meeting where there were poor facilities may nevertheless attract younger members. Groombridge therefore argued that many factors were relevant in discussing success or failure of auxiliaries, and that decline could not be blamed on any one factor, whether it was age, programme or meeting place.

Discussing declining membership, Groombridge compared the decline in WCG membership with that of the Townswomen's Guilds (at 220,000 in 1960, double the membership of 1950) and the Women's Institute with a membership of 452,000 which was 100,000 more than in 1938. The Report commented 'These figures are not quoted for the sake of provocation but because they show that the social climate is not necessarily hostile to women's organisations with educational programmes and an interest in larger social questions.'

On age, Groombridge said that whilst 40% of WCG members were over 60, 15% were under 40 — and pointed out that the whole population was ageing and that those under 30 were unlikely to shop at the Co-op. Whilst over half the WCG branches reported losing members, 30% had increased, either continuously or since their foundation.

It is interesting to note that the 1960 Annual Report said this of Guildswomen: "They have worked for and achieved an expansion in the Co-operative idea and the raising of the standards of life, but because so much has been gained, that is no excuse for present day Co-operative women to rest on their laurels. There are, unfortunately, fields of Co-operative effort in which there is a great need for keen, able and willing workers to win back the enthusiasm, loyalty and trade of Co-operative members and instil in their minds the importance of protecting and fighting for the interests of the many through the strengthening of their own Movement... 1960 has not been a good year either for the Co-operative Movement or our Women's Guild, and so an all-out effort will be attempted this year to regain the old pioneering spirit that built our Movement. There is a great deal of this spirit in our older members, and we call upon them to inspire our newer members to join us in the task ahead .... The situation is one that calls for immediate action, and every Guildswoman is asked to help.

Were branch programmes related to this challenge? After analysing the programmes of all branches for the weeks starting 1.9.59 and 10.1.60, Groombridge concluded that:

8% had programmes which were well balanced and enterprising

13% were purposeful but less well balanced programmes

40% were neither good nor bad

39% had programmes 'either dedicated to the minutiae of routine Guild business or a jollification or both.'

He went on to say that this figure of 39% was too high. The WCG should regard the improvement of branch programmes of urgent importance — a matter of concern to WCG already, of course, as frequent reference in Monthly Bulletins and Annual Reports showed. Recommendations on training for speakers, the setting-up of a speakers panel and using more expert speakers were already being pressed centrally but were not, obviously, implemented by all branches. Or was it the way in which so many subjects for discussion at branch level were selected centrally that was to blame? 1962 Congress at Plymouth passed the following resolution: "This Congress is of the opinion that the subjects for discussion submitted by the Central Committee for District members are out-of-date and old-fashioned so do not attract younger members ...Guild meetings also need reorganisation with the business side kept to a minimum, and new, interesting and up-to-date subjects introduced for discussion.

Of the large percentage of WCG branches that appeared not to understand the role of the Co-operative auxiliary, Groombridge said that such branches may be serving a useful purpose:

...opportunities for people to be neighbourly over a game of whist are important to our communities... Nobody should pretend, however, that they are serving the purposes of Co-operation through education and active citizenship, they are not. Nor does it make much difference that a great deal of money raised playing games and raffling tins of Co-op milk in fact goes to very good causes.

Turning to Co-operative commitment, the Groombridge Report found 59% of WCG branches had discussed local Co-operative society issues within the past month, and attendance at Society members' meetings was good — Groombridge commented here that the 'fate of the auxiliaries is in part the fate of democratic control in an epoch of amalgamation.' As for representation, the Report found one third of WCG branches had at least one member on the Management Committee, and over half the branches had at least one member on the local Society's Education Committee. Groombridge asked if the auxiliaries should be more selfish, suggesting 'some of the best members are not able to give proper service to their branches because they are so busy being useful elsewhere.'

The report was concerned that the WCG did so little to recruit Co-operative employees — 80% of branches having no employee member at all. Groombridge found the WCG more active politically than the other auxiliaries (in contrast to finding WCG proportionally less well represented on societies' committees). This is shown in the following table:-

Association of branches with Co-operative and Labour Party (Source: Groombridge Report, 1960)

Branches affiliated	Women %	Other %
Branches affiliated to Co-operative Party	96	70
Branches sending representatives to Co-operative Party	84	69
Branches having contact with Labour Party	49	42

NB. Membership of auxiliaries in 1959 gives just under 50,000 to WCG, 1,500 to Men's Guild, 150 in BFYC and 4,000 in Mixed Guild.

The Groombridge Report made the important point, overlooked by so many organisations, that older members have the same need for educational stimulation and rights to participate in policy making as younger people. Groombridge went on to say that whilst it was to be regretted that there were not more younger men and women in the auxiliaries, it was 'not reasonable to regret that so many branches consist mainly of the elderly. Their programmes may be as enterprising, their ability to recruit new members as keen, their morale as buoyant and their commitment to Co-operative democracy as active as that of any other branch. It is greatly to the credit of the auxiliary movement that this is so.'

In an interesting chapter entitled 'Influence for and against auxiliary progress' Groombridge, whilst acknowledging the wide range of factors that affects branch progress, offered a rough but perceptive analysis of some of the influences at work. Among his conclusions were that good relations with local Co-operative Education Committees had a beneficial effect on membership trends and programme quality; discussing Co-operative trade had a slightly detrimental effect on membership trends, and that there was a tendency for Co-operative involvement to be associated with decreasing membership and a higher standard of programme.

Groombridge said that good programmes did not by themselves attract and hold members, as other factors might be relevant (e.g. lack of publicity), and that branches which co-operated with other educational and social organisations found their programmes enriched and brought to the notice of potential members. Bad programmes seemed linked to the disproportionate time given to routine business at branch meetings. The WCG branch secretary's or treasurer's length of service did not make any difference to either programme quality or membership trend, but he concluded that both programme quality and membership trend tended to suffer the longer the president had been in office. The following table, taken from the Groombridge Report, gives more information about this issue:

Distribution of Branches by Length of Officers'
service (%) Source: Groombridge Report

Length of service	Secretary	President	Vice Chairman	Treasurer	District/ Section Rep.
Less than 1 year	8	10	20	11	12
1 - 3 years	30	39	51	36	50
4 - 6 years	24	20	15	20	14
7 - 10 years	14	11	7	14	8
more than 10 years	24	20	7	19	16
Totals	938 = 100%	899 = 100%	824 = 100%	886 = 100%	332 = 100%

The second part of the Groombridge Report went on to make recommendations, but as we will next discuss the Guild's own modernisation document, less space will be given to them than to his analysis of the problem.

Groombridge argued that the decline of the auxiliaries matters to the Co-operative Movement, and to the country as a whole. He felt branches should realise there was more at stake than gaining new members. 'More efficient and more democratic Co-operative trading and a more civilized Britain dedicated rather to Co-operative virtues than to aggressive personal ambition will not be built on a foundation of beetle drives and bingo,' he concluded tartly.

Groombridge's recommendations (which actually take up half the Report) included:

Recruitment — As the population is ageing and their needs as consumers were being largely ignored, recruiting older adults could be seen as an achievement in itself.

Programmes — Groombridge was critical of WCG meetings for starting with a Co-operative song, and because the Guild encouraged branches to read the Monthly Bulletin out loud at meetings. He was also critical of the presentation of branch programmes, with speakers made to sound cliquey (e.g. District Speaker) and their title obscure. (For example, 'The world we live in' or 'Women under the Rainbow Flag.') More and better publicity was urged, with more society involvement — giving information on the auxiliaries to new members for example.

Meetings — The Report suggested that whilst viewed separately, rituals within meetings did little harm. (e.g. roll call, reading the Bulletin, singing 'Happy Birthday dear Sister' to those with birthdays), they 'conjure up a remote and uncongenial world.' Subscriptions needed to be higher — he suggested 10s. p.a. for the WCG instead of the then current 4s. (2/6d. to Head Office). Social activities should be a by-product not main programme ingredients.

The auxiliaries should act as consumer associations and special events linking trade and the auxiliaries held. Groombridge felt the responsibilities of branch secretary were too diffuse — she should be the chief administrative officer of the branch, helped by the treasurer, by a membership secretary, a programme secretary and greater involvement of members.

This summary does not do justice to 40 pages of detailed recommendations, but the WCG response is more important. The November 1960 Bulletin urged all branches to order a copy of the Groombridge Report in order to study and discuss it thoroughly. It is interesting to note that this same Bulletin had a 'Round the Branches' section reporting on activities in seven branches — five concerned social activities, one a member becoming a JP and the other congratulating Herne Bay (Kent) on its interesting programme and reports in the local paper.

The Guild's Reaction to Groombridge

Congress in 1961 passed a resolution urging all Co-operative Management and Education Committees to study the Groombridge Report and to implement its recommendations 'especially with regard to publicity and to the provision of adequate and comfortable accommodation.' Groombridge was discussed at Sectional Conferences in the Spring of 1961, whilst discussion in branches included consideration of the Guild policy statement 'Co-operative versus Chains, Cartels and Combines.'

Groombridge was published as the serious problems facing the whole Co-operative Movement were also being debated.

The 1962 Congress held in Skegness passed a long resolution under Plans for Co-operative Progress appealing to all active co-operators, Co-operative officials and employees to work to ensure a future role for the Movement within the community. Recommendations included amalgamation among small retail societies, switching uneconomic factories over to production of goods in demand and taking the lead in design, packaging and competitive pricing.

This same Congress carried some important resolutions on Guild matters. One proposed by Central Committee was for a compulsory levy of 1s. per member to be raised by Branches to be sent to Head Office; this followed defeat of the attempt at the 1961 Congress in Portsmouth to raise subscriptions from 4s. to 6s. per annum.

Most important of all, Congress resolved that: "This Congress is of the opinion that the time has come to modernise the Constitution, Rules and Methods of the Women's Co-operative Guild. It therefore empowers the Central Committee to set up a Commission forthwith to prepare a plan for submission to Congress in 1963. The personnel of the Commission to consist of adequate representation from Central Committee, Sectional Council and District Committee levels, with power to co-opt Guild members and to invite suggestions from Guilds."

Yet in 1962, we also learn from the Annual Report, about Co-operative involvement in practice. This varied from visits to CWS factories and demonstrations at branch meetings to lobbying the CWS on shoe-fitting and on dress-sizing. Although the problems of factored goods was explained, the Guild felt these 'did not meet the needs of the middle-aged women whose statistics normally change on reaching maturity.' The May 1962 Bulletin explains this problem in more detail. Standard sizing of 36" bust and 38" hips do not meet the needs of many over 40s who seek 36" bust and 40" hip clothing. 'We would like to know,' says the Bulletin 'whether 36″ bust with 40″ hips is a fairly common sizing for women of 40 years and over.' 1963 saw the Guild running a 'Come Co-operative Shopping' campaign including factory visits and a panel of 183 speakers.

The 1962 Annual Report looked at the Movement's response to Groombridge when it discussed NJAC matters. Reporting on the good response to Groombridge, it reported the appointment by the Co-operative Union's Education Executive of a full-time officer on auxiliary affairs who would act as secretary to the NJAC. The report expressed disappointment however with the Movement's response to Groombridge on more finance and better accommodation.

Movement for Moderns

This Report[19] was the Guild's response to Groombridge, and set up in response to the 1962 Resolution outlined above. The report was prepared by 11 guildswomen.

The Modernisation Committee met six times. They tried to see the Guild as others see it, and tried to determine what sort of organisation would appeal to the woman co-operator of today — probably coping with a job, able to bring the world into her living room by flicking a switch, used to electrical labour saving devices, wooed by advertisers and instructed by women's magazines, 'the woman who is, in fact, a very far cry from the pioneers of 1883 and even the pre-war Guildswomen of 1939.'

The crucial paragraph in this introductory section of the Report says: "In our opinion the Guild member of today, better educated, and with greater opportunities than her predecessor of eighty years ago, is an intelligent woman, capable of assessing a situation and coming to a decision without the need of restrictive rules and binding traditional practices. She needs an organisation which recognises this fact and provides her with scope for exercising her judgement and ability and pursuing her interests.

An up-to-date organisation which not only meets the needs of today but is capable of rapid and early adaptation to the changing needs of the years to come."

The first recommendation was a change of name — 'as belief in Co-operation bring us together and is the mainspring of all our activities the name should be THE CO-OPERATIVE WOMEN'S GUILD.

201

With hindsight, was this right? One could argue that 1963 saw the Co-operative Movement on the threshold of decline, the women's movement on the threshold of success. It is not without significance that it is Virago Press that re-published the early books of the Guild (Letters from 'Maternity' and 'Life as we have known it'). The Guild's interests were already wide: they had debated issue after issue of fundamental importance to women, and were often involved in radical political campaigns in advance of the Co-operative Movement, the Trades Union Movement and the Labour Movement. Perhaps, if as they responded to Groombridge, and rejected the auxiliaries own working party's recommendations on a merger, they had become more explicitly aligned with the radical women's movement and not the Co-operative Movement which was beginning to lose its philosophical base as it fought to maintain its trading position — perhaps the Guild would then have had a better chance of growth.

But then it would no longer have been a Co-operative auxiliary, the necessity of which Groombridge had argued so cogently. The alternative, which Lady Fisher would have liked to have seen, was the Guild putting up a stronger fight on behalf of the Co-operative philosophy.

The next major recommendation concerns Aims and Objects

As at 1948

The object of the Guild is to promote a new social order in which Co-operation shall replace capitalism and women have equal opportunities with men. For this purpose it seeks to organise women for the study and practice of:-

1. Co-operation and other methods of social reform.
2. Improved conditions of domestic life.
3. And with this object in view to work with and support the Co-operative Party, provided that the policy of the Co-operative Party is not inconsistent with the policy of the Guild as declared by the Guild Congress.

From 1963

The objects of the Co-operative Women's Guild are:-

(a) To promote through the expansion of Co-operation such conditions of life as will ensure for all people equal opportunities for full and free development.

(b) To educate women in the principles and practice of Co-operation in order that they shall be loyal members of their societies and play a full part in the control of the Co-operative Movement.

(c) To encourage and prepare women to take part in local, national and international affairs.

(d) To work for the establishment of world peace.

(e) To provide social, cultural and recreational activities through which members may live a full and interesting life.

Turning to Guild structure, whilst retaining the levels of branch, district, section and Central Committee, the report suggests a need for better liaison and a change in duties and responsibilities of District and Section. As Sections were already represented on the Central Committee, so in future branches should be represented on District, and District on Section.

Examining each level in turn, the Report said that there was no better advertisement for the Guild than an active, well-run branch, which should carry out the objects of the Guild by close co-operation with the local Co-operative society; training its members to play a full part in the administration of the Co-operative Movement; participating in local, national and international affairs: organising educational, social and cultural activities and stimulating members' interest in the organisation to enable women to make the fullest possible contribution to the community.

The need for planned programmes was stressed, saying 'nothing could be less attractive to new members than dreary, haphazard meetings.' Branch programmes must carry out Guild purposes, and 'should be linked to a national theme (for example; Co-operative products, housing, health, education, consumer protection and other current topics) to be prepared annually by the Central Committee. Other recommendations included planning programmes in advance and allowing for membership participation, meetings should be given continuity to ensure that action (such as Resolutions or letters to MPs or local press, or pressure on local authorities) stemmed from deliberations. Other activities should include visits to factories, local authority meetings, art galleries and society meetings, whilst attendance at LEA or Co-operative classes for serious subjects or subjects like keep-fit, dressmaking or choral singing should be accepted as ways of providing education, cultural and recreational activities.

Branch procedure should be brisk and businesslike, not so formal that members felt there was no time to express their views, nor so cumbersome that it became ineffective. Some rules then binding on all branches should in future be left to individual branches to decide, such as attendance qualifications for officials. Traditional rituals (criticised by Groombridge) such as Roll Call and the opening song were also to be left to the branch's discretion.

Branch officials were urged to foster a sense of belonging by encouraging participation in District and Sectional activities as well in the local society. The Branch Treasurer should take over the keeping of accounts from the Secretary. Assistant Secretary, Minute Secretary, Membership Secretary, or Social Secretary should be appointed according to branch requirements. Branch committees should meet regularly and plan the programme for branch approval — 'no Branch should be a one-man band.' Training facilities for branch officials received a great deal of attention, and should include practical training in such matters as letter-writing, minute writing, book-keeping and conducting meetings. A briefing conference on Guild policy and programme should be held at least once a year by District for Branch Secretaries and Presidents with other members invited to attend as observers. The Report was keen to ensure that branches publicised the Guild as widely as possible.

To expand, branches need to make sure all members were involved in presenting 'an image of an enthusiastic, energetic, friendly organisation,' with branch meetings having an attractive and purposeful programme and being efficiently run, fostering friendship and understanding, and being held in comfortable meeting rooms.

As ever, Rule 24 promoted most controversy. This Rule barred from office those engaged in business in competition with the Co-operative society and (whilst welcoming persons of any political persuasion as Guild members, subject to branch approval) anyone not a member of the Co-operative or Labour Parties could not hold office or be Congress delegate. Rule 24 also says 'Furthermore a Communist person shall not attend any meeting or conferene as a delegate especially at the Guild's expense.' A majority of the members of the Modernisation Commission wanted to see this rule go. They argued that a 'take-over' by any pressure group could only come about through the apathy of those who allowed themselves to be taken over, and doubted if there were 'many Guild branches where rows of Tories, Liberals, Communists or Fascists, clutching their party membership cards are waiting to assume office and transform the Guild overnight.' Arguing that no woman may join a Branch without the consent of the Branch, the majority report said if there was to be political discrimination it should be at the lowest level of refusal of membership, not in the refusal of democratic rights to accepted members.

Joan Baker and Ada Hill submitted a minority report putting forward the case for retaining Rule 24. The authors asked 'Do you wish to see the Guild Committees bolstered by an influx of women politically opposed to the aims, purposes and policy of the Co-operative Party, to which the Branches are affiliated and on the National Committee of which Party we have representation? ...The strength and purpose of our Guild cannot be nurtured and made to prosper by the dilution of our ideals.'

Who won? The "Daily Herald" tells us in its report from the 1963 Guild Congress in Birmingham headed 'Ban on Tories and Communists stays.'[20] Despite pressure from the platform, and the presence of Russian, Hungarian and Red Chinese delegates, Congress refused to have officers other than those belonging to the Co-operative or Labour Parties.

The "Manchester Guardian" quoted Commission member Mrs. Elsie Lawn, who said that there were adequate safeguards against political takeovers, whilst Mrs. Ruby Vincent of Portsea Island was applauded when she said "I plead with you not to have a Tory chairman in your Guild room."[21]

Congress also rejected the Commission's recommendation that affiliation to the Co-operative Party should cease to be compulsory for branches.

Turning to Districts, the Report said District Committees should encourage joint activities between Branches, be in continuous contact with branches, and should study and possibly improve branch programmes before forwarding these to Head Office for information. Closer contact would be established if each branch was directly represented on a District Council. District used to be a group elected to serve as speakers when invited by branches, but co-ordination and helping branches were now the major tasks.

The new District Councils were to consist of a representative from each branch, a Secretary elected by branches and an Executive Committee elected by and from the Council. Districts were to be smaller, with a maximum of 25 branches, and their functions were to include organising activities for all branches within their area; maintaining existing branches and opening new ones; helping branches to incorporate national themes in their programmes; encouraging branch involvement in the local Society, and ensuring branch officials received training, including being briefed on Guild policy. Guildswomen would have to be members of a branch for six months to be eligible to serve on a District Council and for two years to serve as a District Secretary.

Turning to Section, closer liaison between District and Section was seen as necessary, as District activities needed to be co-ordinated. Central Committee was drawn from Section personnel and this was the level at which intensive training in public speaking was needed. Sectional Councils would consist of one representative from each District, elected by branches in that District and a Sectional Secretary elected by branches in the Section. Duties of Sectional Council would include supervision and co-ordination of work of Districts within the area, promotion of activities in the Section in accordance with the policy laid down at Congress, organisation of Spring and Autumn Sectional Conferences plus one other event. They were to hold at least four Council meetings annually. Sectional Council members were to be trained as leaders of a democratic organisation, as public speakers, and as discussion group leaders. To serve on Sectional Council, two years membership of District Council was necessary, and two years on Sectional Council was needed to stand as Sectional Secretary.

Discussing Central Committee, the Report says this was the executive body of the Guild and should therefore change its name to National Executive Committee. It would, as before, be made up of one representative from each Section, and functions should include:- to provide national leadership; to select subjects for national programme themes (including planning the programmes in detail and advising Sections, District and Branches of their roles); to secure maximum national publicity and maintain the public image of the Guild as a forceful organisation of well-informed women; to maintain closer contact with the Co-operative Movement at national level as well as with other women's organisations, government departments and other national bodies in accordance with Guild policy, and to be responsible for Guild finance. Finally, 'to be the driving force in the Guild and a source of inspiration and enthusiasm to Branches, Districts and Sections.' More frequent meetings were recommended, together with formation of sub-committees with the right to call in specialists. To be eligible for service on the National Executive, two-years service on a Sectional Council was needed, and the limit of service should be increased from three to five years to give

206

greater continuity.

Despite arguments for change, the Commission felt it was preferable for the National President to be elected by the National Executive Committee but recommended that, to ease her work load, the status of Vice-President should be raised and greater use made of her services. Head Office should deal with the engagement of both President and Vice-President so they could cover a maximum of meetings with the minimum of trouble. The office of Treasurer should be abolished as accounts must be dealt with by Head Office.

On administration, the relatively low pay (i.e. below the minimum salary of a local education secretary) of the General Secretary was noted, although seen as outside the scope of the Report. The work of the part-time fieldworkers was praised. However, 'Organiser' was preferred to 'fieldworker.' Retirement for all employees at 65 and the introduction of a superannuation scheme was recommended.

The suggestion of a biennial Congress was rejected as an annual Congress was seen as essential. However, it was becoming unrealistic to expect invitations from societies who could face a bill of £1,000, and a Congress levy of £1.10s. per branch was therefore recommended. Recommendations about Congress included papers on subjects to be selected by the National Executive from suggestions submitted from branches; provision for emergency resolutions, no branch to be permitted to submit more than one resolution, and that branches should elect their delegates (i.e. not select by rota).

Increased subscriptions of 12s. per year was recommended, with 5s. going to Head Office, 1s. going to Sectional Council, and 1s. going to District Council.

Lastly came recommendations to gain publicity for the Guild's work and promoting 'an image of an up-to-date go-ahead body of women; determined, enthusiastic, successful, well-informed, efficient, following discussion with action, and ready to take up any challenge.' Apart from the defeat over Rule 24, these radical recommendations printed as 'Movement for Moderns' were accepted by the Guild.

The Guild and its Members
But let us end this survey of the years 1952-63 by reminding ourselves how much the Guild meant to its members, despite setbacks, criticisms and the obvious need for reform.

Take the Toy Project of 1962, which led to 5,000 toys, mostly made but a few bought, being given at Christmas to children in need - 4,000 going on a float loaned by the London Co-operative Society to Save the Children Fund offices whilst a further 1,000 went to Family Service Units (some guildswomen also offered holidays to children in families being helped by FSU).

Take the 11,000 signatures collected within four weeks only for the Guild's own anti-nuclear petition presented by Harriet Slater, MP to the House of Commons on 20 February 1962. Turn back to 1957, and remember the Guild's participation in the three-week Festival of Women in Wembley of which the 1957 Annual Report said 'The many tributes we received acknowledged that of the activities of the Women's Organisations in the Festival, none could compare with the part we played.' The Guild stand arranged by the CWS Publicity Department contained dolls dressed in national costume and guildswomen in attendance wore national costumes on the special Guild Days. Visitors were entertained by choirs, drama groups, music and, on the last day, there was an International Pageant with '212 performers in costumes of 28 different countries and carrying the flags of their country together with rainbow flags and led by the "Spirit of Co-operation".' The Pageant was described as 'truly magnificent' as well as having gone off without a hitch.

Some members who filled in our questionnaire had joined the Guild in the 1950s. What did the Guild mean to them? Mrs. Cockle of Newbold Verdon, Leicester, talks of the way her Guild has served the local Society (e.g. by attending members' meetings) and the community (e.g. with concerts for the over-60s in the village). Mrs. Iris Kell of North Shields mentions friendship, social activities and educational tours to factories.

Mrs. Ivy Watson of Lowestoft found learning about the Guild and, as branch secretary, helping to make the branch active, happy and purposeful. She says Guild contests are good to bring out talents of members, and she is now working with other members to design and make a Guild banner for the centenary and says

'The Guild has made my life fuller and I think made me a better person. Long may it continue.' She also recalls many educational visits (e.g. to prison, lighthouse and Co-operative factories), as well as recalling a Hallowe'en Party where 'dressed up as witches we got got some strange looks walking home in our gear.'

Lastly, let us repeat the questions asked by a member new to the Guild in 1961. Mrs. Marjorie Britland of Shipley won first prize in the Women's Co-operative Guild Aims and Objects competition and her winning entry was printed in 'Woman's Outlook.'[22] She asks: "Why are we so short of new recruits? Ask yourself these questions.

Have you asked them to join? I was a co-operator for ten years before anyone asked me. Are you sure a young woman would feel welcome at your branch meeting? ...Whatever her social standing, education, colour or creed? Would she be encouraged to state her new ideas? Helped to overcome her initial shyness at doing this? Are you quite sure there are no petty jealousies amongst your members? Are you certain your branch meetings never degenerate into a tea-up gossip rather than an intelligent discussion of Guild business?

"When you can answer yes, honestly yes, to all these questions perhaps the Guild will begin to rise from its present moribund condition. No re-wording of the rules, no re-statement of the Aims will help. Nothing more will help except that each member puts a little more effort into being a guildswoman.''

Notes to Chapter 7

1. B. Groombridge, Report on the Co-operative Auxiliaries (Co-operative College Paper No.7, Loughborough 1970).
2. CWG, Movement for Moderns (Report of Modernisation Commission 1963).
3. *Daily Herald,* 13th November 1956.
4. *Daily Herald,* 23rd May 1952.
5. *Manchester Guardian,* 13th November 1953.
6. *Daily Herald,* 17th May 1956.
7. J. Bailey, The British Co-operative Movement (1955).
8. *The Times,* 19th March 1953.
9. Bailey, op.cit.
10. Bailey, op.cit.
11. Groombridge Report, op.cit.
12. *Co-operative News,* 21st November 1953.
13. Groombridge, op.cit.
14. Movement for Moderns, op.cit.
15. Report of the National Joint Auxiliaries Working Party on the Future of the Auxiliaries, 'Co-operative Consumer', Spring 1960.
16. *Daily Telegraph,* 1st December 1958.
17. NJAC Report, op.cit.
18. Groombridge Report, op.cit.
19. Movement for Moderns, op.cit.
20. *Daily Herald,* 16th May 1963.
21. *Manchester Guardian,* 16th May 1963.
22. *Woman's Outlook,* September 1961.

CHAPTER 8

THE DIFFICULT YEARS: 1963-1982

Membership of the Co-operative Women's Guild, as it faced the challenge of implementing the recommendations of Movement for Moderns[1], was 38,380 in about 1,400 branches. During the period under review, membership fell to 13,709 in 578 branches by 1981. Explanations for the decline will be discussed in the next chapter which will contain a concluding discussion of the Guild, and look forward to its future as it faces the second century of life.

However, if we measure the Guild's role only in terms of membership we miss other strands in the story. We need to recognise the contribution of the Guild's leaders, especially the National Presidents, and the dedicated work of the General Secretary in increasingly difficult conditions. Conditions so difficult, indeed, that Kathleen Kempton found herself breaking Guild rules. The rules said she should retire at 65. Only at 70, and after changing the Rules so that a non-member can become General Secretary, is she able at the 1983 Centenary Congress to retire.

Above all, the Guild gave an enormous amount of pleasure and satisfaction to thousands of women up and down the country. This chapter will look more briefly than earlier chapters at Guild campaigns, financial or administrative problems and at international activities. Instead, more space is given to the voices of the guildswomen who wrote or talked to us in order to share their experiences and views of their guild membership.

One major change in the Guild has been the way the central leadership and General Secretary have become less directive. Contrasting her pre- and post-war Guild experiences, Mrs. Olive Davies, born in 1897 who joined the Guild in 1928 in Harrow and is now active in 'retirement' in Sussex talked of Eleanor Barton (General Secretary 1925 to 1937) as a very good General Secretary who was very strict. They could not be strict after the war in case they lost members — 'they had to change tactics after the war' she told us. Her place in this section is earned because of her post-retirement success. Moving to West Sussex, hardly the mecca of Co-operation, she was Sussex District Secretary 1975-1980 and five new branches were opened in that period!

Olive's success in the mid 1970s had its roots in the 1967 Congress decision giving Districts responsibility for opening new branches when the Guild could no longer afford to employ part-time fieldworkers. In 1980, 41 branches closed and 10 new ones opened. At about the same time, in Brighton's Co-operative Society's Annual Report and Accounts, we read that District Secretary Olive Davies has co-ordinated events so that 'each branch is able to consciously feel a part of the wider Co-operative Movement.'

But the success of Olive Davies, and others like her, could not halt the steady decline in the number of branches. The specific reasons for branches closing change over time. In 1963 the Annual Report related reduced membership to the increased subscription. The 1964 Annual Report talked of areas with older branches disappearing and the need to replace them with branches in new towns and on new estates. The five Guild organisers worked together in Harlow New Town — three new branches opened, although one closed due to lack of a meeting place, said the 1964 Annual Report, which also reported that the National Executive Committee had set up a Membership Sub-Committee. Their recommendation that steps should be taken to open special branches for young women 'caused a great deal of controversy' said the 1964 Annual Report, although there was general support at the special meetings of District Secretaries and Presidents organised by each Section. The report continues 'The appeal to young members to volunteer to open and lead such branches has not so far met with a very great response but progress is being made in some areas.' The 1966 Annual Report talks of some Branches closing down because no-one would become Secretary or Chairman, a theme which recurs throughout this period and contrasts with the competition for office in the earlier years of the Guild. Lady Fisher said that her branch in Birmingham kept its membership up until the 1960s when women went out to work to buy material things in the 'never had it so good era.'

In 1966 the organiser scheme was working well with 17 local societies participating in a scheme to split the salary and expenses three ways for a three-month period, i.e. Guild, Co-operative Society and Education Executive of the Co-operative Union.

By 1967, the four organisers having been dispensed with, fewer new branches were opened than for many years. Apart from redevelopment in city centres the 1967 Annual Report related the decline in membership to difficulties faced by the Co-operative Movement (for example withdrawal of society grants and loss of meeting rooms, problems that were to worsen over the years as more and more retail societies amalgamated).

From 1968, the Co-operative Union Education Executive offered support to auxiliaries in the form of an Adviser Scheme; 11 guildswomen took the one week training course at the Co-operative College. Each Adviser was to help two branches near her home and try to open a new one. By 1971 there were not enough potential advisers to be trained.

Membership was discussed by Mrs. Edna Shotton in her Presidential address to the 1975 Annual Congress at Paignton. She surveyed the year of office which included handing over an Inshore Lifecraft to the Royal National Lifeboat Institution on behalf of the Guild, seeing the Guild discuss its theme of Housing and the Environment, the choice of Eva Dodds as President of the Co-operative Union Congress for International Women's Year, and reviewed the Guild's concern with a wide range of International issues. She went on to say:

My greatest disappointment has been the continued decline in membership and the closure of branches. I am conscious of the difficulties which branches are facing, loss of rooms, shop closures and increased transport costs, but I make no apology for urging every guildswoman once again to make a special effort to increase membership in 1975, by strengthening existing branches and opening new ones .... The situation is extremely serious, we cannot continue to be an important organisation doing valuable work if our voice is too weak to be heard. We cannot carry out our policies if we are drained of finance. In short, if we continue on the downward slope we shall surely die and this is unthinkable. Our work is as vitally necessary now as it was when we were formed. Are we to see the work and sacrifices of our predecessors wasted? Please treat this matter with the greatest urgency.

1977 saw seven District Secretaries going on a Co-operative Union Education Department course on opening new Branches, but the Annual Report was back to explaining the decline, citing lack of officials, lack of meeting places, and the closing of local Co-operative shops as reason for Branch closures.

By 1980 inflation was also blamed, with staggering rises in room rentals given as a common reason for closure.

In the 1981 Annual Report, the last available, increased subscriptions were a further explanation for declining membership — 13,709 on 31st December 1981, compared with 15,645 in 1980. Is there a way of halting this decline? The answer to this, the most fundamental question facing the Guild in its Centenary year, will be discussed in the next chapter, as we turn now to look at other aspects of the Guild's administration in this period.

Finance, Staffing and Office Accommodation

The link between finance and membership has been stressed before. Increased subscription loses members. Declining membership loses income. Reduced income restricts the work of the Guild. 1962 saw the end of the printed Monthly Bulletin and its replacement was a duplicated monthly newsletter. The 1963 Annual Report, the first carrying the new name, Co-operative Women's Guild, also reflected a change of style. It had a modern cover, with a coloured stripe, as opposed to Annual Report covers and format that had varied little since 1883. 1970 saw the last of these printed reports, as in 1971 the first Annual Report to be duplicated was available. Apologising for lateness, unusual format and extreme brevity, the point was made that a shorter report 'may, perhaps be more carefully read and duplicating will help to conserve our slender resources.' The Report went on to say 'It is always useful to be able to make a virtue out of necessity and if a brief review of a full year's work produces more questions and discussions at Congress we shall feel, whilst still expressing deep regret, that we have turned adversity to good account.' A changed format for the Annual Report was not the only major change in 1971. This was the year the Guild bought its own home: 342 Hoe Street, Walthamstow, London, E.17.

In 1964 the Guild were granted a new lease for their office in Pioneer House, Gray's Inn Road, London by the London Co-operative Society Political Committee and they had used the Guild Office Fund to pay for it to be redecorated. In 1968 Pioneer House was sold. It was obvious that a new lease was unlikely to be granted in 1971. Luckily they were able to purchase the house in Hoe Street, that had previously been a local Labour Party Headquarters. Building work was necessary to make it comply with the Shops, Offices and Railways Act, but the Guild moved in on 19th August 1971, and on 16th September the official opening took place. The ceremony was performed by Baroness Fisher, a former National President and the first guildswoman to sit in the House of Lords.

The purchase price came from the Guild Office Fund of £10,400 and the Guild Project Fund for the years 1969-72 which was added to the Office Fund to enable the purchase and renovation of the Guild's new home and allowed for some money to go into a Maintenance Fund. The advantages of owning their own offices were obvious, and the importance to the Guild's income of being able to let rooms for office or meeting use is often mentioned in later Annual Reports.

The effects of financial problems on the Guild's work is touched on in most Annual Reports in this period. 1964 saw a deficit of £1,086 on an annual budget of £24,655, despite administrative savings which included reduced spending in postage following the closure of the Sales Department. The deficit was reduced to £181 in 1965 — at a cost which included cutting all training courses and cutting down printing costs. In 1966 the NEC took no action on many matters in order to save money. The deficit was up to £815 in 1969, in a period of rising costs, especially for Congress which was actually costing half as much again as the special Congress levy paid by all branches. By 1976 we find the Guild in a healthier state, mainly because the CWS grant rose from £900 in 1971 to £1,200 in 1972 and reached £5,000 by 1975 (although this was complicated by the fact it was covenanted, but the Guild could not reclaim tax).

The major and perhaps most devastating economy that led to this 1976 balance of income over expenditure was a reduction in staffing, sometimes planned and sometimes accidental.

When Kathleen Kempton took over as General Secretary in 1963 the Guild's Head Office employed eight staff. Over the years the staff dwindled, and Kathleen Kempton related how tough it had been for her. She told us she felt that she had been spending too much time typing and duplicating and not enough time speaking, planning or getting publicity for the Guild.

By 1970 Joan Baker, then Assistant Secretary, went to be Secretary of the Mary MacArthur Home, leaving the Office with four staff, two of whom were only 17. The office could not cope with the same volume of work, leading to complaints of delays and failure to answer mail.

The 1971 Annual Report shows an even worse problem: one General Secretary working with a full-time and one part-time person. Deciding to employ an Assistant Secretary, the post was advertised in the Branch Newsletter, "Co-operative News," local newspapers and trade union journals — leading to only one tentative enquiry! A young graduate was appointed in 1974 but she did not stay and Kathleen Kempton was left, aided only by Diane Crook and Daisy Codd, although guildswomen volunteers were invaluable in helping to keep the office going.

1978 was the year when Kathleen Kempton should have retired but as no one applied for the job she became Acting General Secretary. In 1978 Jeannette Gould joined the Guild as Assistant Secretary/Development Officer. Her job was seen as partly to be in Head Office, partly spending time in the field opening new branches. Diane Crook left in 1978 after seven years but rejoined in 1981. Luckily guildswoman Mrs. Kitty Spooner joined the staff, together with a junior.

In 1980 Jeannette Gould left, and her useful innovation was then dropped, although revised by Angela Hardy, "on loan" from the Co-operative Union Education Department in 1983. This was a newsletter supplement called Information Exchange which dealt in depth with one topic such as organisations for the elderly or International Year of the Disabled; or suggested various ways to follow up Guild resolutions, or looked at current legislation.

Head Office was manned by Kathleen Kempton and volunteers only towards the end of the period covered by this chapter. Her spirit is summed up in the way she starts the September/October 1980 Branch Newsletter: 'Despite financial problems and lack of staff Guild work must go on and I am doing my best to cope.' And the Newsletter shows Guild work *was* going on: it dealt with finance, the 1981 Congress, the Rules Revision Committee, National Contests, Christmas Draw, Demonstration Day, Death Grant Petition and sales of diaries and the rainbow scarf.

Special Funds

The Guild maintained large numbers of small funds for specific

Two aspects of the Cost of Living Campaign in 1970. The National Executive visit to 10 Downing Street included (left to right) Mrs. Phyllis Gard, Mrs. Florence Francis, Renee Short, M.P., Lady Fisher, Mrs. Hannah Arrandale, Mrs. Joan Young and Mrs. Winifred Liversedge.

Above: Members of the Guild who attended the mass lobby of the House of Commons.

Guild members' submissions to a "Handicrafts for the Home" contest organised by Ipswich District.

Members of the
National Executive
visited the
headquarters of the
Royal National
Lifeboat
Institution when an
inshore lifeboat
was presented in
1974.

A delegation of
North-Vietnamese,
South Vietnamese
and Laotian
women visiting
Congress at
Margate.

purposes. Let us look at them at the beginning and end of the period of this chapter:-

	Name of Fund	1963	1981
	Guild Office Fund	4,980	15,535
	Centenary Fund	—	3,167
1	Exchange Fund	1,727	963
	Guild Education Fund	—	(89)
2	Margaret Llewelyn Davies Fund	1,914	652
3	Development Fund	—	350
	Political Fund	625	—
	Relief Fund	232	—
	Presidents International Fund	119	—
4	Eleanor Barton Fund	499	—
	Zanzibar Fund	159	—
	Aid to British Guyana Fund	225	—
	Special International Fund	4	—
5	Cecily Cook Memorial Fund	1,345	—
	Co-operative Shopping Campaign Fund	31	—
	TOTAL	11,865	22,692

1 used for international exchanges ... 2 used to send Guildswomen to International Conferences ... 3 rest of a special grant (1978) from the Co-operative Union to spend on development work in 4 areas ... 4 used for scholarships (to Co-operative College events) for prizewinners (eg 1963 Song Contest) ... 5 Sent in 1966 to equip a library in a Co-operative College in Tanzania.

The number of funds was much reduced in recent years, and the Guild concentrated on single projects, raising significant sums for a wide range of charities:
1967 over £7,000 was raised for Co-op/Oxfam Botswana Project.
1972/3 Project was for Royal National Lifeboat Institution — £5,000 collected.
1976/7 Muscular Dystrophy — over £5,000 collected.
In contrast, there was a tendency for fund raising for the Guild's own needs to be undertaken with less enthusiasm:
1969 — £3,143 — half for Guild Office Fund, rest for Margaret Llewelyn Davies Fund.
1969/72 — Appeal for Guild Office Fund — £25,000 target but only £3,378 collected in first year.
1973/4 Project was Guild Education Project — £2,000 collected — £4,890 in the three years to 1976/7.

In 1977 it was decided to share National Project Funds between a Guild objective and a named charity. For 1977/8 it would be the Chest, Heart and Stroke Foundation and just under £4,000 was shared between the Guild and this charity. The current Project is the Guild's Centenary Fund.

The charitable work of the Guild was seen as very important by many guildswomen. Mrs. Lydia Middleton who joined the Guild in 1925 and is still active in Walthamstow Branch said

she felt the collection of money for projects was one of the Guild's greatest achievements, and that she regretted the fact that the Guild 'did not broadcast what they did, like other women's organisations do.'

Miss Violet Herlock, who joined the Guild in 1968 and is now District Secretary at Colchester wrote to say they had collected £1,300 for Annual Projects, and Mrs. Margaret Jackson of Manningtree branch wrote that guildswomen have organised and manned stalls for local charities. Most guildswomen saw fund raising as one task among many. Mrs. Garrod of Newton Road Guild, Ipswich, wrote:

as a Treasurer it is the challenge of giving the best possible benefits to the members whilst still supporting charities of all kinds; and showing a healthy bank balance — all on the small amounts from draws, Bring and Buys, etc; and practising Co-operation in the true sense of the word.

Even in the early days when Central Committee gave no encouragement to raising money, branches obviously gained great satisfaction out of charitable work. Mrs. Rosina Prewett, Guild member since 1944, included

help we have given to children and elderly in our city. Washing, repairing and supplying clothing to a home for orphan and unwanted children until it closed. Knitting children's clothing for the WRVS, knitting and crocheting blankets for local elderly people's homes and hospitals. She went on to write that 'When the Guild branch opened 90 years ago, the members made chemises and pinafores for children of Muller's orphanage.'

Changing the Rules

We ended the last chapter by examining the changes in Guild Rules and organisation that followed the 1963 publication Movement for Moderns. The next major set of rule changes were recommended in the 'Rules Revision Report'[2] — discussed at the 1981 Congress which was held at Middleton Tower. The 1981 Annual Report says 'The report of the Rules Revision Committee gave rise to much debate, but less changes than were expected.' The most important were those giving greater freedom to the Branches.

This relaxation of the Rules was described by Mrs. Olive Davies, member since 1928, as 'going over the top.'

The Rules Revision Committee was set up in accordance with a Resolution passed at the 1980 Congress which began 'in looking ahead to the social changes to be expected as we move into the new decade of the 1980s, this Congress of the Co-operative Women's Guild recognises it is now seventeen years since there was a comprehensive revision of Guild Rules.' Sections each elected a representative, and Mrs. Doris Dan, National President was Chairman.

In its introduction the Report says the basic structure and restrictive practices date back to time long past, when women were less well educated, had less access to information, were less self-confident — rules had needed to be tight and continuous so that members felt secure. The recommended Rule changes were designed to be flexible enough to appeal 'to the new generation of younger women whom we must attract if we are to survive.'

Only minor revision of the Aims and Objectives was suggested, although the report wanted to see them as frontispiece to the new Rule Book rather than merely as Rule 1, which is how they appear in the Guild's new Rule Book.

The most radical suggestions on structure were in fact rejected by Congress. These would have set up Local Joint Councils to replace District Councils, to be related geographically to Co-operative Society Members' Relations Committees as well as to Co-operative Members' Councils or Joint Auxiliaries Councils. Regions would have replaced Sections. The 1981 defeat of these changes means the original structure of the Guild thus survives, although restrictions on continuous office holding have gone — victim to difficulties of finding people to fill their positions. Only service on the NEC remains restricted to a maximum of five years.

One further radical change not agreed was that branches and not the NEC should elect the National President. It was however accepted that Branches should be free to run themselves to suit local circumstances. Branches were offered 'self-determination' according to the Rules Revision Report — 'freed from red tape' to quote Kathleen Kempton — free to decide what officers were needed, as well as their own branch rules and regulations.

The other two major changes accepted were that a General Secretary from outside the Guild could be appointed and that

219

membership subscriptions should rise to 20p per month, with £1.50 annually going to Head Office.

As in 1963, the Rule which said members of political parties other than the Labour or Co-operative Parties could not hold office or act as Congress Delegate, and prevented Communists from attending any meeting or conference as a delegate, was controversial. Rules Revision Committee wanted to delete it. Congress agreed. But it did not receive the two-thirds majority required and so remains in the Rule Book, as Rule 24, complete with the sentence that members engaged in business in competition with the Co-operative society are not eligible for office.

Links with the Rest of the Co-operative Movement

Relations with the Co-operative Movement seemed to have been amicable over the years discussed in this chapter, with frequent meetings with CWS directors, stronger links with the Co-operative Union Education Executive and Department, as well as a few more women reaching top positions within the Movement.

For example, Eva Dodds became the second woman ever to be elected President of the Co-operative Union Congress in 1975, International Women's Year. Soon after Mrs. Dodds' election as a CWS Director, Mary Stott, a former editor of "Woman's Outlook", wrote in "The Guardian" that she was 'so far removed from the unkind popular image of the dowdy fat woman shopping at the fuddy-duddy Co-op that it is natural she is enthusiastic about the new set-up, about the Co-op's new design policy.'[3] By 1981, there were two women directors of the CWS, but there were only 106 members of boards of directors compared to 462 in 1963. There were 143 education/member relations committee members in 1981 compared to 462 and 626 respectively in 1963. This reduction reflects crucial changes: the decline in Guild membership was being matched by a decline in the number of Co-operative societies.

The problems of the Co-operative Movement stayed on the Congress Agenda. For example, 1964 saw Congress declare its opposition to Stamp Trading, seeing it as 'evidence of increasing competition in retail trading, for which the consumer alone will pay.' At the Guild Congress at Skegness in 1972 four resolutions concerned the Co-operative Movement. The first, whilst recognising the fact that large societies were essential, said that 'financial and trading problems must not be allowed to obscure the fact that a Co-operative society is owned by the members and that as owners they have the right to consideration, information and trading facilities,' and Congress called on directors and officials to ensure that membership participation remained a priority. The second resolution expressed concern that the Co-operative Union had reduced the Education Executive's expenditure by 25%. The third resolution expressed alarm at the continual decline in educational provisions for the Movement and called on members to oppose the closure of Education Departments by being 'vigilant in their own society, attending society meetings and making their voices heard.' The last resolution urged the CWS to lead the way in cutting food and fuel prices.

In 1982 Congress called on the government to give more support to the Co-operative Development Agency and for 'guild branches to take the initiative in their own area by contacting Co-operatives in their own area and urging a joint approach to the local authority calling for the establishment of a local Co-operative Development Agency.' This is an important resolution, as it recognises the development of the 'new' Co-operatives which will be discussed in the next chapter. The second resolution passed by the 1982 Congress, whilst recognising the problems of retail Co-operative societies, argued that the 'caring, sharing Co-op' had a duty to provide reasonable shopping facilities for its members, and that this should include shops in inner city and/or rural areas in addition to hypermarkets and superstores.

Apart from good relationships with the Co-operative Union Education Department, the fact that the Department had a staff member with special responsibility for auxiliary development was helpful, as was the closer relationship with the Association of Education Secretaries. There was growing flexibility for branch programmes in this period, but each year the National Executive determined a Programme Theme, and the Co-operative Union Education Department often prepared discussion notes for these themes (for use by the other auxiliaries as well as the CWG). National Themes over this period were varied. The 1964/5 themes were 'State Education' and 'Home and Family.' 1966 saw 'Hands Across the World' which was common to all auxiliaries and 'Women in a Man's

World' which was purely a Guild subject. The 1966 report voiced disappointment that 'numbers of branches completely ignore the themes and in these cases it would seem that programme planning is very much at fault.' Following the Groombridge[4] recommendations, programme themes were designed to be dealt with over a period and provide opportunities for member participation and action.

In subsequent years, one theme only was selected (for example 1968 Regional Societies; 1971 Co-operative Auxiliaries; 1974 Housing and the Environment; 1978 Women's Rights and 1981 Labelled Disabled). The 1979-80 theme was Democracy in Danger. Discussion notes were produced by the N.C.J.A.C. and, longer than most discussion notes, ran to 27 pages, with Kathleen Kempton sending it out with three additional pages of CWG notes which raised stimulating and pertinent questions. These included questions about changes in the Co-operative Movement; the problems of the adult auxiliaries (especially compared to the attractions to the young of groups like Oxfam or Shelter): the need to build bridges at grass roots level with the new Co-operatives and also raised questions about other aspects of democracy such as local authorities. However this was 'not a very popular theme' according to the 1980 Annual Report, and Head Office was left with 'a considerable supply of notes.' This attitude at branch level seems consistent with Lady Fisher's views that the Guild did not fight hard enough for the Co-operative Movement.

A most depressing feature of the Co-operative links related to the Co-operative Press. Looking at old press cuttings of the Guild, the loss of the "Daily Herald" is brought forcibly home. But at least the Co-operative Press was able to cover Co-operative matters nationally through "Reynolds' News" (which became the "Sunday Citizen" in 1962) and closed completely in 1967. Biggest blow of all to the Guild was the loss of "Woman's Outlook" in 1967. By then monthly, it had a broad appeal with its fiction, problem page and regular contributions by journalists such as Ursula Bloom and James Norbury. It gave space to the Guild and its activities, and its letter pages often reflected Guild concerns. It also outlined important episodes in the Guild's history such as the Ben Jones Fund[5] or the Divorce law campaign.[6] Nevertheless the "Co-operative News," which was instrumental in the Guild's very formation and had generously covered Guild and women's topics continued, as it continues today, to be an outlet for Guild news (edited now by Mrs. Lily Howe).

The Guild received generous financial support from the Co-operative Union in this period, and from the CWS. The Co-operative Union published three relevant reports. In 1972 they published the Report of the Study Group on the Situation and Role of Women in the Co-operative Movement[7] which, whilst recognising that women were not accorded equality with men in the Movement, rejected reserved places on committees and talked instead of the need for an evolution in attitudes. Other, more specific, recommendations included young married women to be attracted by trading policy and by facilities for young children; the Co-operative College should run family holiday and women's courses and female staff should be encouraged to aspire to promotion.

In 1975 the Union published their Working Party Report on Developing Lay Leadership[8] which was concerned with problems such as the large number of uncontested elections within the Co-operative Movement and the fact that the interests of members and employees do not always coincide. Recommendations included that there should be a more unified structure for the three adult Guilds and that there should be a Confederation of Auxiliary members in which the Adult Guilds and Woodcraft Folk retained their separate identities. It recommended three development officers, one for women (Guild, Young Women's Groups and Other Women's activities); one for the mixed Guilds and Community work and one for children and youth work.

Thirdly, and perhaps most important, was the Report of the Working Party on Auxiliary Development and Reorganisation,[9] set up in 1980 and accepted at the 1981 Education Convention. Kathleen Kempton spoke in the debate and in her speech alluded to the decline of Guild membership and emphasised that a similar decline was to be found in the number of member relations committees, full time officials, retail shops and so on. It was therefore inappropriate, she argued, to focus attention solely on the problem of the auxiliaries; the essential requirement was to build them up so they could play their part in 'salvaging democracy within the Co-operative Movement.'

Although passed, there was token rather than enthusiastic support for the report, according to Member Education

Development Officer (Auxiliaries) Peter Gormley,[10] and indeed there were no funds for the developments the working party suggested. It was an imaginative report, seeing the auxiliaries involved in a wide range of activities such as encouraging consumer groups, developing society membership, furthering relationships with schools and most important of all promoting the formation of new Co-operatives among groups affected by the economic recession, such as young people, women workers, the unemployed over 50 and minority ethnic groups. Let us hope it is only in abeyance and has not yet been buried!

Campaigns and Concerns

Not surprisingly, in a period of declining membership there are more examples, in the Annual Reports of this period, of working with other organisations. For example, in 1970 the Guild was represented at a meeting convened by the National Federation of Women's Institutes to discuss the Countryside Project (for better understanding between town and country dwellers), which the Carnegie Trust was to fund. The 1971 Annual Report said explicitly that much of their work was carried out in association with other bodies, and lists those organisations with which they had been actively involved, including the National Commission for Women, the Women's Group on Public Welfare, the British Standards Institution, the Women's Advisory Committee, the National Council of Women, the Council for Educational Advance and the National Joint Committee of Working Women's Organisations. Organisations supported in 1971, halfway through the period under review, included the National Peace Council, the National Council for Civil Liberties, the Socialist Medical Association, the Council for Children's Welfare, the Abortion Law Reform Association, the Birth Control Campaign and the National Council for the Single Woman and her Dependants. Here we see the Guild working on a wide range of issues, as well as following up the 1971 Congress resolutions which covered topics as diverse as ever.

In addition 1971 saw the Guild active in the Cost of Living Campaign and acting against the Common Market as well as social service cuts. The interests of the Guild remained constant around the central concern for the welfare of the family and the role of the mother. From an initial interest in maternity alone came a developing interest in an ever widening range of health and welfare issues. This is as true of the inter-war years as it is of post-war Guild activity. The extent to which the broadening of interest stretched the Guild's resources too far is discussed in our concluding chapter.

Names were submitted for a wide range of public bodies, including Gas and Electricity Consumer Councils, Hospital Management Boards and Transport Users Committees.

1971 was also a year of lighter activity. There was the Champion Co-operative Housewives Contest, for example, as well as the Leisure time Crafts Contest and Branch publicity Contest. The pleasure these lighter events gave to Guild members is an important and positive aspect of branch life. Mrs. Rosina Prewett writes that

Birthday parties have caused many laughable instances too numerous to record, but still give the members happy memories when we have a "Sing, Say or Pay" afternoon. We still have a few members well over 80 years with 60 years membership.

Before picking out a few specific campaigns, let us look at one issue: corporal punishment. In 1939 the Guild's Congress had passed the following resolution: 'That in view of the renewed fervour of some of the magistrates and judges for flogging, we demand the abolition of the law which allows flogging, and call for legislation to be introduced immediately, such legislation to include the abolition of birching of juveniles and young persons in remand homes.'

In 1965, the Co-operative Party debated the same issue at their Blackpool Conference. Before conference was a resolution which said that punishments meted out in the courts for crimes of violence were not sufficient in their severity and that a review of these punishments should take place at an early date. (The Guild's own resolutions to the Co-operative Party Conference that year were on mental health and comprehensive education.)

The Guild's Assistant General Secretary, Mrs. Joan Baker, was Guild representative on the National Committee of the Co-operative Party. According to the "Manchester Guardian" Joan Baker appealed passionately on behalf of the platform for rejection of the call for heavier punishment, saying the resolution was 'more worthy of a Tory women's conference' and that crimes of violence should be reduced by attacking the root causes of violence through improving housing and welfare schemes.

Mrs. Hilda Wickens, JP, from Birmingham, Guild National President 1969/70 supported the motion, saying that on the magistrates bench she was often distressed at her inability to pass severer sentences on persons found guilty of violence ....
'Youths should be set to work at unpleasant jobs, such as the clearing of midden heaps, and their wages should go to the victims of their violence,' she said.

The resolution was passed and in 1982 the Guild itself passed a resolution expressing deep concern at the increasing number of serious crimes against persons in the street and calling for additional uniformed policemen and policewomen in the street; stricter discipline for young offenders; enforcing the law that parents are responsible for youngsters under 18 found guilty of vandalism, and the re-introduction of the birch for persons convicted of crimes of violence. The resolution asked members to exert pressure on MPs 'to ensure the speedy introduction of legislation so that all citizens will be able to walk the streets with freedom and in safety.'

It would be easy to criticise the resolution, and certainly many guildswomen argued against it. Nevertheless, given the age structure of the Guild and the reality of the fears relating to street crime, it shows a real concern for how many women actually feel. It is also an example of how an early concern for the protection of women and children, which included the demand for women police officers, widened into a more general concern for law and order issues.

The other 1982 Resolutions covered the familiar, wide range — on world peace, unemployment, the rating system, charities and VAT, recycling of waste, preserving the countryside, banning smoking in public places, deploring the payment of Family Allowances 4-weekly, deploring the plight of the pensioners, opposing changes in the financing of the NHS, protecting those disadvantaged by cuts in the Social Services, against prescription charges, and calling on Guild branches to submit names of capable women willing to serve on major national committees. The resolutions opposed the National Front and sensational journalism and supported a peaceful settlement in the Falklands and legislation on glue sniffing. Looking back to 1963 we find an equally wide range of resolutions. Some of the battles of that year are virtually won, for example they wanted unrestricted hospital visiting for children, and urged legislation against racial discrimination.

Sadly, many of those 1963 resolutions could appear virtually unchanged in 1983 — deploring the money wasted on armaments, deploring the failure to provide adequate finance for the health service, urging an increase in unemployment benefit and arguing that householders should be encouraged to carry out measures to increase safety in the home by means of Improvement Grants: these are just four examples of issues as relevant today as 20 years ago.

Guild work goes beyond passing resolutions at Congress. What was the Guild doing, say in 1969, with a membership of 30,000? Sectional conferences discussed Social Security in the spring and Children in the autumn. Co-operative loyalty took many forms. Lady Fisher recalled the year when deprived children was the theme. At Sectional conference one of the speakers was from the Family Service Units and it was decided to combine listening to the talk with a practical expression of support for the needy families helped by the Family Service Units. Everyone who came was asked to bring a tin — a tin of Co-operative food. The speaker expected to go home with a bag of groceries: such was the response that 300 women presented him with tins of food and he had to hire a van! Lady Fisher told us that there was no doubt that for many of the families it would be the first time they would have had a tin from the Co-op in their home.

The National Programme Theme for 1968/9 — A Charter for Children — proved popular, involving Branches in speakers, visits, weekend schools, day conferences and film shows. Practically 2,000 copies of the discussion notes prepared by the Co-operative Union Education Department were disposed of (to just over 1,000 Branches).

The 1968/9 National Speakers Forum had been a great success, but the Novices Speakers Forum promoted in 1969/70 attracted a much reduced entry. Thousands of entries were received for the handicrafts contest, which was designed to link with the Programme Theme as the entries were to be for children 0-5, with five classes: knitted garments, crocheted garments, sewn garments, toys, and pram and cot sets. In addition Sections asked each District to prepare a dressed doll which would be presented at Congress as a gift for needy children. Many Districts promoted local contests, the best doll being kept for Congress, others being presented locally so gaining valuable publicity. There was a Programme Planning competition that year, as well as Training Courses for District Executive Members. Also held was a Sectional Council Members Training Course with speakers including an NSPCC Inspector, and a Children's Officer. A training course for Treasurers, 'in readiness for decimal book-keeping', was being planned.

Two major innovations that year were, first, a weekend school for young guildswomen and, secondly, a tri-partite weekend conference. Three groups of members were invited: Young Guildswomen, Magistrates and Women on Co-operative Boards and Education Committees. The theme was education and Mrs. Renee Short, MP gave the opening address. Young members then discussed comprehensive education with Margaret Miles; magistrates discussed children in trouble with Mrs. Millie Miller, MP and women on Boards and Education Committees dealt with consumer education with Alma Williams of the Consumers Association.

In addition to all this activity, the Panel of Speakers was circulated again to Branches and refresher courses held by Sections for those on the Panel of Tutors. And that was not all. In the pages headed Citizenship we read of representation and involvement in a wide range of issues — Submitting nominations for Regional Hospital Boards and Hospital Management Committees, supporting Abortion Law Reform, being represented on the Executive Committee of the Women's National Cancer Control Campaign by Mrs. F. Shalloe, acting as one of the sponsors of the Women's International League for Peace and Freedom, a weekend conference on Chemical and Biological Warfare, as well as involvement in issues as diverse as road safety, equal pay and the distribution of pre-packed solid fuel.

This chapter as a whole deals with a period of decline for the Guild but it is hoped this survey of one year selected at random will show how much constructive and enjoyable work was undertaken.

It is sad to note from the 1975 Annual Report that the Guild was not represented on the National Consumer Council when it was set up, despite over 90 years work on consumer issues, although representation was later gained.

This section ends by looking at ways the Guild participated in International Women's Year, 1975, of which the Annual Report said, 'The Year has ended but the fight still goes on, until the goal of complete equality is reached.' Branches and Districts

Other 1967 international activities included an invitation for a Guildswoman (Mrs. Iris Flett went) to join a British delegation to the USSR with all expenses paid.

Two guildswomen visited Hungary and two separate visits were made to Poland (Mrs. Ivy Beresford attending a School on Social Aspects of Urban Co-operatives in Poland and Mrs. Norah Willis representing the Guild at the Congress of the Polish Co-operative Women's Organisation). A UNESCO travel grant enabled Joan Baker and Joan Lamb to undertake a Study Tour of Guyana. The Guild, that same year, records involvement with the British Council for Peace in Vietnam, Medical Aid for Vietnam, the Anti Apartheid Committee, the Movement for Colonial Freedom; the liaison Committee for Women's Peace Groups; Women of Asia, the United Nations Association and UNICEF.

Jumping forward 10 years, the 1977 Annual Report had a section on Peace and International Activities which recorded continued support for the Women's Disarmament Campaign, and the campaign against the Neutron bomb. Support for the London Co-operative Society's stand against South African goods was given. A party of 16 Guild members went on a tour to East Germany. The General Secretary represented the Co-operative Union on the ICA Women's Committee.

This level of activity and concern continued. In 1981 the Peace and International Section contains information about support for CND and the campaign for World Disarmament. Views were expressed to the government on disarmament, nuclear weapons, Cruise missiles and other topics. The NEC attended a meeting organised by the Liaison Committee for Women Peace Groups on International Women's Day. The Guild was in contact with the women of the African National Congress and demonstrated concern for the women of Chile through affiliation to the Chile Solidarity Campaign.

We turn from this brief survey of international concern to review how guildswomen felt about the Guild in the years leading up to the Centenary.

Guildswomen Speak

We have examined Guild activities at home and abroad in the 1963-1982 period, showing a wide — possibly over-extended — range of activities. Through interviews, letters and replies to our joined in local activities. Nationally, over 2,000 members joined the service and rally at Westminster. The service was held at Westminster Abbey (an Abbey decorated with flowers given and arranged by Co-operative societies in Greater London and with trumpets played by members of the Royal Military School of Music). The speakers at the Rally in Central Hall afterwards included Judith Hart, MP and Mrs. Muriel Russell, JP.

International Work and Concerns

The CWG had formed the ICWG and been the most active Guild supporting it. It was they who had led the fight to maintain its independent existence but as Muriel Russell pointed out to the authors, few countries had Guilds on the English model. During International Women's Year the International Co-operative Alliance (ICA) published 'International Women's Year — Women and the Co-operative Movement.'[12] Muriel Russell, who worked within the ICA Secretariat from 1965-1978 wrote an article on the 'Promotion of World-Wide Women's Co-operative Interests' in which she traced the development of the ICA Women's Co-operative Advisory Council from 1964 to the 1969 enquiry which strengthened the status of the newly constituted Women's Committee, which then became an integral part of ICA. She described the main concerns of women co-operators as the role of the consumer, the burdens of women in rural areas and the needs of women in developing countries. The ICA Women's Committee without funds of its own had a duty to promote schemes and programmes which will change the 'attitude of complacency that accepts that in the nature of things men occupy the overwhelming majority of offices.' Muriel Russell was later to announce that over £230,000 had been collected worldwide for the ICA's 'Buy a Bucket of Water Campaign.'[13]

Turning back to the CWG, what was its own international work in this period? In 1967, the Guild raised £7,000 for the Co-operative/Oxfam Botswana Project. Caravans set off from Ipswich, London, Newcastle and Plymouth for the 17-day journey to Congress in Morecambe, where the High Commissioner for Botswana Mr. D. Mokama visited the caravans. "Woman's Outlook" shows Mary Wilson, wife of the Prime Minister, with Mr. Mokama, Norah Willis and Lord Oram, among others, watching the London caravan leave Trafalgar Square.[14]

questionnaire, we now look at the Guild through the eyes of just a few of those guildswomen kind enough to send in their impressions of the Guild.

Mrs. Wilson of Manchester, only joined the Guild in 1969, when she was already 56, and she wrote to say of Gorton Guild

we are a very happy Guild although our members are steadily getting less. I am always sorry that I didn't join them much sooner than I did, but I had young children and went out to work. Like so many others she has particularly warm memories of being entertained by other Guilds — after a fun packed day, all ended well with a real Guild get-together at Southport, they gave us tea and really entertained us, it was such a happy evening, we all look back and wish we could have those kind of days once more.

Regret at decline in branch membership does not stop members enjoying Guild life. Mrs. Jones, nearing 80, looks back at 48 years membership in Birmingham, and says she has most enjoyed

Speakers on all subjects, friendship of members, Guild business and Newsletters from Head Office, and goes on to write 'we are a small Guild, but we enjoy our meetings and take a full part in events arranged by District Committee.'

Newer members contributed similar comments. Mrs. Dorothy Porter from Lincoln, after five years in the Guild wrote of

The companionship of fellow Guilders of all ages, and their willingness to help others in real need.

Mrs. Edna Swift who joined the Guild at the age of 50 only 4½ years ago writes about

meeting people, making new friends and taking an active part such as President of Chester-le-Street Branch Committee and District Secretary for North West Durham

Mrs. Rosamund Foster who joined in 1966 says her major interests as a Guild member have been

educational side, companionship.

Mrs. Folley from Royston in Hertfordshire also picks out

friendship of members, whilst also writing of her enjoyment derived from being on branch committee and attending Congress, church services and rallies.

Guildswomen show their resourcefulness too. Mrs. Ida Bailey from Stoke-on-Trent joined the Guild in 1964, and recalls preparing the Guildroom for a Birthday Party Celebration.

*Just got tables prepared, sausage rolls, mince pies nicely
warming in oven. Guests arrived — having a celebration sherry,
when whop — all the lights and electricity fused for the night.
Made frantic rush to home, collected torches and candles, and
had a marvellous time by candlelight and never cease to talk
about it. Marvellous how Guildswomen can cope with most
situations, particularly as this was in November and darned cold
weather. Jackets and coats soon donned and fingers blown to
warmth.*

Mrs. Harriet Arrandale from Manchester, who joined the
Guild much earlier, in 1946, showed personal resourcefulness in
a similar situation. She was visiting a branch in Derbyshire, to
speak on 'Nursing through the Ages.' They met in a room over
old stables, but

*the new neon lights would not work so candles had to be bought.
These gave a poor light and did nothing to discourage the mice,
so to fit into the atmosphere I abandoned the talk on 'Nursing
through the Ages' and we all told ghost stories instead.*

Mrs. Irene Hickman from Birmingham, who joined the
Guild in 1959 tells of work for local charities, friendship and
committee work, but her most interesting story arose from a
visit to her son in Perth, Western Australia. Invited out to
dinner, her hostess had a book, written by a neighbour, which
concerned a CWG branch in Road End, Birmingham! The
author's mother had founded that Branch some 60 years
before, and as she was a bad writer this author had at the age of
10, attended meetings and written the minutes. She writes of the
author, F.B. Vickers, who based his novel[15] on his childhood
memories, that

*he was thrilled to meet me in his lovely garden under the almond
tree with doves above. He talked about the Guild and all it
meant to his mother and him. On leaving he signed the book and
gave me a lovely letter to take back to Road End Guild. How
strange I should pick that book up on the other side of the
world?*

Many Guildswomen wrote of what the Guild meant to them.
Mrs. Ivy McCann of Hyde Branch, 21 years a member, wrote
that she had gained confidence in herself from the Guild. A
younger member, Jan Taylor of Kidlington, who joined in 1967
aged 29 elaborated. She wrote of

*gaining confidence (personal) that enabled me to be Chairman
of my Branch and later serve on the Education Committee and
also become District Treasurer and then Secretary. I enjoy
organising and this is something I would not have been able to*

do outside the family and home had my confidence not been strengthened by listening to other women LIKE MYSELF speaking out and having convictions regarding their principles.

This book has often dwelt on the Guild's efforts to recruit younger women like Mrs. Taylor — better meeting places, more efficiency, more interesting programmes — but why did Mrs. Taylor join before her 30th birthday? She writes

I would never have joined the Guild (although I always had Co-operative principles) if a friend had not suffered from post-natal depression (has anyone a better reason!) and we just had to get her out and about again.

Mrs. Toghill of Bath, a member for 27 years, says that when she first heard of the Guild she did not know what it was or what it entailed but after a year she was asked to be Secretary and she gained in confidence, becoming a member of District and Section as well as serving on local Co-operative Society Committees and as she says

members learn to help other people and also one makes lots of friends.

This theme is repeated. Mrs. Cowell of Cambridge had been a Co-operative society member 20 years before joining in 1972. She joined after her husband died and writes

I have made many friends that I otherwise would not have met. She liked the Annual Arts and Crafts Exhibition as it encouraged her to do things she had never done before like making jam or needlework, and she regrets that this aspect of the Guild has lapsed. Mrs. Cowell ends by writing, I have found that it is never too late to learn of something new and useful.

Mrs. Bullard of Welling, Kent, looks back on 44 years in the Westwood Guild — she joined in 1938, when she was 32. She writes how drama classes helped her to speak in public (she is Chairman of her branch and the local over 60s club). She remembers helping to man a post to help those bombed out during the war, and enjoyed craft afternoons as well as speakers and discussions on all sorts of topics.

'We all learned something about our own Co-operative society, politics, education, health and our Commonwealth.' Mrs. Bullard also expresses her pride in the Guild and fears for its future when she writes 'I feel proud to be a Guildswoman and when there is a Conference or rally and one meets Guild Sisters from different areas and different parts of the country it is a meeting of real unity. Alas over the years our membership has declined and it seems that younger women are working and so have no time for Guild meetings. I only hope that this situation

alters during our second century.'

Some of our oldest correspondents were particularly interested in education. Mrs. E. H. Treese, born in 1893, joined Stanhope Street Branch in 1927. She said she liked

being able to meet educated women and men in other Co-operative organisations and learn about work for birth control, voting rights, becoming member of Parliament, etc. She had welcomed the chance to go to week-end and summer schools and was especially interested to learn about how to run branch, district and sectional meetings.

Mrs. Ella Pamplin, now 83, joined the Guild in 1921, when New Malden Guild met at the Stoneleigh Hall, of which she writes

that hall was indeed a hive of learning. I studied Psychology there as well as going to Guild meetings.

Mrs. Doris Jones of Northfield, Birmingham, also joined the Guild in 1921 (Accrington and Church, Lancashire), but she recalls that several years before joining, she would go to the Guild parties and learn dancing there. She said she learned about the Rochdale Pioneers from the Co-op Library, 'The man who issued the books used to talk to us about them.' Mrs. Jones' letter shows the balance of Guild activities; in Birmingham, where she joined a Guild branch in 1938, she writes that

the branch had 'Speakers, MPs, Councillors, visits to all kinds of places and getting to know all the services of Brum. Twice a year we went to Avoncroft College. Two Guilds shared a coach. A conference in the afternoon, then tea and a discussion. Then a dance. I have always thought that the Co-op Women's Guild tried very hard to get women out of the humdrum life at home, if only for one night a week.

Interest in Guild history is widespread. Mrs. Frances Stabeler of Ashton-in-Makerfield Branch, Wigan, wrote to say she was

just an ordinary Guild member, without any research qualifications, just an obstinate streak making me unable to sit at home in ignorance of some answers to questions I ask.

The question she had set herself was to find the origin of the Guild Motto 'OF WHOLE HEART COMETH HOPE.' Her research took her to London Guild Head Office and Hull University where she looked up Central Committee Minutes to find that on 29th March 1904 the Guild motto 'Of whole Heart Springeth Hope' had been worked into a Banner made by the Royal School of Needlework. With astounding tenacity she traced it to the mediaeval work, 'The Vision of William concerning Piers Plowman.' Mrs. Stabeler's description of the detailed research needed to find the origin of the Guild motto reads like a detective story, but she feels there are still unanswered questions surrounding why it was chosen in the first place.

Mrs. Stabeler's interest in her branch led her to look at early minute books and the following two extracts reflect the continued delight of Guild membership. The Minute book describes a wagonette outing to Lymn in Cheshire in August 1907:

> About 142 people set out for a pleasant afternoon the weather being very favourable. Tea was catered for at The Fox Temperance Hotel, where everyone did justice to a well provided tea. The wagonettes, seven in number, started from Ashton at 1.30pm returning at 7 in the evening everyone being well satisfied. We had a slight loss from our outing owing to the wagonette men charging half fares for children and we had only charged 6d. each.

Mrs. Stabeler was also interested in the way refreshments were recorded in the minutes, together with quantities, costs and member responsibilities for provision and service, down to who was to get the tablecloths. She quotes as an example one social in 1916 when

> they ordered '12 dozen 1d. cakes, 1 ham, one 3 lb. tongue, 8 box loaves, 12 lbs. sugar, 4 lbs. butter, ½ lb. tea, 1 lb. coffee, 5 quarts milk, 1d. tin of mustard and 100 oranges, Mrs. Snowden to get the tea urns.

Mrs. Sylvia Paine was National President in the year this Centenary History was written. She joined the Guild in 1954, when she was just 40. She writes of her particular interest in the Guild as being

> The Loyalty of supporting our own Society, the friendship of being together, the caring for others in need, collecting for the third world victims, providing a gift to a new old people's home, etc. etc. and taking an interest in the handicapped. Everyday interest in current affairs and putting forward resolutions to Congress which we know do reach the appropriate departments of government.

And she looks forward, saying she feels 'there is a future for the CWG as we go into our second century. Women are more united in the things they do and they all have one aim "Peace for All," equality with men and caring for those with needs.'

National Presidential Address

Guildswomen talk to us in other ways too — the CWG publishes each year the Presidential Address given at Congress. Each address has a personal flavour although common themes, such as the need for member involvement and for recruitment, occur. Florence Shalloe, for example, said in Skegness in 1972 that on her election as National President

I felt very honoured and very conscious too of my responsibilities to you all and yet I was also concerned with your responsibilities ...... the best recipe for action is consultation and team work, (and ending) Guild work will never be complete, our work must go on, remembering that the Guild is bigger than the individual.

In a similar vein, but 10 years later, Mrs. Florence Cowlings said in her Presidential Address at Middleton

There is so much we have yet to do as an organisation of socially conscious women ... I plead, let us work together, live up to our Co-operative principles and ideals, working for Peace, the strengthening of our Movement, and always trying to keep that word Co-operation in our minds, so that we do our best to make things better, not only for the Co-operative Movement, but for our country and the rest of the world.

The Presidential Addresses, always interesting to read both for style and content, usually end with a quotation or poem. For example, Mrs. Flossie Wren ended her 1974 Scarborough Address with 'United We Stand! Divided We Fall!' and Mrs. Cissie Brown ended her address at the 1978 Harrogate Congress with one of the early Guild songs:

Be strong in Faith,
Let courage be our watchword
Then all we hope will be a certainty,
Of Whole Heart Cometh Hope.

And last in this section, the final words of Joan Young whose Blackpool address of 1973 still seems relevant:

So let us then face it! We do have a challenge. As an organisation there is much we can do to correct injustice, to oust discrimination in any form, to see every person gets some share of the nation's wealth, and to work for better social and educational facilities, so that as an organisation and also as individuals we are all striving to enrich the quality of life, and to improve and extend the lines of communication for all people from every walk of life. If I could end with a few lines of verse they would be as follows

> *If you could talk with crowds and keep your virtue,*
> *Or walk with Kings nor lose the common touch,*
> *If neither foes nor loving friends can hurt you,*
> *And all men count with you but none too much.*
>   *These lines echo my sentiments so I will close my address by*
> *saying to Guildswomen everywhere 'Fall in at once and close the*
> *ranks follow the flag today, another rainbow lights the sky. It*
> *can also light our way.'*

Guildswomen Share a Joke

We asked for amusing stories — all of them made us laugh, and it is a pity that for reasons of space we can only share four of the stories with our readers.

A very new member who only joined in 1979, Mrs. Margaret Jackson from Manningtree, Essex, writes about a branch outing

> *The Committee booked for the Branch to pay a visit to an*
> *evening's entertainment at Clacton-on-Sea, which consisted of a*
> *meal, followed by a HEN PARTY, with several DRAG*
> *ARTISTS. As the programme reached its peak, and became*
> *more and more revolting, one by one the members crept out,*
> *and gradually, one by one, the rest made their exit to see what*
> *had happened to them all, only to find that they were waiting*
> *outside on the sea front, this was supposed to have been our*
> *Christmas Party for that year, and needless to say it made*
> *headlines in the next week's local newspapers.*

Mrs. Margaret Kendall wrote to tell us about an evening with the Lutterworth Young Wives Group, writing that:

> *It was our weekly Wednesday evening Guild — a very cold and*
> *frosty night in October. Our speaker was most interesting,*
> *giving a talk on her visit to Hong Kong. She had brought*
> *numerous articles to show us and was showing us some jade*
> *jewellery that she had bought when, without batting an eyelid,*
> *she suddenly exclaimed that there was a male streaker outside*
> *the window. The room went deathly quiet, and not one member*
> *of the Guild turned round to look! We were all quite*
> *dumbfounded and didn't quite know what to do — one member*
> *said she would go and report it to the office at the College where*
> *we had our meetings — this she did. By this time the 'streaker'*
> *had disappeared — it was a cold night. The police then came and*
> *asked the inevitable question 'Could anyone recognise him?'*
> *There were of course, shrieks of laughter and the police didn't*
> *really believe us when we said that no-one had looked. They said*
> *he must have been very courageous to have streaked on such a*

bitterly cold night — they never did catch him though —
apparently there had been other sightings in Lutterworth. We
naturally expected our membership to increase.

And last, but by no means least, two stories from Mrs.
Garrod, member of the Newton Road Guild in Ipswich since
1963. First she writes:

I was fascinated by popper beads when they were popular and
on one outing our social secretary was wearing one of the very
long necklaces. They swung to and fro all day and when we
finally stopped for tea at a small restaurant in Norfolk I could
no longer resist the temptation to give a mighty tug at the lovely
loops of beads. Just one snag! They were not poppers and beads
rolled everywhere! Whilst in my horror I couldn't believe my
eyes and was still frantically trying to put them back. I can still
visualise the 29 bottoms all up in the air at once trying to find
and pick up all the beads which had rolled away in all directions.
I paid 50p to have them re-strung and learned my lesson.
Poppers? I could never look at another necklace without
cringing!

And as if that was not enough she tells us that:

Another funny occasion was at a picnic at Flatford when after
enjoying the tea we decided to go in boats on the river. Four of
us went in the last boat — only then did we learn that none of us
could row! One member pulled on a rope at the stern thinking it
would help us to guide (it was actually the tie-up rope!). We
went from one side of the river to the other — disturbing
mosquitoes every time we hit the bank, changed places in mid-
river and finally had to be towed back to base by another boat.
The bridge was filled with folk having hysterics and the boatman
had tears streaming down his face as he helped us out and
chokingly said 'no charge!' The filled bus sang 'for those in peril
on the sea' all the way back to Ipswich. Years ago now but
happy memories.

Notes to Chapter 8

1. CWG, Movement for Moderns, op.cit.
2. CWG, Rules Revision Report, 1981.
3. *Manchester Guardian,* 8th March 1962.
4. B. Groombridge, Report on the Co-operative Auxiliaries (Co-operative College Paper No. 7, Loughborough 1970).
5. *Woman's Outlook,* April 1958.
6. *Woman's Outlook,* May 1967.
7. Co-operative Union Ltd., Report of the Study Group on the Situation and Role of Women in the Co-operative Movement (Manchester 1972).
8. Co-operative Union Ltd., Report of the Working Party on Developing Lay Leadership (Manchester 1975).
9. Co-operative Union Ltd., Report of the Working Party on Auxiliary Development and Reorganisation (Manchester 1981).
10. Personal letter, 7th September 1982.
11. *Manchester Guardian,* 20th April, 1965.
12. M.J. Russell, 'Promotion of World-wide Women's Co-operative Links in International Women's Year — Women and the Co-operative Movement' Review of International Co-operation, Vol. 68, No. 1, 1975.
13. International Co-operative Alliance, Women and Work in Co-operatives Report of the Women Co-operators Conference held in Moscow, 10/11th October 1980.
14. *Woman's Outlook,* May 1967.
15. F.B. Vickers, Without Map or Compass (Sydney 1974).

CHAPTER 9

THE GUILD: YESTERDAY, TODAY AND TOMORROW

The Guild was known as the League for the Spread of Co-operation from 1883 to 1884; until 1963 it was called the Women's Co-operative Guild and from 1963 it has been known as the Co-operative Women's Guild.

As we bring our survey of one of the first organised, radical working class women's movements to a close, it seems appropriate to look first at the links between changes in the modern Co-operative Movement and the difficulties which the Guild has encountered in the post-war decades.

The Guild's 1979 Annual Report has this to say: "In the climate created by the Tory Government the Co-operative Movement today is having a desperate struggle and it is inevitable that this, also, will affect member organisations. As the bitter war in the High Street brings more shopping precinct superstores and out of town hypermarkets the smaller shops, which were so often the focal point for Guild branches, disappear, and Co-operative membership begins to lose its meaning. In these circumstances, however, member organisations such as ours become even more important."

The decline in the number of Co-operative shops is a crucially important aspect of the decline in membership, because they served as a focal point for recruitment and for loyalty to the Movement. Norah Willis is Chairman of London Region C.R.S. She has been elected by the Co-operative Union Central Executive to preside over the 1983 Co-operative Union Congress — only the third woman to receive this honour in 140 years. This election is a tribute to Norah Willis herself, but it is surely also a tribute to the Guild in its Centenary Year. She recalled that her mother would walk miles to the nearest Co-operative shop, and she suggests younger women do not develop this loyalty. Norah Willis also talked of the declining importance of the dividend — her mother had used it to buy school shoes. It has less significance, if any, today.

The change in the number of retail societies has been significant too. The Independent Commission of Enquiry headed by Hugh Gaitskell which reported in 1958 recommended 200-300 societies and not 900 as then existed. There were less than 200 retail societies in existence in 1982, and many of the smaller societies lacked the resources to provide member education. The Annual Report of the Co-operative Union for 1982 said the fragmented structure of the retail Co-operative Movement remained an obstacle to effective development, and emphasised the need for a reduction in the number of societies, some of which 'are seeking to preserve an independence which is of relevance only in historic terms and which has no commercial justification in 1982'. The problem of retaining member interest and member participation in the fewer, larger societies has already been mentioned. As Kathleen Kempton said, 'people ask me — Why belong to the Co-op? I can only answer — ideals'.

The Guild always understood the need to maintain trade and to trade efficiently. Nevertheless, there has always been a tendency for there to be tension between the men in the Movement concerned for commercial success, and the women more concerned with the philosophy of Co-operation. Yet early on they sought to influence goods stocked by local Co-op shops and this continued.

Michael Dent, who worked as a Buyer, first for London Co-operative Society (and later for South Suburban Society) recalls resisting demands for certain types of women's clothing to be stocked. He says the guildswomen represented only a small proportion of customers, yet tried to persuade the buying staff to buy 'even more fuddy duddy clothes'. Michael Dent also feels the Guilds had an influence out of all proportion to their numbers when they successfully delayed the closing of small local shops. A reversal of this argument could be put that the potential of the Guild to mobilise its members and therefore loyal shoppers was never recognised by the Movement.

Former General Secretary, Mabel Ridealgh, is just one of the large number of guildswomen who say they believe members no longer feel they "belong" to the Movement. Lady Fisher remains convinced that the decline in Co-operative trade might have been slowed down had management listened to guildswomen. She recalled asking CWS Directors, when she was National President in 1959-60, to end the large number of brand names of Co-operative produce, for example Wheatsheaf, Desbeau, Waveney and so on. Instead she argued that "Co-op" should appear on everything sold. Whilst critical of management attitudes, Lady Fisher also feels that the Guild is partly responsible, suggesting that they lost standing with the Co-operative Movement when they became involved in such a wide range of issues which involved working with many other bodies some of which "used" the Guild — they got 'side tracked completely' she says.

The Guild was at its most successful when it fought on specific issues and gave those issues its virtually undivided attention. The way it has now diversified means the taking up of such a wide range of issues that none or few can be successfully followed through. This is one possible explanation of the Guild's post-war decline — in terms of both members and influence.

Fewer shops and fewer societies also meant more difficulties in finding meeting rooms. Traditionally, most Co-operative societies provided a meeting room for branches, or helped by making a contribution towards meeting room costs — a growing problem as rent and other hire charges rise and as Co-operative societies close meeting rooms and, often, reduce spending on education and member relations work.

Fewer shops means less opportunity to display Guild material and less direct contact with shoppers. Fewer shops has led to fewer people joining a Co-operative society and hence the Guild. Even with fewer societies there seems to be apathy and difficulty in getting people to stand for election for committees — this is a similar problem in the Guild itself where unwillingness of members to take office in the Branch is often a reason for Branch closure. Co-operative committee work is of increasing interest to employees of the Movement, and it is interesting to note the relatively low proportion of women in key Co-operative management positions.

Nevertheless Roy Garratt, Co-operative Union Librarian, who is often asked to judge a Programme Competition in Manchester District, says he has consistently noted the prevalence of Co-operative themes, and the number of speakers from societies under whose auspices the Guilds operate.

In contrast, Mrs. Joyce Trickey has strong views on the Co-operative aspect of the Guild today. She was a CWG member from 1948 to 1972, and in 1981 joined the newly formed branch in Chester. She recalls how locally the original Guild took a great interest in the society, 'and was the cause of many a

242

lively Quarterly Meeting, and was a link between the local Board of Management and members. I know, as a member of the Board, their views were treated with respect'. Mrs. Trickey's branch in Chester was closed down in 1972, when the increasing age of members made it difficult to get committee members. Mrs. Trickey says she was the youngest member when she joined that Guild in 1948 (aged 30) and the youngest when the Branch closed in 1972 (aged 54). She is the only member of the old Guild who has joined the new Guild formed in 1981 by the Birkenhead Member Relations Committee. She writes that to her, the new Branch is

> *a cross between an Old People's Club and a Townswomen's Guild — it is not a Co-op Guild as I understand it (maybe I'm prejudiced) and does not function the same — very few of the members are even members of the society. In the old Guild the emphasis was on education, we were always kept well acquainted with current affairs, trade matters local and national, and loyalty to the local society was of paramount importance. Of course we cannot expect the latter to apply today as under CRS there is no encouragement to be loyal. We have no stamps even now. In Chester .... we have to travel about 15 miles to the nearest Departmental Store .... I know business today is very difficult, and margins are small and the price policy is very keen and inducements for loyalty to the Movement are not easy to find, but I do feel membership should be made worthwhile. The Guilds must ensure, in spite of enlarged and more remote societies, that the principles of Co-operation are maintained.*

This is in complete contrast to the early years of the Guild when the relationship with local Co-operative shops was close. Also relevant is the move from small shops where communication between customers was encouraged to supermarkets and hypermarkets which are inevitably more impersonal.

This section is not trying to "blame" the Co-operative Movement for the Guild's decline, but to recognise the relationship between the problems faced by the small auxiliary and the great Movement to which it relates. The report[1] of The Working Party on Auxiliary Development presented to the Education Convention was not implemented due to lack of finance. But the Co-operative Union continues to support the Guild financially, and in many other ways and Peter Gormley, Member Education Development Officer (Auxiliaries) and other Union officials are also involved.

Advice and support given to the Guild goes beyond help with programme materials. For example, during the centenary year, with its many events to be organised and co-ordinated, Angela Hardy was "lent" to the Guild by the Union's Education Department to help with the administrative work.

The CWS is also generous with its financial support and the 1982 Annual Report to Congress of the Education Executive says a welcome feature of the year, for the auxiliaries, has been the support and help provided by Co-operative Retail Services (CRS) which contrasted with the national trend of reduced or static provision of grants and facilities. It does not seem likely that the Guild can win any more support from the traditional Co-operative Movement. Nevertheless if the Guild can adjust to the challenge of the new Co-operative Movement in a more positive way than it met the challenge of the new feminist movement, it could be of benefit to old and new. It would also fit in with founder member Mary Lawrenson's early plans for women's productive Co-operatives discussed in Chapter 1.

New Forms of Co-operation
December 1981 saw the publication of two items about the "new" Co-operatives. The Co-operative Union published a leaflet setting out its interest in the "new forms of Co-operation which are emerging in Britain including workers' Co-operatives, housing Co-operatives, credit Co-operatives, food Co-operatives and other common ownership enterprises". Where possible and appropriate, it says, the Union has given advice and information to such societies on legal, procedural or other matters. The leaflet also identifies other sources of help to the new Co-operatives such as the Co-operative Development Agency.

The "Co-operative News" reported that the First Neighbourhood Co-operative Nursery based in East London was in contact with the CWG, and that members of the new Co-operative attended a social of the Hoe Street, Walthamstow, Branch whilst guildswomen had offered to help at the nursery and collect toys. A year after this report the authors spoke to Councillor Anne Smith, one of the organisers of the Co-operative. The community day nursery is still operating, although not yet able to open for full days. The Co-operative has 22 members, but larger numbers use the centre and attend meetings.

What are the current links with the Guild? Head Office helps them by duplicating the information they need to get to parents and members. Members of the Co-operative Nursery have talked about their aims and objectives at CWG branch meetings. Anne Smith told us how much she felt she had benefited from mixing with the older women from the local Guild branch, 'women who have done it all before', as she described them. The experience and expertise of guildswomen is obviously valued by those running the Co-operative Nursery in East London.

As a result of the current disastrous economic climate and consequent unemployment there is an upsurge in new Co-operatives. Women faced with no employment opportunities are taking initiatives in their local communities. It may be a response to discrimination in employment, or sometimes be related to the increasing number of single parent families unable to manage on social security. Encouragement of local Co-operatives by the Local Authority is often part of a policy of inner city regeneration. Examples are small Co-operatives involved in cleaning, typing, jewellery, selling food, selling fast food or producing children's wear — usually with creche facilities as an integral part of the operation. They face problems: for example, how can they produce competitively priced children's clothing *and* pay decent wages — is there the danger of the 'sweat shop' resurfacing? These self-help groups and small retail and producer Co-operatives need help — can the CWG share their experiences and in so doing regenerate the Guild as well as helping to spread Co-operation in line with their very earliest aim?

The Co-operative Family
The early chapters in the book have shown how family connections influenced so many of the Guild's earliest pioneers. Here we look — impressionistically and not systematically — at the effect of growing up in a home where mum was an active member of the Guild.

Judy Kirby is a freelance journalist who whilst not politically involved 'could never vote Tory'. She wrote to say she would like to help with our book 'as I am sure my mother would want me to'. Her mother, Elsie Kirby, has been an active member of Canning Town branch for a great number of years

The Guild played quite a part in our lives as my mother was quite political in her way and had been part of the abortion law reform movement (even though she had 11 children of her own).

245

Of these 11, two died at birth, one as a child, and I was by far
the youngest, having been born when my mother was well over
40.

She also recalls her mother telling her, when she was still a
child, that women should not be forced to have children they did
not want. She remembers being taken on marches and to
meetings as a kid, as well as going on the regular "chara"
outings to the sea. These could be quite boozy affairs, but they
only drank Guinness! She talked about her mother's
compassion and how the Guild played an educational and
intellectual role for women who had no education, making
them aware of problems outside the home.

Mrs. Lydia Barlow of Birmingham who will be 90 in the
Guild's centenary year, joined the Guild in 1933. Her mother
was the first member to receive the Freedom of the Branch
(granted after 25 years of service), and she herself, in 1957, was
the last member to receive that honour. (Honouring members
for long service in this way was discontinued because with an
ageing membership it was felt to be becoming too
commonplace. It is therefore interesting to note that in 1981
Congress passed a resolution calling for the introduction of 'an
Honorary Membership Scheme for long standing members no
longer able to take part in meetings'.) That Mrs. Barlow and her
mother shared this distinction in this particular way is perhaps
unique, but many other daughters followed their mothers into
the Guild.

Mrs. Gladys Lynam from Alfreton, Derby, was a Guild
member for 40 years until the branch closed for lack of a
meeting room. She wrote that she came of a good Co-operative
family, her railwayman father having "got a pittance from the
railway Lords."

Mrs. Joyce Trickey wrote from Chester to say that her mother
was a founder member of the Chester Branch in 1920-21, and
she and her sister were members. She joined in 1948 when her
mother was presented with the Freedom of the Guild and her
sister was Branch Treasurer; she later became Assistant
Secretary, resigning after 6 years in office in order to care for her
mother. Mrs. Trickey points out

I could never understand why other members did not bring their
daughters into the organisation.

Some, of course, did. Norah Willis is one of today's leading
women co-operators. Her mother, who was a founder member

of Barkingside Branch, took her to Branch meetings when she was a child, and she joined the Guild herself when she married. Mrs. Willis recalls how her mother would often talk of what was done in the 1930s and 1940s, and that her mother had felt that much of what had been achieved was being whittled away, leaving younger women with a lot to fight for, still. Other guildswomen who wrote to us had come from Co-operative families.

Mrs. Morfydd Owen of Falmouth, born in 1904, was influenced by her mother and her mother-in-law; she has been an active guild member for 56 years. She writes

At an early age I knew the value of the Co-op. divi, having a mother who was a very strong believer in the Co-op stores. What a heritage they handed to me when they took me to the Guild in 1926. It was at the Guild I learned the wisdom that has been my inspiration even at this age now.

She saw that the Guild was different from other movements, especially in the fight for maternity benefits, and she is proud that 'still the movement fights, especially for women's rights'. Mrs. Owen is obviously keen to encourage young members, and she says she has enjoyed every Guild meeting to this day, especially when she sees young members come with their news and outlook. She says she feels

honoured and proud to be a Guild member, and that she feels she has helped to build up a movement in which young members look at us with astonishment and she hopes to encourage them to follow in 'our footsteps'.

But growing up in a Co-operative family is no guarantee that Co-operative ideals are passed on. Mrs. Justice of Cheam is certainly herself not a Labour voter but she talked to us, with affectionate admiration, about her mother and the Guild. Her mother joined Worcester Park branch in 1930, from strong moral convictions, linked to those of Mrs. Justice's father who had been 'kicked out of jobs for standing up for the working man.' When Mrs. Justice went along to Branch meetings during the last war she felt there were more middle-class than working-class women. She recalled how everything came from the Co-op — weekly grocery order, coal, milk, and all her clothes. Mrs. Justice's mother, Mrs. Mason, who was born in 1898, joined the Guild in 1935, and obviously regrets the closure of Worcester Park Branch in the 1960s. She writes about the lovely atmosphere and how members helped each other. She felt the Guild gave members the confidence to stand up for their rights.

She recalls the hard life of the old days, when husbands and wives were separated in the workhouse and the difficulties of managing financially. But she also talks of happy days, packing the children on the back seats of coaches for outings, for example. She writes about

sisters sharing troubles and ends, *Oh happy days. A jolly crowd. We didn't have much money but I'm sure we were happier in those days.*

And what about sons of guildswomen? Olive Davies' son became a member of a Co-operative drama group — and then spent a life time earning a living in the theatre.

Two sons of active guildswomen could not be further apart in the political spectrum.

The first is Laurie Pavitt, MP, a member of the Co-operative Party's Parliamentary Group. Talking to him, his commitment to Co-operative ideals, so strong in the household where he grew up, are still with him, as is the moral courage he attributed to his mother's generation over the White Poppy Campaign. He worked as National Secretary to the 18-25 age group auxiliary, the British Federation of Young Co-operators, and as adviser on Co-operative development in Asia before becoming an MP. How does he recall growing up in a Co-operative household? He writes:

My main recollections of a Co-operative household are, of course, so many they would fill a book in themselves. For example, coming home from school at the age of nine or ten I would find the parlour filled with women wearing funny hats, drinking cups of tea provided by my mother who was the National President in 1934. This could be the local district Guild Committee. This was a very important time for my brother, when aged 23, was killed in a cycle accident coming away from a Co-operative Youth Movement event, and the fact that my mother was so fully engaged the following year in Guild affairs helped her to overcome her loss.

Laurie Pavitt's childhood led on to a lifetime devoted to the Co-operative and Labour Movements, and he is now MP for Brent South.

The Conservative MP for Brent North is Dr. Rhodes Boyson. Politically apart, they share a similar background. Dr. Rhodes Boyson wrote to say:

My mother was a member of the Guild for many years, and was President or Chairman of the Haslingden Co-operative Women's Guild for a long period. I was a director of the

The 1975 International Women's Year Service in Westminster Abbey. The Rainbow Flag being carried down the nave flanked by Mrs. Daisy Codd (left) and Mrs. Diane Crook of Head Office Staff.

Delegates foregather for the 1977 Congress at Southport.

Lady Fisher cuts the Rainbow ribbon at the official opening of the Guild Head Office, Walthamstow, in September 1971. Mrs. Florence Tobin, National President, accompanies her.

In a lighter vein. Part of a display of over 100 exquisitely dressed dolls given by Guild Districts as gifts for needy children at the 1970 Scarborough Congress. Below: Members of Darlington branches commandeered the famous Chitty-Chitty Bang-Bang for a parade depicting 150 years of fashion.

Haslingden Co-operative Society for six years and wrote its history in its centenary year.

Some Conclusions

The Guild membership grew from 195 in 1884 to an astounding 87,246 in 1939, falling to 49,222 in 1941. There was a post-war rise to 62,411 in 1949, but it was down to 13,709 in 1981. We have already looked at the decline in relation to the Co-operative Movement and now turn to other contributing factors.

One important strand is that of the role of women in society. The first chapter in this book has looked at the limited opportunities for women during the Guild's first years. It was that lack of opportunity that attracted middle-class women like Margaret Llewelyn Davies and Lilian Harris as well as working-class women to the Guild. Were the problems of recruitment that faced the pioneers more acute than those facing Guild leaders today? Guild literature places strong emphasis on the need to attract younger women to balance the high average age of the current membership. But how young were the earliest recruits? Women married later in life in the 19th century than they do now, and young members may *never* have played a significant part in the CWG. Mrs. Ethel Mewis of Watford, National President in 1979, talked about the age at which women might join the Guild today. Those with young families are not interested, women in their forties whose children are grown up tend to be looking for paid employment, and are unwilling, like so many women, to go to evening meetings for fear of being out alone at night — the mid-fifties are therefore the major age group that could be recruited.

And if younger women are to be recruited, says Norah Willis, existing members will have to forget the past and never say 'we tried that' or 'it did not work'.

Mrs. Mabel Ridealgh, National President 1941-42, member of Parliament 1945-51, and Guild General Secretary 1953-63 suggested several reasons for the loss of members and difficulties of recruitment. 'Women are also able to get about and spread their wings' she said, preparing at the age of 84 for a winter holiday in the Canary Islands.

Women are working, have freer attitudes, new openings and a higher standard of living.

Women have educational opportunities not available before, changing the nature of, and need for, the educational role of the Guild which was of such vital importance at its foundations and

249

indeed until well after the First World War.

Mrs. Joan Mallinson now lives in Putney but she joined the Shepherds Bush Guild in 1945 at the age of 25, before the birth of her first baby and before the 1945 election. She writes:

My background was respectable working-class, first generation grammar school, leaving at matriculation and entering the usual clerical "safe" job. My appreciation of the encouragement of the elder women who trained me to take minutes, speak in public and, at the same time, gave me hints in child rearing remains with me after all these years. To talk with them was to experience living history long before "History Workshop".

Was Mrs. Mallinson's acceptance by older branch members the exception or the rule? Mrs. Joyce Butler was MP for Wood Green from 1955 to 1979. Her support to Guild officers and of Guild campaigns is acknowledged time and again in Guild Annual Reports. She too joined as a young woman, writing:

In the immediate post-war years I was Secretary of the Bowes Park Women's Guild and thoroughly enjoyed it, more particularly as my children were small and I had no worries about bringing them to Guild meetings .... the Guild is still 'ideal for young mothers who so often find — even today — that they are suddenly cut off from effective political activity when their first baby arrives. Unfortunately the present day separation of age groups has also militated against young mothers feeling welcome among older women, and vice versa, unlike the Bowes Park days when older and younger members were able to meet together without undue hassle. In my view, present day age-separation has been rather more responsible for preventing some older Guilds renewing themselves with a natural intake of younger women than the more commonly-held view that younger women cannot manage afternoon meetings because they are out at work.

Jeannette Gould who was Assistant General Secretary from 1978 to 1980 felt there were significant differences between older and younger members; that the older ones were political, younger ones being virtually non-political. Overall, she found a failure within the Guild to see that the world had changed.

This view is shared by Mrs. Olive Waterman from Croydon, who joined the Guild at the age of 30 in 1930. Now, after over 40 years in the Guild and ten years as branch President Mrs. Waterman has resigned. What was the cause of her disillusionment? She writes:

I have come to the reluctant conclusion that it is a waste of time and that members are no longer bothered about such matters.

*Indeed it has actually been said more than once in my Guild,
"We must not be political". Again and again I have stressed the
point that by joining the Guild they have made a political
decision — that is, they have declared themselves to be for Co-
operation rather than competition. It has got me nowhere. In
fact, although it is against the rules, we have members who are
not even shareholders.*

*There is no question but that it is a dying movement and
deserves to be so. The management of the various regions seem
to have become undemocratic and no account is taken of the
wishes of the members. The whole conception of 'Co-operation'
has gone. Whoever heard of an ordinary commercial business
paying dividend to non-shareholders?* **We** *do! Young women
today demand something more positive and relevant to their
own considerable problems. We do not offer them anything ....
But in spite of all the disappointment in recent years, I shall
always remember with gratitude and affection the many
splendid and highly intelligent women of the past who worked so
hard and with such dedication for the principles of the Co-
operative Movement.*

Mrs. Doris Hajou is a District Secretary, living in Cheshunt
and a relative newcomer to the Guild, having joined in 1976
when her Branch was formed by members of the Education
Committee of Enfield Highway Society and local guildswomen
handing out leaflets in the local Co-operative store. They have a
recruiting problem, she writes, saying:

*ours is an evening guild and the climate is such now that ladies
are afraid to venture out at night. Unfortunately the Guild has
got an "older woman's image". I am 55 and some of our
members are younger but some of the Guilds in my District are
celebrating their 84th and 75th birthdays but are not replacing
members who for obvious reasons are leaving.*

Is the difficulty of recruitment linked to factors other than the
changing position of women and changes within the
Co-operative Movement? Would it not be more realistic to look
at the totality of family life than the position of women? The
fact that men and women share more of their leisure, and that
the leisure pattern in itself is more home centred, for example?
When working-class women grasped the opportunity to get out
of the house when the Guild began they were leaving a home full
of a drudgery totally unknown today.

One Guild member, quoted in the book "Life as we have
known it"[2] wrote that most of her lectures and addresses had
been thought out 'When my hands have been busy in household

duties, in the wash tub, when baking or doing out my rooms', and Virginia Woolf, having been an observer at the 1913 Conference writes in the same book that whilst trying to imagine the lives of the women speaking at Congress:

> *One could not be Mrs. Giles of Durham because one's body had never stood at the wash tub, one's hands had never wrung and scrubbed and chopped up whatever meat it may be that makes a miner's supper .... They did not stroll through the house and say — that cover must go to the wash, or those sheets need changing. They plunged their arms in hot water and scrubbed the clothes themselves. In consequence their bodies were thick set and muscular, their hands were large, and they had the slow emphatic gestures of people who were often stiff and fall tired in a heap on hardbacked chairs.*

Now, for many, that drudgery is over and the home a place for shared leisure and a joint interest in home making. Joyce Mallinson tells how she came to live in Putney in 1954, after 9 years in the Guild and:

> *tried to organise a Branch on this Local Authority Estate. More married women were working outside the home (to help pay higher rents and buy the new consumer goods!). Few had time for meetings and leisure activities were home centred to make their flats as desirable as the television was suggesting. This coincided with a new prosperity where the chain stores were more attractive than the Co-op store, loyalty to which was becoming eroded.*

If the relative attraction of the meeting room compared to home had shifted, was it because the Guild had ceased to be fighting the battles younger women wish to fight — or are young women choosing to fight elsewhere?

Many of the early campaigns the Guild fought and won are behind us; better maternity facilities, abortion, free contraception, a national health service, and despite a 1982 resolution calling for more women to be represented on public bodies, the situation is far different than when that kind of plea first appeared on Congress agenda, albeit not different enough.

Sheila Rowbotham in her book "Hidden from History" says that women fight for positions from which they can change things.[3] Once there (for example, on a Committee or in Parliament), success is defined in terms of recognition and approval of the very power structure they opposed. But this does not appear to be true of the Guild as a whole or its leaders who have held to radical, and often unpopular, policies throughout its first hundred years.

Nevertheless, with the arrival of the 1945-51 Labour Governments and to a slightly lesser extent in 1964-1970 and 1974-1979 the Guild saw many of its battles won. Congress resolutions became policy in a way early Guild leaders may well not have ever imagined possible.

Mrs. Joan Mallinson, quoted earlier, writes that
the irony is that the Guild was the victim of its own achievement. It contributes vastly to the opening of opportunities for women. She writes that *she does not feel she could have taken her chance to take courses at London University's Extra Mural and External Departments without 'the solid groundwork I'd learned in that shabby Methodist Hall earlier on'.* However, she goes on to say: *The Guild seemed irrelevant — it looked as if many of the objects had been achieved with the acceptance of the welfare state by all political parties ... younger women saw a different battleground.*

It is a further complicated aspect of this story that the battles won are now having to be fought again, as unemployment soars, the value of social security benefits is eroded and the level of social services, especially the NHS, decline rapidly — all under attack by a government led, irony of ironies, by Britain's first woman Prime Minister.

Mrs. Joan Powell of Hyde Co-operative Women's Guild, Manchester, who joined the Guild in 1942 when she was 23, writes that what interested her most during her Guild membership was
campaigning when I was younger — we were a campaigning Organisation then.

Mrs. Edna Owens of Birmingham was a guildswoman from 1950-1955 and says:
As a member of the Women's Guild I found it a stimulating afternoon quite a cut above the average females' afternoon groups .... Something has happened and quite a lot of the magic has gone. It seems to be more loyalty than anything that holds Guilds together now. After a break I rejoined the National Guild of Co-operators and fail to see why the Women's Guilds wish to remain exclusive.

Mrs. Norah Willis is convinced there is still a role for the Guild, as she told us there are issues only women know how to fight for. This remark is perhaps an echo of the Guild's 1976 Annual Report which pointed out that founder members of the

Guild lacked education and leisure but "they fought tenaciously for what is now taken for granted. Today there is vandalism, pollution, unemployment, threat of a nuclear war and hunger in the third world, to spur us on to renewed efforts to achieve our aims and objects".

One problem for any organisation is the relationship between branches and Head Office. We have already discussed the fact that branches seemed readier to collect for charities than support Head Office, a characteristic shared with the Townswomen's Guild, according to its Jubilee History.[4] Muriel Russell, J.P., formerly Women's Officer with ICA, commented on this aspect — a "them" and "us" feeling.

Laurie Pavitt, MP, an affectionate observer of the Guild for so long, talks of personal power struggles and even feuds, of rivalry between sections, as well as between Branch, District and Section — suggesting a clash of "strong personalities". This of course would be equally true of any lively, radical, democratic organisation. He talked with admiration of the Guild's structure — 'built to last', he said.

If there are battles still to be won, is the Guild, despite a declining and ageing membership, fit enough to fight? Perhaps from self-doubts, or for fear of competition from other women's organisations there has been a diversification which seems to have taken over from early stress on education for citizenship and Co-operation. The handicraft work, for example, gives an enormous amount of pleasure, and goods made are usually given to a most worthy cause, but the organisation and judging of such a large number of competitions may have well used resources which in a period of constraint could have been better deployed.

Some members make no mention of this side of Guild life. For example, Mrs. May Truscott of Plymouth, now aged 81, who joined the Guild in 1929 at the age of 28, wrote to say of her membership of Devonport Branch:

The Co-operative Guild appealed to me as a woman where I could meet and join with other women like myself. A Co-operator, a democrat, a housewife and mother. Meeting other women interested in the working and development of the Co-operative Movement. To help create conscious Co-operation and to spread the knowledge of Co-operative Principles. To assist toward universal application to human affairs. To enjoy speakers on all subjects, and lectures, and to enter in healthy discussions. Keeping the meetings alive by enthusiasm and dedication, which could be presided over by a factory worker, a teacher, an office worker or housewife. Nothing to prevent her wearing the Presidential Chain. To enjoy a fellowship. To laugh, to build, to serve for truth and justice. This is their purpose and their aim.

Mrs. Doris Smith, who is 88 joined the Guild in 1935 in St. Ann's, Nottingham and told of her interest in the Guild in lighter vein. Whilst mentioning being Secretary, President and Congress delegate, she writes about handicraft classes, entertaining, elocution, and a concert party which entertained in hospitals and clubs around Nottingham. Mrs. Smith also writes, as did many guildswomen of the Branch Birthday Party.

Our Guild birthday rally are events I shall remember as hard days work but great fun to see all the guests arrive and welcome them. Also to receive the Board of Directors. We have catered for 200 visitors in days gone by.

Mrs. Morfydd Owen from Falmouth, looking back on guild membership that began in 1929 when she was 25, says:

I cannot put into words the memorable comradeship in good and sorrowful years.

Yet Olive Davies of West Sussex says of younger women joining,

most join thinking we are cheaper than the Women's Institute or Townswomen's Guild. Many come and go. They were more keen then than now.

Mrs. Mary Newman who is Branch Secretary at Wallsend, joined the Guild in 1946 when she was 32, and recalls, from her 36 years of membership, entertaining wounded soldiers after the war, fancy dress and competitions but whilst looking forward to the Branch's 99th Birthday in 1983 says:

things are not the same now, we have all merged together.

An organisation that meant so much, even in such different ways, to so many people must still have a role to play. Mrs. Ethel Mewis feels there is no quick answer, but that there cannot be a good Guild branch without good officers, and Miss Violet Horlock, District Secretary from Manningtree, Essex, who joined the Guild in 1968 when she was already 60, but has had 15 years full of activity and interest, is also concerned with leadership, writing:

How difficult I feel it is going to be to get officers to take over the leadership in time to come. Please be like myself, never be afraid to take the plunge, one will never please everyone.

Given the diversity of activity and the link with the Co-operative Movement the Guild does stay different from other women's organisations. But it does still work with them — as it began to do much earlier. The Guild is represented on the National Commission for Women and, more important in its history, with the National Joint Committee of Working Women's organisations which brings together women from the Co-operative, Trades Union and Labour Movements. The Guild used to be affiliated to the National Council of Women but left, feeling the co-ordinating bodies were 'all doing the same things,' to quote Kathleen Kempton. Several Committees where guildswomen used to meet with representatives of other women's organisations have disappeared (e.g. B.S.I. Women's Advisory Committee).

Kathleen Kempton talks of the way in which more specialist groups have taken over some of the issues on which the Guild was closely involved — she gave Child Poverty Action Group and the National Council for Civil Liberties as examples. The Guild is still associating itself with new co-ordinating bodies, and has recently become interested in the national organisation for Community Associations. There are also women's groups linked to the Co-operative Movement that are not necessarily linked to the CWG. Norwest Pioneers Co-operative Society, for instance, has a Ladies Club which was formed after a Guild branch closed, initiated by 2 or 3 staff from the local grocery branch store.

The Guild has enabled many women to do much they would otherwise not have achieved. That could come from skills passed on, confidence instilled and in an even more practical way! Norah Willis recalls she could not have attended a College Course if branch members had not met her children from school and cooked regularly for her family. This kind of mutual self-help and support must, surely, have a future in a society where individualism, competition and privatisation are so stressed.

Joan Mallinson wrote that Guild members were always a minority of working-class women 'but their influence on the Co-operative Retail Movement, the Labour Party and the work they did so competently for both movements was out of all proportion to their membership'.

Joyce Butler sees its value in the way the Guild represented the needs of working women generally, but especially those not eligible for membership of other weighty pressure groups. She also sees the Guild as more effective than the Labour Party's women's sections and more independent and international than many other labour/socialist groups.

This international role of the Guild has, perhaps, been too little stressed in this book. The extent to which Guild members travelled, individually or in groups, and welcomed women from all over the world to Congress, meetings, Head Office and their homes is evidence of this internationalism. Joyce Butler mentions the practical side to the main Congress resolutions on International issues and on peace. Their independence is shown in early battles such as when they refused the Co-operative Union grant rather than compromise their principles and change their divorce policy. Another example is that whilst accepting hospitality from Eastern Europe they did not hesitate to pass critical resolutions as in 1956 deploring Soviet intervention in Hungary.

Some last comments on the Guild before passing on to the Second century. First on the competence of the Guild as an organisation. The 1958 Congress was held at Blackpool with 1,038 delegates and 2,000 at the Civic Reception. There was a high standard of debate and business-like administration and visitors from home and abroad told the officers again and again, how rare it was to see such a large Congress so ably conducted, and delegates so well behaved, and knowledgeable of Congress procedures, so the 1959 Annual Report informs us. No doubt the 1983 Congress will be equally impressive.

Peter Gormley, the Co-operative Union's Member Education Development Officer (Auxiliaries) writes:

I personally feel that the CWG still fulfills a needed service for its members, and has a valid role to play. The threats, challenges and discrimination facing the world, specific countries, and sections of the Community, which faced the Guild in previous decades still exist, and the task of confronting them still remains.

One way in which the Guild still helps those whom it has helped since the early days is the help extended to strikers. In the early years, the help was varied, including collection of money and offering holidays to the children of strikers. Now, it is the Guild office offering office facilities to local strike committees which is the clearest expression of this continued concern for comrades in trouble.

And lastly on the Guild's political role, Joyce Butler writes:

In retrospect I feel that the mere fact that the Guild existed and continued to work through increasingly difficult times was more

important than anything else. While, undoubtedly, its special
campaigns were valuable, it is as a symbol of the whole Co-
operative idea that the Guild has its special place in history. And
I am sure that for many Labour Members of Parliament,
particularly, perhaps, those from the industrial areas and the
North of England, the Women's Guild was their point of
reference to the whole Co-operative philosophy. They knew
their own constituency Guilds, they knew the women in them,
and from them and from the local Co-op shop they had a better
idea of what Co-operation was all about than from any amount
of reading Co-op pamphlets or books.

Mrs. Olive Waterman, who resigned from the Guild at the age
of 82 because of its lack of commitment to Co-operative
principles shares the view of Lady Fisher, who deeply regrets
the way in which the Co-operative Movement is no longer an
equal partner in the Labour Party — Trade Union — Co-
operative alliance. Mrs. Waterman wrote to say:

To me the Co-operative Movement is an inseparable part of the
socialist movement. I do not see how anyone can think
otherwise.

The Future

As this book is written, plans for Centenary celebrations are
being made in branches up and down the country, as well as at
Head Office. A service in Westminster Abbey, to be attended by
Her Majesty the Queen, the Centenary Congress, Centenary
souvenirs, Centenary Pageant, Picnic Day, Centenary Contests
and this very book are part of national plans. Church services,
decorative flower beds and banners form part of local
arrangements. The second century of Guild enterprise and
initiative has begun.

Norah Willis, active guildswoman, member of the Co-
operative Union Central Executive and president elect of the
1983 Co-operative Union Congress, looks with good heart to
the future. She identifies two major challenges ahead. One is the
rapid reduction of retail Co-operative Societies. The current
plan is for only 25 societies in two years, which means fewer
places for lay people and a role for the Guild in ensuring that
guildswomen continue to make their valuable contribution to
Co-operative development and management in the coming
years as they have done in the past.

Indeed, Norah Willis feels that the reduced democratic
participation within the Co-operative Movement makes this
role ever important, to ensure that member participation and

democratic rights are maintained.

She is equally concerned at the way in which the social services are being whittled away, providing the Guild with an opportunity to reassert its past authority in the area of family welfare.

We end by looking hopefully into the future. The overall aim of this book has been to enable Guild members and others to share the excitement of the foundation of the Guild, to appreciate the progress made in this first hundred years, and be aware of the challenges of the future.

We hope the book has given the same sense of involvement to its readers as it has to the authors, and will do to future historians of the Co-operative Women's Guild.

Notes to Chapter 9

1. Co-operative Union Ltd., Report of the Working Party on Auxiliary Development and Reorganisation (Manchester 1981).
2. M.L. Davies, Life as we have known it. (originally published in 1931 and reprinted by Virago Press 1977).
3. S. Rowbotham, Hidden from History (1974).
4. M. Stott, Organisation Woman: The Story of the National Union of Townswomen's Guilds (1978). See also O. Banks, Faces of Feminism (Oxford 1981).

THE STORY OF THE MRS. BEN JONES GUILD CONVALESCENT FUND

The story of the Ben Jones Guild Convalescent Fund is told in the April 1958 issue of "Woman's Outlook" as follows:

'One of the greatest ambitions of Mrs. Ben Jones was that the Women's Co-operative Guild should have resources for helping its members — busy housewives and mothers — in times of illness. Mrs. Jones knew that many of her fellow-guildswomen, when they became ill, struggled with looking after their families for as long as they could before they were eventually forced to stay in bed.

More often than not they would get up again before they were fully recovered, to carry on looking after their households: they could not afford to go away for a rest and change of air, and to have help in their homes while they were away.

Mrs. Jones, a pioneer member of the guild, was national president for six years, and an able and tireless worker; she gained the deep respect and affection of all who knew her and worked with her. Unfortunately, she died when she was only 44 years of age, in 1895, and the Guild suffered a sad loss with her death.

To perpetuate her memory, and to help fulfil her ambition, the Mrs. Ben Jones Convalescent Fund was started, and Mr. Jones gave £100 to it as the first donation.

Since the start of the fund in 1895, many thousands of guildswomen have gained benefit from it. The object is to provide a change of air for convalescents where it is necessary, and the fund works in several ways.

It can provide grants to pay for board and lodgings and fares, in the case of members who have friends or relatives willing to receive them if the cost of their food is paid for.

In cases of convalescence after serious illness, or where medical supervision and nursing are necessary, members can stay at Co-operative convalescent homes. Where convalescent homes and personal friends are not available, guild members living by the sea or in the country are often willing to receive convalescents for a small payment.

The fund will also assist with grants for fares alone, and with expenses incurred by the need to have someone in to care for the home during the convalescent's absence.

The fund benefits in many ways by the special efforts of guildswomen, apart from its normal means of income from donations and subscriptions.

Often proceeds from branch social activities, such as raffles, concerts, entertainments and harvest sales are donated to the fund; freedom members of guild branches, normally exempt from paying subscriptions, often provide donations. Some societies, too, make donations annually.

All contributions are pooled and the fund is for the assistance of every member of the guild.

The fund committee, composed of all the sectional secretaries and the general secretary, meets annually at Congress, and also considers all applications for benefit at intervals throughout the year. Applications are submitted on behalf of members by their branches.

At the Guild's annual congress before and after business, guildswomen from all parts of the country crowd round the "Evergreen Book" which is kept in memory of former guildswomen.

It was started in 1903 and the first name entered is that of Mrs. Ben Jones, herself. Today there are more than 4,000 entries. The book is kept at the Guild's head office, but is usually on show at Congress.

First secretary of the Mrs. Ben Jones Convalescent Fund was Mrs. Abbott, to whom the fund owes its sound business-like foundation. She resigned in 1905 and Miss Catherine Webb was elected to continue the good work. She resigned in 1930, and was followed by Mrs. M. J. Pidgeon.

The present secretary, Mrs. Mary Corrigan has been secretary since 1941, when Mrs. Pidgeon resigned.

But of course the story did not end in 1958. Annual Reports each carry at least a page of information about the Fund and its accounts. The fund has always been in a healthy state. At the 1958 Congress Mrs. Jones' son presented to the Fund a gold brooch given by the WCG to mark her six years as National President. Fund Secretary Mrs. Mary Corrigan wrote that it was a welcome link with the Guild, and that 'it is also a reminder that in an age of so much destruction ordinary women, quietly and without fuss, keep alive the spirit of self-help and mutual aid which inspired the early guild pioneers'.

The 1962 Annual Report looked at the income and expenditure of the Fund in the years 1941 to 1962. Subscriptions amounted to £32,647 and £25,085 was paid out. The total working costs of the Fund were only £3,900 for the period, including printing, stationery and the Secretary's Honorarium (only £109 in 1961 and a mere £200 in 1981).

The fund had its problems. In 1963 the Annual Report notes the decline of Hostesses willing to look after convalescent members — there were only three, in Blackpool and Ramsgate that year. It meant that members often had to find their own accommodation, often with friends and relatives. This 1963 Report was Mary Corrigan's last. She writes that her feelings were mixed, in relinquishing the post, but that the heavy daily mail, travelling and speaking the work entailed, had been too much for her — it was an office she took up in 1941. Mary Corrigan was replaced by Mrs. Ellen Brooks who was Chairman during Mary Corrigan's 23 years as Secretary. Mrs. Gladys Robertson took over as Secretary in 1973, and her period of office ended in 1976. In that year, the fund's donations were £705, but interest on invested funds of over £11,000 gave a total income of just over £2,000, with the demand for grants particularly low that year at £140. The Annual Report is used in 1976 to remind members that the endowed beds in three convalescent homes are under used in winter. In 1977 Elsie Lawn was elected Fund Secretary — it is interesting to note that whereas no one wanted to apply for the post of General Secretary, eight applied to be Secretary of the Fund. In the next year Elsie Lawn became ill and Mrs. Jessie Anderson took over, becoming Secretary of the Fund in 1979. Although the 1978 Report stressed that it was important for branches to be kept informed of the Ben Jones Fund work, and pointed out that Council members — all of whom are Sectional Secretaries — should talk to branches, the Fund was in a healthy state.

The 1981 Annual Report shows payments of £1,343 of which £523 were grants to members and £600 was a payment for the Endowment of a bed at the Mary McArthur Home. Expenses totalled £625 giving total payments of £1,968, compared to receipts of £2,486 (of which £727 was in the form of donations). The Fund had over £17,000 invested. In her Report on 1981 (during which year the grant to members was raised from £20 to £30), Honorary Secretary Mrs. Jessie Anderson expresses pleasure that the Fund was in a sound financial position, but regretted that so many donations are sent in memory of members who have passed away.

The Ben Jones Fund is a good example of the self-help and support side of the Guild's work. It might be questioned now whether the £17,000 capital (compared with the £20,000 capital of the whole Guild in a year when their current income and expenditure was over £29,000), is the best use of scarce resources. Nevertheless the Fund is an enduring symbol of the Guild's humanitarianism.

BIOGRAPHICAL NOTES

This Appendix gives brief notes of the lives of some former and contemporary guildswomen. More information about those marked ★ is given in the "Dictionary of Labour Biography" edited by J. Bellamy and J. Saville (Macmillan. Vol.I 1972; Vol.II 1974).

Dowager Lady Alice Acland ★

Born in 1849, Mrs. Acland (later Lady Acland) lectured widely with her husband on Co-operation. She started the Women's Corner in the "Co-operative News" in 1883 which led directly to the foundation of the Guild. She was the first Secretary of the Guild but retired in 1884 due to ill health. She was National President from 1884-1886 and was presented with the Freedom of the Guild in May 1931. She died in 1936.

Eleanor Barton ★

Born in 1872, Mrs. Barton joined the Brightside & Carbrook Co-operative Society, Sheffield. She was a Director from 1917-1925 and served on its Education Committee from 1917-1925. She joined the Guild in 1901 and was Secretary of the Hillsbury Branch for 17 years; a member of the Central Committee from 1912 and in 1920, National Treasurer in 1913 and National President in 1914. She was Assistant Secretary of the Guild from 1921 until 1925 when she was elected General Secretary holding that post until retiring in 1937. She was also a Sheffield Councillor and stood three times as a Parliamentary candidate. She was the first woman to become a Director of the Co-operative Newspaper Publishing Society, now Co-operative Press. A committed pacifist, she drafted the Guild's Peace Pledge Card. On leaving England to live with relatives in New Zealand she wrote regularly to the Guild, the letters being read at Congress and printed in the Bulletin. A Memorial Fund was set up after her death in 1960.

Margaret Bondfield ★

Whilst better known for her work with the Labour Party, as an MP and as the first woman to hold government office, as well as a Trade Union official, she also made a vital contribution to the Guild. In 1912 the Central Committee set up a sub-committee to watch and promote new legislation, and Margaret Bondfield was its chairman. This Committee played a major role in the maternity campaigns. She joined the Guild in 1911 and her most important role was her involvement in pressing for improved maternity care, and for a Ministry of Health.

Joyce Butler

Mrs. Butler was born in 1910 and joined the Bowes Park Branch of the CWG in 1946, later moving to the Wood Green Branch. She held the office of branch secretary, and went on to become Labour and Co-operative MP for Wood Green from 1955 to 1979.

Cecily Cook ★

Mrs. Cook was a keen suffragette and trade unionist. She joined the Earlsfield Branch of the CWG in the 1920s, later moving to the Marylebone Branch. She worked with Clement Attlee in general elections between the wars, and for the ILP between 1924 and 1932. Her responsibilities with the ILP included preparing weekly notes for speakers and she also wrote extensively. She worked in the Head Office of the Guild from 1933-1938, but following her defeat in the election for General Secretary she was asked to leave, returning as the elected General Secretary in 1940. She was awarded an OBE in 1943. She retired from the post of General Secretary in 1953 and was granted the Freedom of the Guild in 1954. In 1951 she became President of the ICWG. She is remembered by members as an intellectual; an able woman with a keen eye for young guildswomen with leadership potential. A Memorial Fund was set up after her death in 1962.

Olive Davies
Born in 1897, Mrs. Davies joined the Guild in 1928 when her husband was an active trade unionist. She became branch chairman in 1930 and was elected to the Education Committee of Watford Co-operative Society. In 1944 she was the first woman to be appointed as a full time Education Officer, of the Watford Co-operative Society, an office she already held on a voluntary basis. On retirement to Sussex, Mrs. Davies remained in the Guild, and became District Secretary, a post held until 1981.

A Honora Enfield ★
Miss Enfield was born in 1882 and went to Somerville College, Oxford, even before women were awarded degrees. In 1917 she became private secretary to Margaret Llewelyn Davies and was elected as General Secretary in 1922. She was particularly active and effective in the Guild's campaigns for improved maternity services. She was involved in the setting up of the ICWG in 1921, and was its Secretary from 1921. She left the Guild in 1925 to continue her work with the International Guild. She was a gifted linguist and a committed pacifist. She died in 1935.

Baroness Fisher, JP
Doris Fisher was born in 1919 and joined the CWG in Birmingham; her mother was caretaker of the Northfield Co-operative hall where the branch met. She became Branch Secretary and later District Secretary, Sectional Secretary and then a member of the Central Committee. She was National President 1961/2. She was a Birmingham Councillor from 1952-1974, and was Labour MP for Ladywood from 1970-1974. She has been a magistrate since 1961 and was a Director of Ten Acres & Stirchley Co-operative Society. She was made a life Peeress in 1974 and is now a junior Whip in the House of Lords. She was a member of the General Medical Council 1974-1979, and a member of Warrington New Town Development Corporation 1974-1981.

Mrs. Caroline S. Ganley, JP
Mrs. Ganley was a product of the suffragette movement. She served as a Director of the London Co-operative Society for 28 years and was its President four times. She was Co-operative MP for Battersea South from 1945-1951. She wrote an outline history of the Guild from 1922-1950 which is in Hull University Library. Laurie Pavitt, MP, who is the source of information for these notes, described her as "one of the truly great co-operators of this century". She died in 1965.

Lilian Harris
Lilian Harris was the daughter of a wealthy Bradford banker, who moved to Kirkby Lonsdale in 1850. It was here that Miss Llewelyn Davies first met and

introduced Miss Harris to the work of the Guild; they remained life-long friends and colleagues. Miss Harris was Cashier of the Guild in 1893, and Assistant Secretary from 1902 until 1921. As well as contributing substantially to the Guild's administration, Miss Harris was the author of articles and papers on economic and social topics. Miss Harris retired from the Guild office in 1921. She died in 1949.

Mrs. Benjamin Jones
In her early life Mrs. Jones lived in Lancashire. Her marriage brought her into close touch with the Co-operative Movement. In 1884 she became Secretary of the Norwood Branch, one of the Guild's first outposts. Mrs. Jones was a member of the first Central Committee and she was the Guild's President from 1886 to 1891. Mrs. Jones died in May 1894. The Mrs. Jones Convalescent Fund described in Appendix I was set up in her memory.

Kathleen Kempton
Kathleen Kempton was born in 1912 and was a member of the Woodcraft Folk at age 13. She joined the St. Helier Branch of the Guild when she was 21. She became Branch President and attended her first Congress in 1938. She was active at District level and joined the Guild office staff in 1944. She became Assistant Secretary in 1953 and was elected General Secretary in 1963. She is to retire from this post at the Centenary Congress in 1983.

Mrs. Mary Lawrenson
Mary Lawrenson was a founder member of the Guild, and its General Secretary from 1885-9. She was a gifted speaker and her inspiring speeches contributed greatly to early branch formation. The Guild set up a 'Comfort Fund' to help her in her declining years. Known to guildswomen as the "Guild Mother", she died in 1943 aged 92.

Margaret Llewelyn Davies ★
Margaret Llewelyn Davies was born in 1861. She became Secretary of the Marylebone Branch of the Guild in 1886 and was elected to the Guild's Central Committee in 1888, becoming General Secretary in the following year, a post which she held until her retirement in 1921. Apart from her contribution to the development of the Guild in England, Miss Llewelyn Davies helped to found the International Women's Co-operative Guild in Basle in 1921. Miss Llewelyn Davies retired from the Guild in 1921. She died in 1944, leaving an estate of over £23,000 with bequests which included £1,000 to the International Co-operative Alliance and £500 each to the Peace Pledge Union and the War Resisters International. After her death a Memorial Fund was set up. A Memorial Meeting was held on 15th June 1944 at the CWS Assembly Hall in Leman Street. The July Bulletin described the meeting as 'not a service of mourning not even of great sorrow. Rather that there was a spirit of thanksgiving for a noble life of service and gratitude for the privilege of having known her and shared in the work she had inspired'.

Mrs. Mabel Ridealgh
Mrs. Ridealgh was born in 1898 and joined the Guild in 1920, in Enfield in North London. She immediately became an active member and was National President in 1941/2 at the age of only 44. She worked with Labour MPs during the war and from 1945 to 1950 was MP for Ilford North. She was General Secretary of the Guild from 1953 to 1963. She travelled widely and

represented the Guild on the National Joint Committee of Working Women until 1970. She remains a member of her local branch and although ill health prevents her from attending its meetings, takes a keen interest in the branch as well as in the Guild nationally.

Muriel Russell, JP

Mrs. Russell was born in 1917 and joined the Ponders End Branch in 1943. She spent a year studying at the Co-operative College. She was elected to the Board of the Enfield Highway Co-operative Society in 1948 and remains a member. She became a JP in 1950 and from 1965 to 1978 held the post of Women's Officer with the International Co-operative Alliance. She has been a member of the Southern Sectional Board of the Co-operative Union since 1973 and is now a member of the Guild's South East Section Committee.

Miss Catherine Webb

Miss Webb was born in 1859. She founded and became the first Secretary of the Guild's Battersea Branch. She chaired the Guild's first conference in 1886. Miss Webb pressed for the participation of women in Co-operative administration. She became a member of the Central Board of the Co-operative Union. Miss Webb wrote the Guild history, ''The Woman with the Basket''. She died in 1947.

Mrs. Norah Willis

Mrs. Willis was born in 1924 and joined South Hainault Branch of the Guild in 1945. She was Branch Secretary within a year, and went on to hold all offices at branch, district and sectional level except that of Sectional Secretary. She spent five years as an NEC member and was National Vice President in 1968/9. She is a member of the Central Executive of the Co-operative Union and Chairman of its Development Committee. She is Chairman of London Region CRS. A former Essex County Councillor, Norah Willis has been Chairman of London Transport Users' Consultative Committee, and is a member of Barkingside Branch of the Guild. In 1983 Mrs. Willis presides over the Co-operative Union Congress.

Mrs. Vaughan Nash

Mrs. Vaughan Nash (nee Shore Smith) became friends with Miss Llewelyn Davies when they attended Co-operative meetings together in East London in the 1880s. Miss Llewelyn Davies referred to her as 'friend and counsellor'. Mrs. Vaughan Nash succeeded Amy Sharp as editor of the ''Corner'' in 1896. Mrs. Nash played an important part in interpreting the Guild's role in its early days. According to Catherine Webb, 'she wrote much of its earlier literature, and brought out the significance of women as consumers'.

SOME FACTS ABOUT THE GUILD

Membership

Year	Number of Members	Number of Branches
1891-1892	4-5,000	98
1899-1900	12,809	273
1909-1910	25,942	521
1919-1920	44,500	783
1929-1930	66,566	1395
1935	77,807	1615
1939	87,246	1819
1945	51,392	1671
1950	59,666	1574
1955	52,914	1640
1960	46,495	1442
1965	35,619	1298
1970 (Postal Strike)		
1971	26,059	946
1975	21,029	761
1980	15,645	618
1981	13,709	578

National Presidents with years of office, and Congress at which they presided.
(Annual Congresses did not commence until 1893.)

Years	Name	Congress
1884 & 1885	Mrs. Alice S.Acland	—
1886 to 1892	Mrs. Benjamin Jones	—
1892/93	Miss E. A.Tournier	Leicester
1893/94	Mrs. Ashworth	Doncaster
1894/95	Mrs. Ashworth	London
1895/96	Mrs. Adams	Burnley
1896/97	Mrs. Bury	Sunderland
1897/98	Miss Reddish	Derby
1898/99	Mrs. Carr	Plymouth
1899/1900	Mrs. Adam Deans	Woolwich
1900/01	Mrs. Hodgett	Blackpool
1901/02	Mrs. Boothman	Newcastle
1902/03	Mrs. Green	Lincoln
1903/04	Mrs. McBlain	Gloucester
1904/05	Mrs. Bury	Sheffield
1905/06	Mrs. Gasson	Ipswich
1906/07	Mrs. Carr	Darlington
1907/08	Mrs. Hodgett	Burton-on-Trent
1908/09	Mrs. Bury	Oldham
1909/10	Miss Gration	Oxford
1910/11	Mrs. Harris	Bristol
1911/12	Mrs. Blair	Hull
1912/13	Mrs. Wimhurst	Newcastle
1913/14	Mrs. Essery	Birmingham

1914/15	Mrs. Eleanor Barton	Liverpool
1915/16	Mrs. Found	London
1916/17	Mrs. Wilkins	Torquay
1917/18	Mrs. Booth	Bradford
1918/19	Mrs. J. Hood	Middlesbrough
1919/20	Mrs. Williams	Derby
1920/21	Mrs. Ferguson	Manchester
1921/22	Mrs. Dewsbury	Portsmouth
1922/23	Mrs. Prosser	Cardiff
1923/24	Mrs. Allen	Leeds
1924/25	Mrs. Matthews	Cambridge
1925/26	Mrs. Webster	Newcastle
1926/27	Mrs. Bird, JP	Leicester
1927/28	Mrs. Bedhall	Plymouth
1928/29	Mrs. Taylor	Stoke-on-Trent
1929/30	Mrs. Hewitson	Bournemouth
1930/31	Mrs. Mellis	Cheltenham
1931/32	Mrs. Priestley	York
1932/33	Mrs. Beavan	London
1933/34	Mrs. Pavitt	West Hartlepool
1934/35	Mrs. Merchant	Birmingham
1935/36	Mrs. McKay	Bristol
1936/37	Mrs. McPhail	New Brighton
1937/38	Mrs. Dale	Southampton
1938/39	Mrs. E. E. Williams	Hull
1939/40	Mrs. I. Thorley	Great Yarmouth
1940/41	Mrs. K. Chadwick	Middlesbrough
1941/42	Mrs. Mabel Ridealgh	Lincoln
1942/43	Mrs. E. Thirwell	London
1943/44	Mrs. E. Webb }	Newcastle ★
1944/45	Mrs. H. Matt-Lewis	
1945/46	Mrs. C. Bamber	Torquay
1946/47	Mrs. G. Lloyd	Blackpool
1947/48	Mrs. R. Pearson	Great Yarmouth
1948/49	Mrs. R. Stonehouse	Margate
1949/50	Mrs. L. Brett	Sheffield
1950/51	Mrs. L. Maddaford	Southend
1951/52	Mrs. E. Baxendale	Scarborough
1952/53	Mrs. E. M. Price	Morecambe
1953/54	Mrs. F. Hall	Brighton
1954/55	Mrs. C. I. Stuart	Bristol
1955/56	Mrs. M. Ewan, JP	Newcastle
1956/57	Mrs. Ethel Bradley	Leicester
1957/58	Mrs. Doris Schofield	Blackpool
1958/59	Mrs. Susan Lowes	London
1959/60	Mrs. Doris Fitter	Plymouth
1960/61	Mrs. Kathleen Owen	Portsmouth
1961/62	Cllr. Mrs. Doris Fisher, JP	Skegness
1962/63	Mrs. F. Annely	Birmingham

★ No Annual Conference held 1944 — war-time conditions.

1963/64	Mrs. Joan Baker	Whitley Bay
1964/65	Mrs. Mary Lewis	Cleethorpes
1965/66	Mrs. Ivy Beresford	Margate
1966/67	Mrs. Emma Chatterton, JP	Margate
1967/68	Mrs. Iris Fleet	Morecambe
1968/69	Cllr. Mrs. Teresa Hinchey	Southend-on-Sea
1969/70	Mrs. Hilda Wickens, JP	Torquay
1970/71	Cllr. Mrs. Winifred Liversidge, JP	Scarborough
1971/72	Mrs. Florence Shalloe	Margate
1972/73	Mrs. Joan Young, JP	Skegness
1973/74	Mrs. Flossie Wren	Blackpool
1974/75	Mrs. Edna Shotton	Scarborough
1975/76	Cllr. Mrs. Sarah Cowey, JP	Paignton
1976/77	Mrs. Ethel Mewis	Great Yarmouth
1977/78	Mrs. Cissie Brown	Southport
1978/79	Mrs. Ivy Harris	Harrogate
1979/80	Miss Martha Blunt	Eastbourne
1980/81	Mrs. Doris Dan	Skegness
1981/82	Mrs. Florence Cowings	Bracklesham Bay Holiday Camp
1982/83	Mrs. Sylvia Paine	Middleton Towers
1983/84		Worthing

General Secretaries:

1883/84	Mrs. Alice Acland	
1884/85	Miss Allen	
1885/89	Mrs. Mary Lawrenson	
1889/1921	Miss Margaret Llewelyn Davies	
1921/25	Miss A. Honora Enfield	
1925/37	Mrs. Eleanor Barton	
1937/40	Miss Rose Simpson	
1940/53	Mrs. Cecily Cook, O.B.E.	
1953/63	Mrs. Mabel Ridealgh	
1963/83	Mrs. Kathleen Kempton	

SOURCES OF INFORMATION

In writing this centenary history we have made extensive use of material published by the Guild itself. Special mention should be made of the Annual Reports, which provide basic information and suggest reasons for administrative and policy developments. Three manuscript sources were consulted — Minutes of the Central Committee, the papers of Margaret Llewelyn Davies and Mary Lawrenson, held respectively by Hull University, the London School of Economics and the Co-operative Union. Newspaper and journal literature provided many important insights into the Guild's history and particular use was made of the "Co-operative News", "Woman's Outlook", the "Daily Herald" and the "Manchester Guardian". A collection of newspaper cuttings relevant to the Guild is held by the Fawcett Library. We have also benefited from the personal recollections and interpretations of many guildswomen and other friends of the Co-operative Movement.

Microfilming of many valuable Guild records has been undertaken by Microform Ltd., East Ardsley, Wakefield, Yorkshire.

CO-OPERATIVE GLOSSARY

CENTRAL BOARD
See United Board

CENTRAL EXECUTIVE
See United Board

CO-OPERATIVE COLLEGE
The staff- and member-training college of the British Co-operative Movement. Founded in 1919 and operated by the Co-operative Union. Originally in Manchester, it is now at Stanford Hall, Loughborough, Leics., which is also the headquarters of the Union's Education Dept.

CO-OPERATIVE CONGRESS
The annual conference of the Co-operative Movement. Organised by the Co-operative Union, the Congress is attended by delegates from the retail societies, the CWS and other member-societies of the Union. The Congress is the final authority on national Co-operative policy.

"CO-OPERATIVE NEWS"
The official weekly newspaper of the Co-operative Movement founded in 1871. Published by the Co-operative Press Ltd.

CO-OPERATIVE PARTY
The political arm of the Co-operative Movement and a department of the Co-operative Union. The Co-operative Party is represented in the Westminster and European Parliaments and on many municipal councils. The Party has an electoral agreement with the Labour Party to put forward joint candidates.

CO-OPERATIVE UNION
National federation of the Consumer Co-operative Movement. Formed 1869, it acts as the co-ordinator, adviser and spokesman for retail, wholesale and other forms of Co-operation with the exception of agricultural co-operatives.

CO-OPERATIVE UNION SECTIONS
To be distinguished from the sectional structure of the Women's Guild. For administrative purposes the Union is divided into areas called Sections e.g. Southern Section, Scottish Section etc. Co-operatives in each Section democratically elect a Sectional Board which is concerned with all circumstances affecting the welfare of societies in the area.

CO-OPERATIVE WHOLESALE SOCIETY
The wholesaling and manufacturing organisation of the Co-operative Movement. Founded in 1863 by retail co-operative societies which are its shareholders. The Co-operative Bank and Co-operative Insurance Society are wholly owned subsidiaries of the CWS.

EDUCATION EXECUTIVE
A special committee of the Co-operative Union responsible for the services of the Union's Education Department to co-operative societies and for the operation of the Co-operative College.

UNITED BOARD and CENTRAL BOARD
Former principal committees of the Co-operative Union which have been replaced by the CENTRAL EXECUTIVE which comprises representatives of the retail societies, the CWS and co-operative productive societies. The Central Executive carries out the decisions of the Co-operative Congress and immediate matters of policy.

"WOMAN'S OUTLOOK"
Founded in 1919 by Annie Bamford Tomlinson, daughter of Samuel Bamford, Editor of the "Co-operative News". In addition Mrs. Bamford Tomlinson founded "Our Circle", the Co-operative children's magazine, and edited both "Woman's Outlook" and the women's pages of the "Co-operative News". She was succeeded as editor of "Woman's Outlook" by Mary Stott (nee Waddington) who later became a noted "Guardian" women's columnist, Nora Crossley and Jean Nicholson. "Woman's Outlook" closed in 1967.

BAILEY, Jack
National Secretary of the Co-operative Party from 1942 to 1962. Prolific writer on Co-operative subjects. President of Co-operative Congress in 1964, knighted in 1965.

BAMFORD, Samuel
Appointed Editor of the "Co-operative News" in 1875 and as such exerted considerable influence in the Co-operative Movement.

GREENWOOD, Abraham
1824-1911 A founder and first President of the CWS. Also a founder and director of the Co-operative Insurance Society and a founder and chairman of the Co-operative Newspaper Co. (now the Co-operative Press) publishers of the "Co-operative News".

MACARTHUR, Mary
1880-1921 Outstanding trade union organiser and campaigner for women's rights. Her work is commemorated by the Mary MacArthur Home for Working Women.

NEALE, Edward Vansittart
1810-1892 Christian Socialist and first General Secretary of the Co-operative Union. Outstanding Co-operative leader and propagandist.

INDEX

NAMES

SUBJECTS

278